CONCURRENT MARKETING

CONCURRENT MARKETING

Integrating Product, Sales, and Service

■

Frank V. Cespedes

■

Harvard Business School Press

Boston, Massachusetts

Library of Congress Cataloging-in-Publication Data
    Cespedes, Frank V.
      Concurrent marketing : integrating product, sales, and service /
    by Frank V. Cespedes.
          p.   cm.
      Includes index.
      ISBN 0-87584-444-8
      1. Marketing—Management.   2. Sales management.   I. Title.
    HF5415.13.C468   1995
    658.8—dc20   95-4325
                                                               CIP

The paper used in this publication meets the requirements of the American National
Standard for Permanence of Paper for Printed Library Materials Z39.49-1984.

FOR ELIZABETH AND HELEN

Contents

■

Preface

■

The past decade has witnessed dramatic and often wrenching changes in the production philosophies and capabilities of companies around the world, in the supply chain and distribution arrangements that condition competition, and in information sources about buyer behavior. This book concerns the implications of those changes for firms' marketing activities. Specifically, it reports the findings of a study of companies grappling with new marketing requirements, and it provides managers with guidance and recommendations that can help them meet the challenges posed by market developments.

In so doing, the book addresses, and often dissents from current conventional wisdom about, a number of wider organizational issues: the place and purpose of functional expertise in the conduct of cross-functional tasks; the role and limits of incentives in achieving required coordination; the relationship between individual and organizational learning; the management of the corporate information infrastructure relevant to new marketing tasks; the changing nature of selling; and the consequences of reengineering and teamwork initiatives that ignore these issues. But the book had its origins in a seemingly straightforward teaching context.

I began doing research on these issues while teaching at Harvard Business School, many graduates of which become managers in and consultants to industrial, consumer, and service firms. My observation (supported by conversations with former students and their em-

ployers) was that most graduates move into these positions with a
good grounding in strategy theories and market analysis techniques
but with less understanding of necessary interactions among product,
sales, and service groups. Hence, they often lack an appreciation for
the tasks involved in real-world attempts to implement a strategy. In
teaching strategy implementation, I soon found that nearly all existing
literature focused either on product management or sales management or service operations in isolation from one another. Meanwhile,
my own work with companies indicated that developments in many
industries were forcing new interdependencies among these groups.

Although there is little scholarly literature about interdependence
among marketing groups, the business trade press frequently high-
lights it in articles with titles such as "The Gap between Marketing
and Sales" or "Sales versus Service." These articles tend to offer three
types of advice: (1) simply encourage "more communication" between functional units; (2) pay all these groups the same way; and (3)
it is not great products or effective selling but great service that will
motivate customers to beat a path to your door. Yet, as this book reports, there are many complications that arise when companies attempt to follow such advice, other important factors that affect these
groups, and useful alternative approaches available to firms.

To examine the issues more systematically, I conducted a clinical
study of companies trying to adapt to the market changes I had observed. The research focused on firms in four industries: computer
products, telecommunications services, branded consumer package
goods, and medical products. One criterion for choosing these companies was a desire to examine the topic in markets that differ in product technologies, service requirements, and daily account management tasks. Another was a firm's willingness to provide access to
managers and confidential information.

Over the next four years, with the help of research assistants, I
interviewed more than 200 managers at firms in the target industries.
At each company, interviews averaging 90 minutes in length were
conducted with product, sales, and service personnel; management in
other functional areas (e.g., MIS, market research, human resources,
logistics); and (when present in a firm) formal liaison managers. Most
interviews focused on one or more of the following questions: (1)

What are the major issues facing your area in working with sales, service, and/or product groups? (2) What factors determine the relative importance of coordination with each group, the tasks that must be coordinated, and the kinds of conflicts or opportunities that arise? (3) What mechanisms exist in your firm for managing these joint tasks, and what is your perception of their strengths and weaknesses? (4) In practice, how do things most often "get done" at these interfaces— i.e., what are the informal as well as formal means for managing the required interactions?

Other data included reports and internal company documents supplied by interviewees, personal observation while attending company meetings, numerous customer calls with sales and service personnel, work with senior and functional managers in executive development contexts, the perspectives of consulting firms and research suppliers to these companies, and (for certain aspects of account management) survey data. I also wrote detailed case studies about changing marketing requirements in each industry group (available in Frank V. Cespedes, *Managing Marketing Linkages: Text and Cases* [Englewood Cliffs, N.J.: Prentice Hall, 1995]). Some firms allowed these cases to be published with no disguising of names; others, such as the firm referred to as "Packaged Products Company" in Chapter 5, requested that published materials not identify the company or managers involved.

I adopted this clinical approach due to the dearth of prior research on the topic and because my objective was to identify key issues and approaches, not to test hypotheses from previously identified options. Another objective, essential to obtaining a useful analysis of organizational response to environmental change, was to gain a rich understanding of the history, field tasks, and strategic goals of the companies involved. In turn, this approach yielded managerially relevant examples and experiences, as well as the opportunity to discuss commonalities and differences across market environments.

As the research continued and I began to publish articles about the findings, the broader issues implicated in this topic became more salient and timely. In the business press, downsizing and "the abolition of hierarchy" became common stories and cross-functional teams the prescribed organizational panacea. In academic journals, the changing role of marketing became a focus for discussion. The prevalent themes (in an echo of Marx's famous forecast about the evolution of the communist state) are that market developments mean the "withering away" of middle-management specialist functions and the demise of personal selling in favor of ad hoc "networks" and technological links.

Such forecasts may prove to be true, new words for perennial buyer-seller activities, or a misinterpretation of the impact of market developments on organizational requirements and as ironically wrong as Marx's forecasts about what endures and what withers away. (As Oscar Wilde observed, "Predictions are always risky—especially about the future.") The point is that, without a better understanding of what companies now actually face in their customer-contact activities, all such predictions are largely armchair speculations.

By contrast, this book is rooted in core value creation and delivery tasks in the field. My conclusions are certainly open to disagreement, but I hope to provide executives with a tangible basis for improvement and action.

ACKNOWLEDGMENTS

During the research for this book, many people generously offered advice and support. My biggest debt is to the companies that participated in the study and the many managers who contributed their time, experience, and suggestions. Evidence of their help is found throughout this book in the form of quotes and references to their decisions and actions. During the field work, Marie Bell and Laura Goode worked with me as research assistants.

The Division of Research at Harvard Business School funded much of my field work. I thank Warren McFarlan and Richard Tedlow for their sustained support and advice. Other colleagues at Harvard who made useful suggestions include Christopher Bartlett, Michael Beer, Bob Dolan, Steven Greyser, Linda Hill, John Quelch, Kash Rangan, Walter Salmon, Ben Shapiro, Al Silk, and Bob Simons. Colleagues at other institutions contributed by challenging ideas and offering intellectual leads. Among them were Bob Buzzell of George Mason University, George Day of Wharton, Bernard Jaworski of the

University of Southern California, Thomas Kosnik of Stanford University, Thomas Leigh of the University of Georgia, Nigel Piercy of the University of Wales, Hermann Simon of Johannes Gutenberg Universitat, Gordon Swartz of London Business School, Frederick Webster of Dartmouth, Brown Whittington of Emory University, Lawrence Wortzel of Boston University, and Bob Young of Northeastern University.

Professors E. Raymond Corey of Harvard and Joel Goldhar of the Illinois Institute of Technology read chapters of the book. Ray Corey shared much of his wisdom about field research, while Joel Goldhar provided a cornucopia of suggestions concerning the draft manuscript, for which I am deeply grateful.

I learned much from many people in industry, including Mark Bruneau and Andrew Belt of COBA-M.I.D.; Stephen Haeckel of IBM; Fletcher Hyler of Logical Marketing, who first suggested to me the analogy between concurrent engineering and new marketing requirements; Barbara Jackson of Jackson Associates; Kathleen Mocniak of Leaf, Inc.; Rowland T. Moriarty of Cubex Corporation; Walter Popper of CSC Index; John Post of Hewlett-Packard; Carole Prest of GenRad; Ruthann Salvatore of Duracell; John Walling of Nielsen Marketing Research; and Charles Wilson of Abberton Associates.

Through its work with companies around the world, The Center for Executive Development in Cambridge, Massachusetts, has afforded me access to thousands of managers. Doug Anderson, John Cady, Richard Hamermesh, and Todd Jick of CED have also helped to implement many useful change initiatives.

Many others helped at various stages by their comments on papers, articles, and conference presentations. In particular, I want to thank the editors and reviewers at *Business Horizons, California Management Review, Harvard Business Review, Journal of Consumer Marketing, Journal of Personal Selling & Sales Management, Marketing Research,* and *Sloan Management Review,* where earlier drafts of several of the ideas in this book first appeared.

I also express sincere thanks to the Harvard Business School Press, particularly Carol Franco, Paula Duffy, Susan Blumenthal, Nicola Foster, Liz Hiser, Nindy LeRoy, Lisa Phelan, Barbara Roth, and

Gayle Treadwell. Natalie Greenberg was again a patient editor of my prose. Laurie Fitzgerald provided invaluable secretarial support during a succession of drafts.

Finally, my wife, Bonnie Costello, and my daughters, Elizabeth and Helen, are—serially and concurrently—the deserved recipients of my thanks and love.

Boston, Massachusetts
February 1995

Introduction

■

THE management literature is replete with exhortations concerning faster product development, flexible manufacturing systems, and innovative supply-chain arrangements. But the literature is silent about the impact of these developments on downstream marketing activities, where implementation of such initiatives with customers resides. Meanwhile, quality improvements during the past decade have moved the competitive bottleneck in many firms down the value chain to sales and service. Many companies can and do produce better, faster, and with significantly fewer defects for more market segments. But this does little good if, in its customer contact activities, the firm's marketing system cannot handle (or, in many cases, actively resists) a greater variety of products, services, and markets.

Between 1987 and 1992, for example, IBM cut production cycle times by as much as 50%; it reduced the time needed to produce mainframe computers by 67%, decreased installation time from a week to 16 hours, and substantially improved mean-time-between-failure for these and other products; the company also won the Baldrige quality competition. But these laudable measures did not stop one of the greatest losses in shareholder value in business history. As one executive notes, "It is meaningless how fast and well-built a product is if it doesn't address customer value or if, in the field, marketing units don't sell and service it properly."

IBM's experience was not unrepresentative. The paradigm of continuous improvement has been driving industry investments and managerial attention for the past decade. Through total quality management (TQM) programs, companies have pursued goals such as six sigma, zero defect, and 10-fold reduction of cycle time. The attention and investments have yielded excellent results. A recent survey found that U.S. and European firms have been improving manufacturing cycle time and production defect rates at annual rates of higher than 10% since 1992—improvement rates that were faster than in the previous survey period and significantly higher than those for Japanese firms.[1] Although one cannot generalize about absolute levels of manufacturing performance from these results, it is clear that any remaining quality gap among U.S., European, and Japanese manufacturers is narrowing. Yet, this same survey found that, despite the intensifying rate of improvement on most manufacturing performance indices, overall competitiveness measures for surveyed firms declined. Why? Because key competitive factors are shifting into areas such as customized new product development, rapid product introductions, and performance along the entire supply chain, including postsales service.

Quality remains a strategic issue, but benchmarked quality is now effectively "table stakes" in the competitive arena of many industries. What's needed is analogous to what, in quality circles, is encompassed by the term "concurrent engineering": better integration among the marketing groups that must interact more often, more quickly, and in more depth across more products, markets, and accounts.

This integration goes beyond abstract notions of teamwork or downsizing campaigns aimed at eliminating layers of hierarchy. Indeed, many current teamwork initiatives are unwittingly slowing decision making and diluting necessary functional expertise and accountability. This dilution is especially costly in an environment where shorter product life cycles and increasingly intricate customer-contact tasks make timely decisions and clear functional responsibilities more, not less, important. In some firms, moreover, the development of concurrent marketing capabilities requires a rethinking of ambitious reengineering efforts. Without attention to the interaction of product, sales, and service units—the primary customer-contact groups in most companies—many current reengineering efforts are, unfortunately, technologically sophisticated and expensive versions of garbage-in–garbage-out management exercises. They often accelerate the dissemination of outmoded market and financial data throughout the organization and, via the increase in fixed costs, effectively cement in place business processes that initially appear streamlined but soon are overwhelmed by the more complex requirements of a new market environment.

FOCUS OF THE BOOK

I aim to provide a better understanding of the forces that make concurrent marketing a competitive necessity, of the issues that impede its realization in many firms, how some companies manage these issues, and their wider organizational implications. The book focuses on certain key interfaces between field sales, customer service, and product management groups. It explains what is involved in managing these interfaces in different market environments; it outlines the interdependencies that affect planning and execution of joint marketing activities; it discusses the impact on account management systems and other aspects of a firm's selling efforts; and it provides diagnostic tools for managers interested in improving concurrent marketing at their firms.

Although my focus is on selling as only one part of concurrent marketing, the book examines field sales tasks in some depth, for three reasons. One reason is that, along with production, sales and service are core activities in any profit-seeking organization. But, as Tom Peters has emphasized, in recent years they have also been among "the two most neglected elements of the typical American corporation. . . . [They] must achieve preeminence if we are to become competitive once again."[2]

Another reason is that, whatever else marketing encompasses, it certainly includes selling—getting and keeping customers and the revenues they represent. As the old saying goes, "In most companies, sales is the only revenue-generating function; everything else is a cost center." Value is ultimately created or destroyed at the boundary between the company and its customers. Whether we call the personnel who manage this boundary "salespeople," "agents," "associates," or

Exhibit I-1
The Linkages That Form the Basic Building Blocks for Marketing Efforts

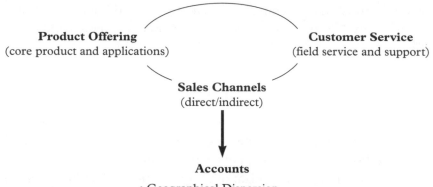

Product Offering
(core product and applications)

Customer Service
(field service and support)

Sales Channels
(direct/indirect)

Accounts
- Geographical Dispersion
- Time-Based Strategies
- New Information Capabilities
- Channel Power Issues
- Shorter Product Life Cycles

(as in many banks) "vice presidents," their customer contact activities are fundamental to business success and now often dependent on their interactions with product and service units in their firms. As Exhibit I-1 indicates, appropriate linkages among these groups constitute basic building blocks in marketing efforts, and the nature of the required linkages is changing because of the forces that influence the account management tasks facing field sales and service personnel.

The third reason for the attention given to field selling activities is that market changes are altering sales management requirements, on the one hand, and organizational requirements in areas beyond sales and marketing, on the other. In recent years it has become fashionable to proclaim that developments in information technology, supply chain arrangements, market fragmentation, and other factors mean "the once-and-for-all death of the salesman."[3] I argue that such a view is not only (as a feisty Mark Twain said about reports of his death) premature; it is also a misunderstanding of sales' role in the emerging competitive environment. Rather than constricting sales tasks, these developments involve salespeople in activities traditionally ascribed to product marketing and other functional groups. This, in turn, alters basic sales-management tasks and, in a more segmented marketplace where speed is important, wider organizational information flows, measurement criteria, incentive systems, human resource policies, and marketing structures.

There *is* a difference between sales and marketing, a difference succinctly captured in Theodore Levitt's classic definition: "Selling is preoccupied with the seller's need to convert his product into cash; marketing with the idea of satisfying the needs of the customer by means of the product and the whole cluster of things associated with creating, delivering, and finally consuming it."[4] Nonetheless, in practice, sales' importance as a source of current cash flows still tends to define the form and substance of most companies' marketing programs. Top managers, some years removed from the realities of actual customer contact, are often unaware of the embedded hard-to-reverse strategic commitments that these field activities represent. As a result, they often develop strategies that cannot be implemented or, worse, are implemented in ways unintended and undesired by senior management. When the factors discussed in this book are coherently integrated, however, the entire company will be focused on customer encounters, and selling will evolve into effective concurrent marketing.

KEY THEMES

Although specific topics are addressed in each chapter, it is worth emphasizing here certain general themes that emerged from my research: the broader organizational challenges facing firms in rapidly changing markets. Some of these issues have received much attention in recent years. But my argument about how to manage the increasingly cross-functional requirements of effective marketing often diverges from prevailing conventional wisdom.

Terms like "teamwork" and "coordination" are value-laden words with positive connotations. Especially before confronting necessary trade-offs and allocating resources, few managers are *against* initiatives aimed at promoting cross-functional coordination. Indeed, it is safe to say that, during the past decade, espoused support for such efforts has become the politically correct attitude in most Western companies. But, as this book indicates, coordination comes at a cost, and different approaches are implicitly choices about the kinds of ongoing marketing issues a firm must monitor and manage.

Further, the examples discussed here indicate that, while companies indeed face new cross-functional requirements in marketing, there is also a continuing need to develop and update specialized expertise in different aspects of customer contact activities. Such expertise is important for achieving scale and scope economies and in-depth knowledge of customers. Such expertise, I also argue, is, in fact, a prerequisite for the higher-level capabilities now required of firms.

How can managers usefully conceptualize and deal with the problems, processes, and options of these cross-cutting competitive requirements? This book develops four themes relevant to this question.

Competency Traps

The traditional alignment of marketing roles and responsibilities assumes a sequential process in which sales and service units execute product management's plans. But certain market factors—the nature of product offerings, market fragmentation, supply chain management initiatives, and accelerated product life cycles—are changing internal organizational requirements. In many business-to-business markets, for example, the adoption of just-in-time inventory systems and broader supply-chain management policies has altered purchasing criteria and buying processes at many accounts and, therefore, sales and service tasks at vendors. In consumer goods markets, changing patterns among retailers in various classes of trade have altered the nature of interactions among brand, sales, and service groups at packaged goods firms in North America and Europe. In both types of businesses, shorter product life cycles and the rapid diffusion of computer technologies and on-line databases have changed the locus of pertinent customer information in the distribution channel and, as a result, organizational interactions at buyer and seller.

There is a domino effect in these developments (see Exhibit I-2). These market factors place more emphasis on a firm's ability to customize product service packages for more diverse customer groups. In turn, this places more value on the seller's ability to generate and maintain timely segment-specific (and, often, account-specific) knowl-

Exhibit I-2
Domino Effect of Market Factors

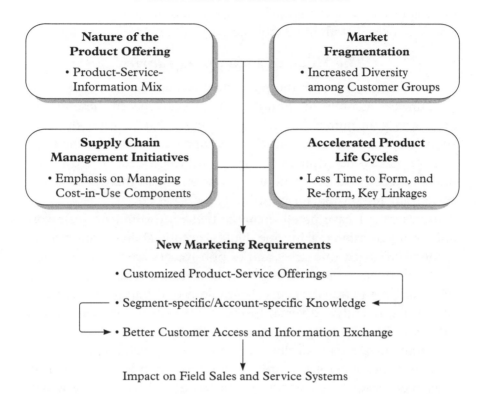

Nature of the Product Offering	Market Fragmentation
• Product-Service-Information Mix	• Increased Diversity among Customer Groups

Supply Chain Management Initiatives	Accelerated Product Life Cycles
• Emphasis on Managing Cost-in-Use Components	• Less Time to Form, and Re-form, Key Linkages

New Marketing Requirements

• Customized Product-Service Offerings

• Segment-specific/Account-specific Knowledge

• Better Customer Access and Information Exchange

Impact on Field Sales and Service Systems

edge throughout the organization. This, in turn again, places new requirements on field sales and service systems where, in most firms, the responsibility for customer access and information exchange lies.

In many companies, however, the current situation is a misfit between market developments and required organizational capabilities. Product, sales, and service units must synchronize their activities in a context where each unit's window on the external environment, its metrics and time horizons, and its information flows differ. Over time, moreover, each unit adopts routines that improve the efficiency of its particular customer contact responsibilities. But, too often, the result is a series of "competency traps" in which each group is unwittingly getting better at "fighting the last war"—developing and executing marketing programs relevant to a previous stage of competition. Further, each unit's established procedures keep the firm from gaining needed experience with new processes. While new alignments may be more appropriate to changing market conditions, competency in each unit is associated with the established alignment.

The Value of Functional Clarity

In this situation, however, the goal is not (as many current approaches to teamwork assume) to eliminate differences between these groups or to assert (in numerous off-site meetings) that "everybody is responsible for customer satisfaction." Multiple efforts across the organization indeed determine customer satisfaction. But in most busy organizations, what everyone is responsible for in theory, no one is specifically responsible for in practice.

Further, as I have noted, many initiatives to stimulate teamwork are slowing decision making and diluting accountability in an environment where speed-to-market and responsiveness are essential. These initiatives often are also hurting basic human-resource capabilities, as teams attempt to transform excellent salespeople into mediocre product managers and vice versa. In the process, necessary expertise is often sacrificed.

I argue that, paradoxically, there is virtue in *separating* and distinguishing functional roles in order to improve the cross-functional coordination needed for concurrent marketing. The key issue is how to link, efficiently and effectively, knowledge, resources, and various sources of customer value that are necessarily located *across* different organizational units in most companies. Doing so requires, first, that managers analyze and understand the continuum of activities at sales interfaces. Because integrating these activities always takes time and scarce resources, moreover, companies must make choices about where and how to attempt linkages along this continuum.

A Linked Triad of Options

At the companies I studied, major initiatives aimed at building concurrent marketing capabilities fell into three categories (see Exhibit I-3): an emphasis on structural devices such as formal liaison units; changes in information systems utilized by product, sales, and service units; and alterations in broader management processes, especially

Exhibit I-3
A Linked Triad of Options

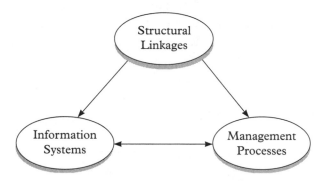

new career paths and training programs. I describe and evaluate the benefits, vulnerabilities, and market environment of each approach, to provide senior executives with a coherent way of assessing the costs, benefits, and ongoing management tasks of each option. I also explain their connections with one another. For example, new structures without the supporting information infrastructure (a common situation facing many multifunctional teams), or new information systems without the appropriate people and organizational processes (the result of many expensive reengineering efforts), will have only limited impact.

I also argue for a redefinition of the role and organization of traditional market research activities. The book explains why "market research" in most firms is really "marketing research," serving the information priorities of product management and often indifferent to the information needs of sales and service personnel. At the same time, changes in the information infrastructure of many industries require closer ties between research and information service (IS) units for timely gathering and disseminating of the data needed for concurrent marketing efforts.

Field Marketing Systems

While market developments require broad organizational changes, they also require companies to decentralize important marketing decisions to local field units. It is increasingly difficult to respond to more segmented markets and customized account demands through general-purpose marketing programs designed at headquarters. Field units must be better informed and more capable because the market is placing more demands and more value on these close-to-the-customer units. Their specific knowledge of customer needs must be upgraded and then integrated coherently with the broader strategic direction supplied by the general knowledge of product managers and top management.[5]

This approach raises a host of training and other human resource management issues that are discussed throughout the book. It also requires that companies pay renewed attention to often neglected basics of their field marketing systems such as the role of account managers, the special product-sales integration needs of big multilocation accounts, the impact of sales compensation and incentives on behavior in the field, and the steps involved in achieving better sales and service coordination with customers. These seemingly tactical issues now have major implications for the strategic management of the firm. Top executives seeking competitive advantage must develop an understanding of, and better organizational linkages with, these field units.

Some years ago, an excellent manager (at a mediocre company) told me that

> Marketing in most companies is conducted as it *should have been* conducted in that industry five to ten years in the past. Because that's the last time that the executives who make the truly important marketing decisions for the firm were out in the field on a regular basis. As a result, they now make these decisions based on an obsolete vision of what's really happening at the company-customer interface.

Research for this book brought home to me the wisdom and organizational realpolitik of his comment. In too many firms, the processes for gathering and interpreting feedback from the field (represented by the solid lines in Exhibit I-4) are either lacking, out-of-date, or limited to the rudimentary and notoriously noisy information of standard salesforce call reports. Especially in fast-changing environments, general managers as well as marketing managers must understand the factors

Exhibit I-4
In the New Marketing Environment, Local Field
Knowledge Must Inform Company Strategy

Company Strategy ⟶ Strategic Marketing ⟶ Tactical Marketing

Definition of Objectives	Product Policy/R&D	Field Sales Activities
Strategic Plans	Pricing Guidelines	Sales Support Activities
Resource Allocations	Competitor Analysis	Local Marketing Programs

involved in building new skills and leveraging existing capabilities in field marketing operations—a vital and visible source of interaction with the marketplace, but also among the most time-constrained and short-term-oriented activities in most companies.

HOW THIS BOOK IS ORGANIZED

Part I discusses the new marketing requirements generated by the changing bases of competition in many industries. Chapter 1 focuses on four factors: changes in what is being sold (nature of the product offering), to whom it is sold (market fragmentation), how it is sold (supply chain management), and under what competitive conditions it is sold (product life-cycle issues). This chapter explains why, in different ways, each development increases coordination requirements among product management, field sales, and customer service groups.

The subsequent chapters in Part I then consider traditional organizational alignments among these groups and issues that affect planning and execution of their increasingly interdependent activities. Chapter 2 discusses typical roles and responsibilities associated with each unit and how their joint activities compose a core marketing "gearbox" in most companies. This chapter also explains the inadequacy of traditional alignments, and explains the need for and nature of concurrent marketing capabilities. Chapter 3 moves beyond formal roles and responsibilities and looks at how managers' time horizons, performance metrics, and information flows affect the functioning of marketing interfaces. These organizational aspects create a series of "marketing dialects"—i.e., differences in how each unit hears, interprets, and articulates the voice of the customer. Managed traditionally, moreover, these dialects give rise to the competency traps noted above.

Part II considers how companies are attempting to alter their organizations in order to build concurrent marketing capabilities. The analysis in Part II is more focused: each chapter discusses a particular case study as a way of evaluating the benefits and vulnerabilities of various linkage devices. Each chapter also provides managers with diagnostic questions useful in considering the applicability of each device. This self-reflection is important because the challenges facing firms are compelling them to make expensive, time-consuming, and often irreversible choices about where and how to attempt linkages along the continuum of marketing tasks discussed in Part I. Taken together, Chapters 4 through 6 outline a coherent way of assessing the costs, benefits, and ongoing management requirements of the major options.

Chapter 4 considers a key tension in organizing marketing activities: how to develop and embed new skills and capabilities in the organization with minimal disruption to the efforts and attention required to maintain current sources of revenue. Using IBM's experience as a running example, it then focuses on a structural device for integrating product, sales, and service activities and the benefits as well as limitations of this approach. Chapter 5 discusses how to make research and information systems more responsive to new marketing demands. Using the experience of a major consumer-packaged goods company as an example, it explains why a linking of market research and information systems has become competitively significant and enumerates the implications for traditional market research activities. Chapter 6 concerns management career paths and training programs. It discusses the connection between individual and organizational learning when market factors simultaneously increase required coordination among functional groups and decrease the time available for utilizing formal coordination mechanisms.

Part III focuses on getting the marketing job done through field sales and service people—the front-line contact with customers in most firms. These chapters probably have the most direct relevance to sales and service managers. But the thrust of my argument is that the seemingly tactical issues discussed in these chapters are increasingly important to the general strategic and organizational capabilities of companies.

Chapter 7 takes up account management systems and the steps involved in building relationships with those customers where concurrent marketing capabilities are most needed. It discusses the role of the account manager, guidelines for clarifying account selection criteria (a key strategic decision in the new marketing environment), and the special coordination challenges posed by major accounts. Chapter 8 examines a core aspect of a company's field marketing system: sales compensation policies. It outlines an analytical process for developing a sales compensation plan, the important choices in setting goals and rewarding results, and the relevance and limits of compensation policies in a healthy and effective sales management system. Chapter 9 focuses on customer service and ways to achieve better sales service coordination. It furnishes a perspective on customer service that stresses its interfunctional requirements, the tasks firms face in their attempts to manage service levels, and a framework for diagnosing customer retention dynamics and the marketing tools relevant to different stages of customer relationships.

The book ends with a chapter that reviews key themes, summarizes lessons learned, and offers advice to managers about how to get started in building concurrent marketing capabilities.

I

New Marketing Requirements

∎

1

The Need for Tighter
Linkages

■

IN most companies, marketing is done by three groups: those who manage the firm's product offerings (brand or advertising managers in consumer goods and services, or product/program managers in industrial goods); those who manage the sales channels (direct and/or indirect channels of distribution); and those responsible for customer service (pre- and postsale services of various kinds). In principle, these groups should interact harmoniously to pursue the overall objectives of the firm. But in practice, there has long been friction among these groups in many companies.

Given this history, one might conclude that such conflict is a nondebilitating cost of doing business. But in recent years a number of factors have made better integration of these activities a prerequisite for effective marketing in many industries. These include changes in: what is being sold (nature of the product offering), to whom it is sold (market fragmentation), how it is sold (supply chain management), and under what competitive conditions it is sold (product life-cycle issues). These changes have been driven by developments in technology, the increased capabilities of flexible production processes, new and better sources of customer information, and the globalization of many heretofore national markets. The result has been an alteration in how customer value is created and delivered and, in the process, the bases of competition and marketing excellence.

NATURE OF THE PRODUCT OFFERING

Traditionally, macroeconomists as well as marketing theorists have distinguished between manufacturing and service businesses. The standard elements of distinction include the following:[1]

MANUFACTURED GOODS	SERVICES
Tangible product	Intangible service
Can be stored by sellers and buyers	Cannot be stored and so is time-dependent
Production precedes consumption	Simultaneous production and consumption
Low customer involvement in production process	High customer involvement in production process
Less variety/customization and information content in transactions between vendor and customer	More variety/customization and information content in transactions between vendor and customer

As the final distinction implies, goods and services occur along a spectrum. Most services contain some goods (the hamburger at the fast-food restaurant), and many manufactured goods have always contained services in the form of support, delivery, and other attributes associated with the "augmented product." But technological and other developments have increased the services content of many manufactured goods while many service businesses have more characteristics of tangible manufactured goods.

Because of microprocessor technology, more services are now stored and so are less time-dependent. On-line database services, for instance, store information and (via expert systems) allow manipulation of that information at different times. Similarly, service production and consumption are now routinely separated in many businesses through electronic links that allow for the export of the service production process from the place of consumer use.

Equally important, more tangible goods producers face new service requirements in product development, production, demand generation, and delivery. In product development, embedded software increases the information content of many products, the ability to customize applications, and the required information content in customer transactions. In production operations, developments in computer-integrated manufacturing allow many broad-line producers to approach the efficiencies of focused producers. Traditionally, the marketer's desire to emphasize a broad product line in order to deal with heterogeneous consumer needs has been limited by the operations manager's desire to maximize throughput and minimize process disruptions by reducing product line variety.[2] But today more firms can accommodate broader product lines at much lower incremental costs and without damage to quality.[3]

For operations managers, this means that variety is cheaper. For marketing managers, the ability to serve more niche markets is increased and, insofar as such capabilities are developed and used by more firms, competitively necessary. And for sales and service managers, a premium is placed on the ability of field personnel to develop and maintain strong account relationships that help the firm anticipate and respond quickly to changing demand patterns in a wider variety of market segments.

One result of these developments is that, more often than not, what companies offer to customers is a product-service-information mix made up of tangible product, service support, information exchange, and active customer involvement in shaping the transaction(s). The nature of the offering requires the close participation of all groups responsible for managing product, service, and actual sale. Each provides a different component of the package offered to customers, and all must interact efficiently and effectively to provide the package. This requirement for customer satisfaction, moreover, is spreading across both high-tech and traditionally low-tech businesses in consumer and industrial markets.

Consider systems integration in the computer business. Motivated by changes in buying behavior and declining hardware margins, many computer vendors are positioning themselves as a single point of contact for the planning, design, and implementation of integrated systems. This process typically means customizing the product for a buyer and (perhaps with third parties) providing the "solution"—i.e., a combination of hardware, software, training, and other support services tailored to the account's business goals. In effect, the seller acts as a general contractor in managing most aspects of design, installation, maintenance, and (in some cases) ongoing operation of the installed system. The seller offers to the customer the ability to manage smoothly its own internal product management, sales, and service functions. In practice, this internal coordination often becomes the de facto responsibility of the relevant account managers, who must work across different product and service units in account planning, product and service development, and ongoing account activities. As one manager noted, "We sell tangible goods but the real product is our company itself. My job is to make my company transparent to the customer and the customer's requirements transparent to the relevant product and service units in my company."

Similar requirements, once the concern mainly of producers of custom-built capital equipment, now face firms in many other industrial markets. At telecommunications firms, network investments in the late 1980s and early 1990s allow development of many new combined voice-data services for various market segments. Conversely, software-defined network features allow commercial customers to track more easily telcom usage patterns in their organizations. This generates more product-sales-service coordination in order to develop and sell appropriate applications to these customers. For medical products firms, group-purchasing arrangements among hospitals and other health care customers have increased buyers' knowledge of comparative terms and conditions among potential suppliers. An executive explained how this affects suppliers' marketing programs:

> Basic services in our business now include on-time delivery, damage-free goods, and efficient order-inquiry routines. Value-added services include custom-designed product labeling, dedicated order-entry specialists, extended warranty plans, and new services in areas such as waste management and safety programs. Basic services get you in the door. But value-added services build the relationship and help to sustain our pricing structure. In turn, we've found that cost-effective development and provision of these services require a multifunctional approach among product, sales, and service personnel in different divisions.

In consumer markets, firms are providing more than the core product. The makers of Lexus and Saturn, and several European car manufacturers now essentially offer consumers an integrated personal transportation package, which includes (in contrast to traditional postsale warranties) emergency roadside service and (in contrast to traditional bargaining procedures at car dealers) the quality of the buying experience itself. Customer satisfaction ratings for Lexus and Saturn are up to 20 percentage points higher than those for traditional auto manufacturers that, since the days of Alfred P. Sloan, have unbundled the product component of the purchase from sales and service. The success of retailers like Benetton, The Gap, and Next is due in part to their ability to help consumers choose already color coordinated outfits. Their value proposition is an apparel package, in addition to clothing value as measured by price, fashion, and other traditional attributes. In turn, this consumer offering depends on a business system that integrates product sourcing, distribution logistics, and in-store merchandising capabilities.

One step up the distribution chain in consumer markets, the fight for shelf space at the retail level of the channel generates analogous marketing requirements. A salient example is the buyer-seller relationships established in recent years between Procter & Gamble (P&G) and certain retail chains. Through on-site account teams and on-line links between its factories and the retailers' stores, P&G has set up customized ordering systems and automated replenishment programs in many product categories. This approach has benefits for both retailer and manufacturer. For retailers, warehouse and back-room inventories can be reduced substantially (from a typical 30 days' worth of detergent, for instance, to as little as 2 days). Further, faster turns of less inventory often allow the retailer to re-order and generate sales before payment to the manufacturer is due, thus providing cash flows without additional working-capital allocations to finance the inventory—a significant buying criterion at many highly leveraged retailers. For manufacturers, such arrangements mean more predictable shipments (with consequent improvements in order accuracy and delivery scheduling), some reduction in promotional deals (which improves production scheduling), and more shelf space and merchandising support.

In these relationships, the manufacturer provides brands but also customized delivery, installation, ongoing information about shelf and merchandising support programs, and other pre- and postsale services. Consumer goods firms rarely use terms like "systems integration" in describing their marketing efforts. But customizing package size, delivery terms, promotions, in-store merchandising, and perhaps advertising for an important account or class of trade is an increasingly prevalent form of systems integration in consumer marketing. From the trade customer's point of view, these services are growing portions of the value-added by a supplier. For the supplier, closer product-sales-service linkages become more important as its offering in the market is a changing product-service-information mix that must reflect increasingly segmented opportunities.

MARKET FRAGMENTATION

Phrases like "micromarketing" and "mass customization" have become familiar themes in the management literature of recent years. Perhaps too familiar. Managers risk losing sight of what is competitively distinctive about these developments versus what is fundamentally old wine in new bottles.

What is *not* new is customer differences and niche marketing. In consumer markets, market segmentation is a truism because people who differ in terms of demographics (age and income), personal attitudes, or life styles are likely to purchase in different ways. In industrial markets, demographic dimensions (industry, company size, location), and situational factors, such as order size or the criticality of a component in the customer's production process, also generate important differences in purchase criteria. Effective marketers have long recognized that this diversity has important implications for patterns of product usage, service preferences, relative price sensitivity, and receptiveness to different types of marketing messages. For decades, product formulas for national brands of coffee, cereals, and other categories have been tailored to regional or ethnic tastes; product applications for industrial equipment have traditionally been tailored for the vertical markets that employ the same core product in different usages. Similarly, standard sales force plans for broad-line suppliers have long been adjusted to deal with a strong regional brand in consumer markets or a strong niche competitor in industrial markets.

What *is* new is the extent, and necessity, of such segmentation because of competitive factors and the tools now available for tracking differences among market groups. Customer heterogeneity may always have been latent in many consumer mass markets and industrial general-purpose markets. But the information search costs associated with locating these differences are now lower and, in many mature product categories, this information is worth more to marketers than in previous decades. Hence, information technology provides the means, and market maturity the motivation, for segmentation at levels of detail that increasingly approach the individual customer. Further, together these forces generate in many industries a self-fulfilling competitive dynamic that erodes traditional sources of competitive advantage.

Before the 1980s in the consumer packaged-goods business, for example, the major sources of product movement data were audits of warehouse withdrawals by participating retailers. Such information was gathered primarily by groups of field auditors who would visit a sample of stores and physically count product. They would return to the same outlets at a later date and repeat the process. By adding in records of retailer (not consumer) purchases between visits, measures of product movement were produced. This information was useful to marketers, but it was aggregated across many different trade and consumer categories and susceptible to important lag effects. The information was gathered every four weeks, and processing the audit reports took another four to six weeks before the data first became available to marketers.

By the mid-1980s, however, the diffusion of computerized retail point-of-sale (POS) systems capable of scanning universal product code (UPC) symbols dramatically altered the quantity, quality, and timeliness of information available. Store sales by UPC are sold by retailers to syndicated research firms that typically supplement this information with audits of in-store conditions as well as retailer and manufacturer advertising and promotion. This information can be used to prepare marketplace reports and analyses by product (UPC-level detail allows breakdown by category, brand, or brand size), mar-

Exhibit 1-1

Market Fragmentation: A Self-Fulfilling Competitive Dynamic

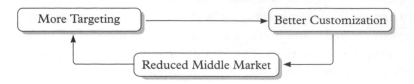

ket (chain, store, or class of trade), merchandising activity (impact of display, ads, extent of local distribution), time (of year or day—important information in many seasonal and impulse items), and other measures such as price point versus competing products.

This detailed information has uncovered many differences in buying behavior and purchase criteria by region, consumer group, class of trade, and account. Among other factors, micromarketing is a response to this information as companies seek to get closer to consumer and trade customers through more effective customization of their marketing programs. In 1994 Coca-Cola's marketing campaign in the United States involved 20 different ads for 20 markets in an effort to address different buying preferences and regional threats made visible by better consumer panel data. Pepsi's Frito-Lay unit, celebrated in *In Search of Excellence* for the meticulous nationwide consistency of its route-sales network and marketing programs, had, by the early 1990s, decentralized into multiple local marketing units in order to address what POS data indicated about the segmented threats and opportunities in its snack foods marketplace.

From a strategic viewpoint, it is important to note that such data are available to all members of the distribution channel and (as syndicated services) to all competitors within a product or retail category. Hence, intelligent use of such information has become a competitive necessity, further accelerating the demassification of markets. New retail formats serve a given segment, in turn prompting producers to tailor their programs by class of trade or individual key account.

The longer-term result is a self-fulfilling competitive dynamic (Exhibit 1-1), in which the increased ability to target customer groups leads to better customization not only of products and services but of vendors' marketing programs as well. Over time, companies are learning what products, services, and marketing tools work (and don't work) for a given segment. The success of these customized offerings reduces the size of the middle market. This, in turn, provides an incentive for growth-seeking firms to do *more* targeting and customization, further reducing the volume and profits available in the middle market.

When this dynamic begins in an industry, the companies usually at biggest risk are the larger established firms. Their installed base of customers typically resides in the shrinking middle market of traditional general-purpose products and services. During the past decade, we have already seen two prominent casualties of this dynamic in commercial and consumer markets: IBM and Sears. During the 1980s, both firms—conventionally acknowledged as "owners" of their middle market customers—were besieged by more and more specialized competitors whose marketing systems were geared to better customization of certain types of apparel, consumer durables, or information products and services. With more data about specific customer groups, the so-called category killers in retailing offered wider and deeper selection of certain goods, and stole market share and consumers from Sears. Value-added resellers and lower-cost microcomputer manufacturers focused on certain segments of the information systems value chain and eroded IBM's once-mighty dominance of the market. Both firms, meanwhile, were for years prisoners of their installed base and the information systems in their heretofore successful marketing. Individually, each competitor seemed small and its specialized segment of the market of only marginal interest to the established giant. In the aggregate, however, these competitors were part of a revolutionary fragmentation of the market and the dissolution of the traditional customer base for the historical leader in each industry.

During the next decade, we are likely to see an acceleration of this dynamic across more industries as the ability to track and understand customer differences increases exponentially. Information-processing costs are dropping dramatically: Intel's Pentium chip, introduced in 1993 and initially sold to OEMs at $1,000 per unit ($300 per unit by early 1995), provided the equivalent processing power that, a decade earlier, required the purchase of a multimillion dollar computer system. Yet, at current trends, it is estimated that in 1998 personal computers will be 65 times *more* powerful than the high-performance models available in 1988. Another estimate is that the cost of communicating a unit of information, taking into account not only the technology involved but its deployment as well, will have dropped by a factor of 100 between 1993 and 2001.[4] In effect, like electricity in the late nineteenth century, information technology is fast becoming embedded in the infrastructure of demand generation and demand fulfillment. As it does, more robust and user-friendly software, interactive media, new modeling techniques, and large-scale databases will make it possible to target customers even more precisely.

For product managers at consumer goods firms, this development means a significant change in their traditional perspective, which focused on a product at a national level and on developing consumer influence through mass-market vehicles such as network television advertising. Now, efforts focus on delivering communications and purchase incentives to targeted trade and consumer groups on a regional, store, or even household basis. For service personnel, this development means increased influence in marketing programs aimed at specific classes of trade and their particular packaging, delivery, and merchandising requirements. For sales managers, these programs often mean more complexities and responsibilities in their customer interactions, e.g., new account management requirements, the need to coordinate multiple sales and service personnel who call on different locations of the same account, and more responsibility for allocating effectively the promotions and other trade-oriented expenditures that now make up the largest component of marketing expenses at most consumer goods firms.

In short, because of these developments, the product, service, and sales functions at such firms have a greater need to work concurrently, while the sales force in particular has more influence on the shape as well as execution of brand-marketing programs. As a senior executive at a leading consumer goods firm noted,

To perform its job, the sales force currently uses marketing input, but increasingly needs marketing skills and marketing support. Conversely, marketing managers currently vie for sales force support in the execution of their brand programs, but increasingly need the local sales unit's input in the development of programs. Along with merchandising [service] personnel, they are organizationally separate but systemically interdependent as the weight and frequency of their joint decisions increase.

There are analogous developments in industrial markets, as commercial customers become more diverse in terms of vertical applications and geographical dispersion, yet more able (through their internal information systems) to coordinate purchasing requirements across heretofore separate buying locations. Industrial business increasingly crosses borders, both before and after the sale. This affects the coordination requirements in planning and implementation among product, field sales, and service groups. The prevalent use of multiple channels of distribution also raises coordination requirements at the industrial company. A manager at a telecommunications firm expressed a marketing reality common to many industrial businesses: "We can no longer target broad industry categories for our products. The value and profits no longer reside, for example, in 'financial services' applications, but in more specific applications aimed at discrete segments like commercial banks versus brokerage firms versus mutual funds companies versus community financial institutions, and so on."

These developments also affect broader organizational requirements. It is difficult to respond to market fragmentation on a centralized basis from headquarters. In the face of multiplying customer diversity, local field units in sales and service must become *better* informed about customer and channel requirements (as well as customers' and resellers' willingness to pay for or support a given application) than upper management or headquarters personnel can possibly be. But field personnel, responding to local conditions, are often less able to perceive and ensure wider scale economies and consistency in company dealings across segments. As one manager commented, "Our central marketing issue is simply stated and difficult to do: we need to decentralize and empower lower levels in the organization while maintaining a coordinated customer interface. This affects how we think about relations among our heretofore separate product, sales, and service units, and between these units and the rest of the organization."

SUPPLY CHAIN MANAGEMENT

"The product is what the product does": it is the total package of benefits customers receive when they make a purchase. As vendors' offerings become a product-service-information mix to an increasingly diverse customer base, buyer-seller relationships are inevitably affected. A major impact is the growing importance of supply-chain management abilities.

Sometimes referred to as "integrated distribution," "pro-listics" (the melding of procurement and logistics), or "time-based competition," the essential concept is this: a company improves its competitiveness by reducing the time it takes to provide customers with products and services. This involves optimizing information and product flows between buyer and seller at as many parts of the supply chain as possible, from the purchase of raw materials through order entry, physical distribution, after-sale service, and replenishment. Several factors make supply chain management more important in designing and implementing marketing activities.

A key factor, spurred by the emphasis on total quality in production, is a change in purchasing processes at many firms (Exhibit 1-2). Traditionally (in most U.S. and European companies) competitive bidding has dominated procurement. The buyer's primary objective was to minimize the prices of acquired goods and services by: (1) working with a large vendor base, both to ensure supply continuity and increase buyer power; (2) frequent shifts in the amount of business given to each supplier in order to limit supplier power and provide "discipline"; and (3) arm's-length, transaction-oriented relationships conducted through short-term (typically annual) contract renewals and rebidding. The crucial aspects of this model are the selection of a sufficient number of qualified vendors and the amount of volume awarded to each vendor. As Raymond Corey noted: "The buyer's primary objective is to have enough vendors to provide effective competition for his business but not more than would allow a meaningful

Exhibit 1-2

Impact of Supply Chain Management on Purchasing

Old Model ———→ New Model

Old Model	New Model
• Competitive Bidding • Price as key criterion in vendor selection	• Cost-in-Use Criteria • Acquisition costs • Possession costs • Usage costs
• Work with Large Vendor Base to Set Up Supply Competition/Increase Buyer Power	• Fewer Suppliers to Cut Monitoring Costs and Increase Quality/ Delivery Standards
• Shift Business Around among Vendors • Signal "discipline" and control over vendor base	• Longer-term Supply Relationships • Improve forecasting and production scheduling

sales potential to each vendor; there has to be a certain 'critical mass' of sales volume available to the vendor to induce low price quotations and to evoke high levels of service if awarded a contract."[5]

But the quality movement has forced a reconsideration of supplier relationships. Quality implies a focus on escalating standards, reducing reject rates and cycle time, and improving cash flow throughout an integrated procurement and production system. From this perspective, the cost and time involved in monitoring many suppliers of a component—largely hidden costs under the old model—are visible and significant. Also, suppliers judged primarily on price often do not focus on pulling substandard parts from the order or on increasing efficiencies along other dimensions of the exchange (delivery schedules). Hence, there has been a shift in many industries to a different model of procurement characterized by: (1) longer-term relationships with fewer suppliers; (2) close interaction among multiple functions (manufacturing, engineering, and logistics as well as sales and purchasing) at both buyer and seller, with suppliers often given the option of redesigning components or orders if warranted; and (3) supplier proximity to allow both rapid just-in-time delivery and to facilitate the

Figure 1-1

Adoption of New Model: Change in Number of Suppliers after Firm Adopted a Supplier Reduction Program

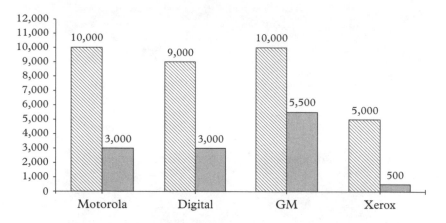

Source: John Emshwiller, "Suppliers Struggle to Improve Quality at Big Firms Slash Their Vendor Rolls," *The Wall Street Journal* (August 16, 1991), B1.

Note: Companies have different ways of counting their supplier base. Some count only direct manufacturing suppliers while others count service and support suppliers as well. Thus, while the numbers are not directly comparable between companies, the magnitude of reductions for a given company remains significant.

closer working relationships aimed at improving product and service quality along the supply chain.

As the data in Figure 1-1 indicate, this has meant a significant reduction in the number of suppliers utilized by major accounts in a variety of industries. Following supply-chain management programs, Xerox reduced the number of its suppliers by 90%, Motorola by 70%, Digital Equipment Corporation by 67%, and General Motors by 45%.[6] Other companies in these industries have followed suit: Ford reduced its vendor base by 45% after a supply chain overhaul during the late 1980s, Texas Instruments by 36%, and Allied-Signal Aerospace by 20%. Across industries, according to a survey conducted by the Center for Advanced Purchasing Studies, the average number of suppliers per procurement category declined by an average of 8% per year from 1988 to 1993. The remaining suppliers are typically those

Exhibit 1-3
Typical Components of Total Cost-in-Use

Acquisition Costs	+	Possession Costs	+	Usage Costs	=	Total Cost-in-Use
Price		Interest		Field Defects		
Paperwork		Storage		Training		
Shopping Time		Quality Control		User Labor		
Expediting		Taxes and Insurance		Product Longevity		
Mistakes in Order		Shrinkage and Obsolescence		Replacement		
Prepurchase Product Evaluation		General Internal Handling		Disposal		

willing and able to meet the supply chain requirements of this buyer-seller relationship. As one manager said, "You must not only build a better mousetrap, but also build a better path to your door, if you want customers to flock there."

For the vendor, a primary goal of such relationships is providing services that affect the cost-in-use and hence the value of doing business with that vendor. This is vital because, in this kind of purchasing, a supplier's value is its ability to improve the revenue potential of the customer, minus the total costs of doing business with that supplier. When a commercial customer purchases a product or service, that customer is always buying into various costs above and beyond the actual purchase price. In the past decade, just-in-time inventory management, activity-based costing procedures, and the benefits some firms have derived from electronic data interchange links with their suppliers have made managers more aware of (and more determined to manage) the below-the-line costs of their vendor relationships. For most companies, these cost-in-use components can be divided into three groups (Exhibit 1-3).

Acquisition costs include not only the selling price but also the paperwork and administrative costs of evaluating products, expediting orders, and correcting mistakes in shipments or delivery. Suppliers with lower prices but poor systems in other order-fulfillment areas entail higher acquisition costs for buyers. In consumer markets, for example, direct product-profit data have alerted retailers to the various product-acquisition costs associated with different suppliers, and have spurred a series of supply chain initiatives.

Possession costs involve financing, storage, inspection, relevant taxes and insurance, shrinkage, and other internal handling costs. For many products, possession costs are substantial and can equal or exceed total acquisition costs. The logistical expenses associated with many health care products typically make up 10–15% of a hospital's operating costs. Food manufacturers' storage and distribution costs were approximately 10% of sales in 1993 while their trade customers spent 3–5% of sales volume on these functions. Buyers and suppliers capable of just-in-time delivery reduce possession costs.

Usage costs are those associated with ongoing utilization of acquired products and services, including field service for repair or customization, internal training and labor costs of users, and (especially as environmental concerns and regulations increase) the costs of product disposal.

An emphasis on supply chain management ultimately aims to lower these costs and, hence, increase the vendor's ability to develop and sustain value-based pricing policies that reflect total systems costs and benefits for customers. For the vendor, implementation of this concept requires product-sales-service linkages along several dimensions.

1. Supply chain management is a multifunctional activity, affecting each element of the marketing mix. In product development, for instance, size and packaging are influenced by logistics costs, in turn, requiring closer coordination between physical distribution groups and product management. For salespeople, important components of customer service *are* the supply chain elements executed by these groups, requiring closer coordination of traditional sales and service activities. One example is sales forecasting: the essence of supply chain management is to reduce costs and optimize product flow throughout the firm's means of going to market. That puts greater pressure on the relative accuracy of forecasts. As one logistics executive noted, "When you look at sales forecasts, you can see that the

function most impacted is [physical] distribution. Inaccurate forecasts mean greater transportation, warehousing, and inventory carrying costs. So it makes sense that we be involved in administering the forecasts. I don't even think of them as forecasts anymore; it's a management planning tool."

More generally, these activities (and, equally important, the increased transparency of these activities to customers) make it necessary that product, sales, and service managers possess what one executive called "systems savvy": skills and tools in supply chain management that make them proficient in the systemwide implications of heretofore functionally driven decisions such as trade promotions, line extensions, or packaging or pricing changes. Quaker Oats Company now includes supply chain efficiencies (in addition to annual sales and/or operating profit performance) as a bonus criterion for nearly 400 managers across product, sales, and service areas.

2. Sales tasks change as supply chain investments seek to move the selling proposition from current transaction/price to longer-term operating value/cost-in-use. This increases required interactions between sales and service groups, on the one hand, and between sales and product management, on the other. This marketing strategy places great emphasis on profitably customizing service to buyers' operations. Yet, critical elements of customer service typically vary by type of customer and, for the same customer, across different phases of the order cycle and account relationship.[7] In most firms, product managers have the cost data, knowledge of planned product introductions, and other information necessary to customize profitably; salespeople have the local account knowledge necessary to know what specific customers actually do and don't value in each area of supply chain management.

As an example of the coordination dimensions involved, consider some of the supply chain activities relevant to different retail formats in a familiar and seemingly "simple" product category: laundry detergents. A packaged goods firm makes the distinctions noted in Exhibit 1-4 for a brand of detergent sold through multiple classes of trade. Note that these differences by customer group affect activities all along this firm's value chain, from the tasks of physical distribution, to the pricing and packaging decisions traditionally handled by brand

Exhibit 1-4

Supply Chain Requirements across Trade Channels: Laundry Products

Trade Segment	Handling	Delivery	Merchandising	Pricing
Club stores	Pallets/shoppable cases with sales-ready fixtures	Direct to store in regularly scheduled/large-order deliveries	Full-pallet displays	Lowest price per use/oz. on all shipments; c. 5% margins
Drug stores	Small cases	Frequent, small-order deliveries	Small displays; six-month lead time necessary for features	HABA = core business with high markups; our product = traffic builder
Convenience stores	Small cases/ on-shelf	To/through wholesaler warehouses	Driven by wholesaler's particular push program	Often a function of store location
Discount/mass merchandisers	Pallets that move well in high-storage system	Drop ship on JIT delivery schedules	Features often involve all brands at same time	Low margins on feature items; variety of everyday margins
Conventional grocery stores	Pallets that move well through system	Regional distribution centers	Display-oriented	Depending on chain and region, a variety of all above

managers, to the in-store shelving tasks performed by merchandising personnel. In the middle—and ultimately responsible for explaining and managing execution of these tasks to the trade buyer—is the salesperson. The senior sales executive for this product group emphasized that "Responding to these differences changes the role of a consumer-goods sales force. Whereas in the past we were often simply the dispatchers of increasingly big trade promotions, we now must understand the particular reseller's economics and operations, act as business managers, and optimize our firm's participation in sensible store marketing programs."

Similarly, in industrial markets, supply chain requirements often depend on the product's place in the commercial customers' production process and service resources. Understanding these differences and activating the relevant alignments along the vendor's supply chain become key aspects of the selling process. In turn, this changes the needed skills in sales, and places greater emphasis on sales-marketing integration.

3. These seemingly tactical changes in how goods and services are sold have strategic consequences. It is difficult for a single vendor to manage all of the many different elements in optimizing cost-in-use for an account or segment. Partnering with other members of the supply chain infrastructure is often economically necessary, and tends to increase the scale and complexity of multiple channel relationships and makes more marketing decisions contingent on the cooperation and abilities of more players throughout the distribution channel(s). For example, as one manager noted, "If you're moving toward shorter lead times, you have to make sure that your transportation vendors, for instance, understand your systems and requirements."

In effect, key elements of competitive strategy in many industries now involve rivalry between competing (and, often, overlapping) channel systems and not just between individual firms. Wal-Mart, for example, competes with other retailers in terms of its supply chain system, not only in terms of price and assortment in its stores. Indeed, Wal-Mart's supply-chain system is the *prerequisite* for its price and assortment advantage over many of its competitors. Northern Telecom supplies telecommunications equipment to different customer groups through very different distribution systems composed of differing channel partners. The result is a tailored logistics system for each segment that maintains the supplier's prices while lowering cost-in-use for each customer group.

These developments make the field's ability to manage such alliances a core marketing capability. But, in many companies, ongoing responsibility for such decisions has traditionally been lodged with lower-level distribution/warehouse managers or customer service managers, who are rarely in a position to monitor or manage the interrelationships outlined here. Similarly, field sales personnel in many companies deal with the consequences of supply chain arrangements, but often lack the broader information and incentives relevant to understanding and managing these systemwide links. One result is that the firm's channel management policies become fragmented or a rationale for maintaining the status quo.[8] Hence, actual implementation of supply-chain management concepts usually requires significant organizational change along three dimensions: relationships among product, sales, and service groups; what sources of information they possess and disseminate to each other; and how the selling process itself works and is evaluated.

PRODUCT LIFE CYCLES

A product's useful life (the period during which it functions before wearing out or before maintenance costs become excessive) is usually different from its economic life (the period during which a product is introduced, grows in sales volume, matures, and then declines in saleability because of technical obsolescence, better substitutes, or changed demand conditions). Product life cycles have traditionally been portrayed as the trajectory of an S-shaped curve, with the stages from introduction to maturity divided into evenly spaced time periods. Marketing scholars have pointed out that there is nothing inevitable about this pattern: the duration of life cycle stages varies greatly among industries and depends upon the level of a product category (TVs), a product form within the category (color TVs), or a brand in a particular form (RCA color TVs). Nonetheless, the paradigmatic product life-cycle curve (Figure 1-2) remains a useful heuristic for discussing the evolution of demand and competition in a marketplace.

Figure 1-2

Paradigmatic Product Life-Cycle Curve

· *Many Exceptions*
· *Not Inevitable*
· *But a Useful Heuristic*

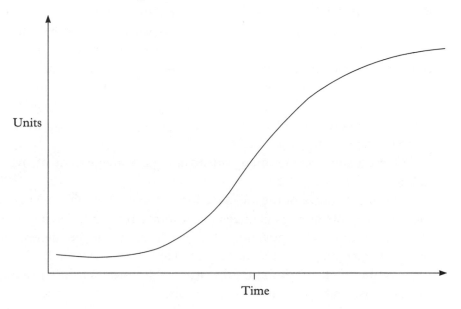

Changes in technology, the diffusion of scientific and technical information around the world, and the growing interdependence of national markets are accelerating product life cycles. Further, this compression in life cycle duration is not restricted to high-tech industries. Indeed, as process technology diffuses throughout industries and as microprocessors become embedded in many low-tech products, life cycles in categories like foodstuffs and consumer durables are compressed.[9] During the 1980s in U.S. food distribution, for example, new store size increased 47% (from an average of 27,200 square feet in 1981 to 40,000 in 1989) while the number of new items introduced annually by manufacturers increased nearly 800% (from about 1,000 in 1981 to more than 9,000 in 1989).[10] One study found that by 1990, buyers at supermarket chains were listening to about 12 presentations of new products weekly and rejecting about two-thirds of them.[11]

Nearly 50% of those surveyed had a policy of deleting one (or more) items for each new item accepted. As one marketing manager told me, "Shelf space is now the Khyber Pass in our industry [and] there is less time available for a product to demonstrate demand."

The market effects of shorter product life cycles typically reinforce the competitive dynamics discussed earlier. Advances in process technology or information systems that less expensively capture differences in purchase criteria among consumer groups reduce the cost differential between new customized goods and existing products in a category. As customers purchase more customized goods, they, in turn, reduce the market and shorten the life cycle for existing goods, further shrinking the cost differential and providing incentives for accelerated repetitions of the cycle.[12]

What do such developments mean for the management of marketing?

1. Over the course of the life cycle for a product or service, marketing requirements alter as changes in customer buying behavior shift the relative competitive advantage that results from a given alignment of marketing strategy and tactics. Such changes affect virtually all aspects of the marketing mix: the breadth of the product line, pricing policies, distribution intensity, the relevance of different promotional vehicles as well as service policies and enhancements.

Making the required changes more frequently, and at a faster pace, increases necessary information flows among product, sales, and service units. An executive at a computer firm said: "Until the 1980s, our business was like the traditional automobile business: five-year model changes. Product management utilized those time horizons for market research and relevant financial projections, and then worked to get other functions to buy into a product plan. [But] market changes now make such plans and forecasts obsolete way before the end date." At telecommunications firms, deregulation and the merging of voice and data technologies have a similar impact on traditional product life cycles, increasing the required interactions among product management and field sales and service units. Similarly, hospital cost-control legislation and new safety concerns have accelerated product life cycles for many types of medical equipment.

2. During its life cycle, moreover, the core product/service design

usually becomes standardized and therefore more easily imitable, new competitors enter, unit prices decline, traditional market segments become saturated, and customers themselves become more sophisticated and demanding. So that, even while total market volume may increase, the margins available to any one competitor are under more pressure as the life cycle moves from growth to maturity. As a consequence, the point in the life cycle at which a firm receives half of its profits from the product is earlier than the point at which it generates half the total revenue it eventually receives from the product. In a larger market with more competitors, moreover, the point at which the initial entrants generate half the total revenues from their offerings is earlier than the point at which they actually sell half of the units that will be sold in that marketplace.

An acceleration of this typical pattern has economic implications that, in abstract form, are outlined in Figure 1-3.[13] As product life cycles shorten, companies have less time to make money in the face of inevitable imitation, more product substitutes, and price pressures. Managing the introductory portion of the curve (the slope to $T_P^{1/2}$ in Figure 1-3) becomes crucial. Time is money in a world where the half-life of a product's total economic value is shortening: the longer it takes the firm to get up to speed in the implementation of its marketing programs, the shorter the window of opportunity to maximize cash flow, profitability, and shareholder value.

3. Shorter life cycles are both a cause and a consequence of more new product development. Innovation—in the form of new products and services and/or augmentation of existing products and services—is critical in this market environment. But for salespeople, new products mean learning about new technologies, establishing relationships with different decision makers in reseller or end-user organizations, using different buying processes and purchase criteria, seeking different sources of information and support from product managers and service personnel—in short, developing ways of selling and marketing often perceived as "alien" to established revenue-generation routines. For salespeople, moreover, new products usually mean developing these new skills while continuing to meet quotas and other short-term performance metrics. A common result is that the imperatives of the latter goal overshadow the longer-term and more risky

Figure 1-3
Economic Implications of Accelerated Product Life
Cycles

What Tends to Happen

- Standardization of Product/Service Design
- Saturation of Traditional Market Segments
- Sophistication of Customers/Resellers

More Competition, Imitation, and Price Pressures

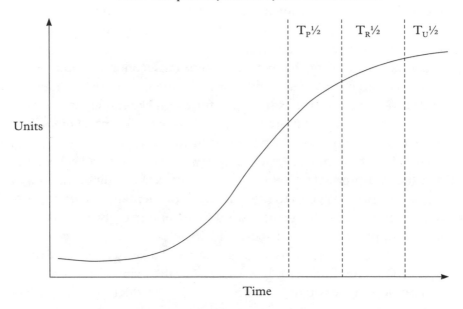

Key: $T_U^{1/2}$ = Time to ½ of total units sold
       $T_R^{1/2}$ = Time to ½ of total revenue received
       $T_P^{1/2}$ = Time to ½ of total profits received

demands of the former, moving sales attention to the familiar rather than the new.

One way to think about the challenge facing many firms is to consider the impact on "channel effectiveness," by which I mean the distribution channel's ability to achieve a critical mass of proficiency with the selling, service, and other key marketing tasks associated with a new product or market segment. For salespeople, this proficiency usually has at least two critical dimensions.

First, they must understand the new product and its potential applications—they must know what they are talking about. Maintaining this base level of knowledge becomes a bigger challenge as more new products are introduced and the offering itself more often involves a product-service-information package intended to optimize cost-in-use for customers.

Second, salespeople must take the risks inherent in dealing with a new product or service versus the established, familiar, "proven" items in their portfolio—they must be *comfortable,* as well as knowledgeable, in talking about the new product or service to their accounts. Without the requisite confort level, the sales channel will stay with the familiar and decreasingly profitable items.

To develop and maintain this knowledge and comfort requires that salespeople work more closely with product and service groups. Hence, even as the other factors discussed in this chapter increase the needed coordination among marketing groups, accelerated product life cycles decrease the time available for establishing and assimilating the necessary skills and linkages. An important measure of marketing efficiency and effectiveness—rarely captured in expense-to-revenue ratios and other common marketing metrics—is the ability to reduce the time required to reach a critical mass of channel effectiveness by accelerating the sales organization's learning curve. For many companies, as subsequent chapters indicate, doing this requires major changes within and between marketing, sales, and service units throughout the firm.

CONCLUSION

These changes in the business environment—which affect what is being sold, to whom it is sold, how it is sold, and under what competitive conditions it is sold—are important in themselves. Each has a significant impact on marketing requirements. Together, they have broader implications for many organizations.

Discussions of shorter product life cycles, market fragmentation, and other factors considered here usually emphasize how companies compete through faster product development, flexible manufacturing systems, or innovative supply arrangements. But little attention has been given to the aggregate impact of such developments on downstream marketing-sales-service activities, where responsibility for customer implementation of such initiatives resides.

Many firms in recent years, however, have realized that there is only limited utility in shortening product development cycles, improving quality, and sinking millions into interlinked manufacturing-distribution systems if, in its downstream activities, the company's marketing-sales-service system cannot handle (or, in some cases, actively resists) a greater variety of products and markets. The cumulative impact of the changes outlined here means unlearning old habits as well as developing new skills while continuing to meet quotas and other near-term goals. In turn, this often means rethinking traditional arrangements among the firm's product management, field sales, and customer service groups.

The next chapters in Part I focus on the traditional roles and responsibilities among these groups and the common organizational factors that affect planning and execution of their increasingly interdependent activities.

2

The Marketing Gearbox: Roles
and Responsibilities

■

AN executive at a consumer products firm described a common situation:

> Our marketing managers operate at a national level and with specific product orientations. They're not as familiar with regional or account differences. Meanwhile, Sales is driven by specific accounts, volume shipments, and trade deals. It's my observation that Marketing and Sales managers *do* talk to each other, but typically when it's clear that they won't hit their numbers. Then, interaction increases significantly.

A senior sales manager at the same firm described product managers as "ivory-tower headquarters theorists, unaware of field realities." A product manager described salespeople as "primarily interested in the deepest deal that moves the most product in the current quarter—regardless of the impact on profitability." Meanwhile, service personnel (in this case, delivery and in-store merchandising personnel) complained that their activities are constantly "disrupted by the ad hoc arrangements that increasingly characterize product sales interactions in a marketplace where trade customers are more powerful and demanding."

Why do such conflicts arise so often among marketing groups, who (as the general manager of this division repeatedly emphasized in speeches and memoranda) "should all be team players because they all work for the same company"? What factors affect their interactions and generate internal differences that have consequences in the marketplace?

In Chapter 1, I discussed developments that are altering marketing requirements in many industries and, in the process, transforming integration needs among product, sales, and service groups. Faced with accelerating change in the marketplace, companies are altering their organizational structures and systems. In practice, however, many of these reengineering initiatives proceed without the participation and perspectives of front-line marketing groups, and attempt to impose cookbook technical "fixes" on the variable features of customer contact activities. The result is too often major investments in technology with less-than-expected returns in customer satisfaction and profits: by one estimate, three out of four reengineering programs have fallen short of their goals.[1] Worse, the result can also be lasting damage to the field morale, expertise, and flexibility needed to deal effectively with new marketing requirements.

To avoid costly mistakes, managers must understand the rationale for the traditional alignment of customer contact activities in their firms. Companies are not clean slates and zero-based approaches to organization are rarely successful. Organizational history is important, and managers who don't understand this history are indeed repeating it: unwittingly "revolutionizing" their way full-circle to new constraints, rather than liberating joint capabilities. At the same time, they must also understand the daily implementation issues caused by market developments at those key interfaces where customer value is ultimately created or destroyed. For these reasons, this chapter and the next move from the external to the internal environment of firms.

This chapter first outlines the roles and responsibilities of product management, sales management, and customer service groups. My focus here is primarily on analyzing each group's day-to-day activities in order to answer fundamental (but often overlooked) questions:

- What do product managers actually *do*?
- What *is* a salesperson?
- What are the components of customer service and how does the

organization of service functions affect product and sales managers?

Next, I examine why the traditional alignment of roles and responsibilities often falters in the face of new integration requirements. Finally, I explain how the joint activities of these groups compose a core marketing "gearbox," whose synchronization is now vital for customer satisfaction, and focus on the need for firms to develop concurrent marketing capabilities.

A CONTINUUM OF ACTIVITIES

Terms like "product manager," "salesperson," and "customer service department" indicate a number of possible roles, depending on the structure and incentives of the marketing organization, the individuals within that organization, and the technical requirements and applications of the product or service offering. Together, however, these positions are usually responsible for a range of activities that move from market research and competitive analysis through the classic "four Ps" of the marketing mix (product policy, pricing, promotion, and place) to the provision of pre- and postsale services. One of the best available empirical studies, based on a sample of nearly 2,200 firms, found that entities labeled Product Marketing, Sales, and Service were, collectively, responsible for these activities in more than 80% of the firms surveyed.[2]

Exhibit 2-1 outlines tasks usually associated with product, sales, and service groups. In business schools and on organization charts, these tasks are usually grouped into separate buckets labeled "brand management" or "distribution." But as the exhibit suggests, these tasks are best viewed as a continuum of activities where one group has primary responsibility and oversight for tasks whose achievement is affected by the plans and actions of another group. Product managers' market research, for example, must be informed by the sales and service activities at accounts. Pricing plans must be implemented by salespeople, and net margins are affected by the type and cost of pre- and postsale services.

In short, product planning without sales and service input, or sales

Exhibit 2-1

**Representative Allocation of Responsibilities along a
Continuum of Activities**

Task Is Primary Responsibility of

Product Management . . . Sales Management . . . Customer Service

- Market Research
  - Competitive Analysis
    - Product Development
      - Product Positioning
        - Advertising/Consumer Communications
          - Packaging
            - Promotions
              - Pricing
                - Account Selection
                  - Personal Selling
                    - Channel Management
                      - Account Management
                        - Applications Development
                          - Physical Distribution
                            - Installation/
                              Merchandising
                              - After-sale
                                Service(s)

actions without product and service support, will be incomplete or contradictory. But in most firms, there is some differentiation of these activities so that specialized expertise in (and, equally important, accountability for) a subset of this continuum can be developed and maintained. What follows is a representative delineation of the roles and responsibilities of each group. This description will help specify the nature of their interdependencies and why, given the forces that are reshaping competition in the external environment, traditional internal alignments along the continuum are under stress.

PRODUCT MANAGEMENT

As an organizational form, product management is thought to have emerged in the United States in the 1920s and 1930s in firms such as DuPont, General Motors, and Procter & Gamble, although vesting individual managers with responsibility for a group of products had been common practice in many U.S. and European department stores since the late nineteenth century.[3] Whatever the precise genealogy, the defining characteristic of product management is a focus on creating strategies, making plans, and monitoring the budgets and programs for one or more branded products or services.

An important motive for establishing such positions is the desire to put one person or group in charge of making a business plan work for an assigned product line. In most companies, accountability and overall responsibility for managing the many tasks required to take a product to market are important. But these qualities are often ephemeral—especially as a company's product line grows larger, more complex, and more diverse. As a result, many top managers appreciate a structure in which "I know who to call if I have a question or problem concerning the marketing of a product line."

Another feature of these positions is the broad-based exposure that individuals receive as they progress through a product management career. In many companies, product management has traditionally been viewed as good preparation for a general management position. In consumer package-goods firms, for instance, product management has historically been a career path that MBAs, entering as assistant product managers, can follow to associate product manager, product manager, product group or category manager before obtaining appointment as general manager for a division.

As a response to market conditions, product management is often seen as one way of managing the differing marketing requirements when a firm has multiple products, many in different stages of their life cycles or with different technical or usage characteristics, flowing through the same distribution channels to a variety of customer groups. In these situations, somebody must manage ongoing trade-offs between maintaining efficient production, satisfying fluctuating demand in different market segments, and motivating the sales force to devote a fair share of its time to each product sold through a common channel. Most product managers try to maximize the return on investments in production assets that are allocated to their products and to maintain a competitive line in the face of changing demand and product substitutes at the end-user level of the marketplace.

Responsibilities

In terms of formal responsibilities, product management positions differ widely—from staff coordinator of assigned products to line manager with profit-and-loss responsibility. But the paradigmatic form of the role is probably that of the traditional brand manager in many consumer goods firms. The following job description, from one leading packaged-goods company, is representative:

> The Product Manager is the primary force behind all programs and recommendations affecting the Brand. The Product Manager assumes broad strategic responsibilities and serves as the company expert in all matters pertaining to the Brand. The Product Manager is responsible for initiating and leading business development programs, executing and controlling the marketing plan, coordinating all department/staff resources, developing strong working relationships with the ad agency, and training/developing the Brand group.

Noteworthy in this job description is the following. First, as the "company expert in all matters pertaining to the Brand," the product manager serves as an information center within the firm for brand-related inquiries and requests, and is expected to have expertise in the consumer research, product development, communications vehicles, and positioning options relevant to the product category. Exhibit 2-2 illustrates why these responsibilities make the role a central "hub of the wheel" one.

Second, while the product manager is designated "the primary force behind all programs and recommendations affecting the Brand," the role—in this firm as in most firms with product management organizations—does not include direct authority over other groups involved in "executing the marketing plan" for the brand. Hence, phrases like "developing strong working relationships" with other groups are used to describe important job realities. As a liaison for different groups over whom they rarely have line authority, product managers must build influence with managers in other areas in order to optimize the attention and resources devoted to their particular products. Indeed, in many companies, overt competition between

Exhibit 2-2
Role of the Product Manager

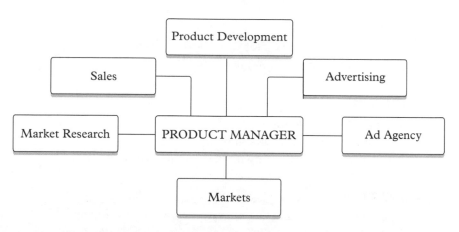

product managers for limited sales, manufacturing, or other resources is an accepted part of "how we do things around here." As studies have repeatedly demonstrated, up-to-date information, skills in persuasion, and a good knowledge of how company budgets are set and resources allocated become important aspects of the product manager's ability to perform.[4]

This aspect of the job is further underscored by the measurement systems of product management positions. In the consumer goods firm mentioned above, the key measures for evaluating product managers are (in order of importance): annual brand-profit contribution, market share, and dollar volume. As one brand manager at this firm noted, "These measures cut across the metrics of other functions such as manufacturing and sales, but are not exactly coincident with either." As a result, she spends much time "lobbying for support" across these functional boundaries. A colleague emphasized that "The way you sell an idea is what distinguishes a good product manager from a poor one. You gain authority by what you recommend rather than by what you decide."

Third, product management's "broad strategic responsibilities" typically mean a daily focus on certain analytical functions concerning the product category, primarily in relation to consumers and competitors. At this firm, for instance, brand managers' major activities are as follows:

- TRACK
  Volume and share trends for category and brand
  Pricing and distribution trends

- ANALYZE
  Consumer purchase patterns
  Consumer and trade promotions
  What-if scenarios regarding marketing-mix decisions

- DEVELOP
  Upcoming year's marketing plan with regard to: positioning of established products, new product introductions, and advertising, packaging, and promotions relevant to both groups of products

In industrial firms, the amount of time dedicated to each task and the allocation of responsibilities often vary from this consumer goods paradigm. Studies indicate that, in general, more time and responsibility for actual product design and development, and less for advertising and promotions, characterize industrial product-management positions.[5] This is not surprising, given the generally greater reliance on media advertising and trade promotions in the marketing budgets of consumer firms.

Industrial product managers also often have a more prominent role than consumer product managers in activities such as assessments of market size, reseller and competitive analyses, applications development, and sales forecasting. In turn, these differences reflect two other characteristics of industrial versus consumer marketing.

One is the derived nature of demand in most industrial markets and, hence, the greater need to track differing forms of product usage throughout the distribution channel. At a maker of industrial components, for example, sales forecasts involve tracking inventory levels and sales movement through distributors and end-user OEMs as well as direct sale accounts since, as one product manager explained, "Demand at our direct accounts will, sooner or later, be affected by sales patterns at their customers and by the inventory available at resellers in the distribution channels for my product."

The other relevant difference concerns the greater availability in most consumer goods markets of syndicated research services and other information sources which, over the years, have provided these firms with much data about market size, consumer behavior, and competitive shares in their product categories. In many industrial markets, by contrast, such data are not yet readily available and so industrial product managers must often do the research themselves.

Like consumer brand managers, however, industrial product managers are usually responsible for formulating product strategies and then achieving the product's contribution or P&L goals by working with other units in the firm. Further, one offshoot of recent market developments is that consumer brand-management positions are beginning to look more like industrial product-management positions. The need to deal with larger, better-informed, and more demanding retailers has caused a shift in the ways brand managers spend their time: more time and attention are being dedicated to product development, sales forecasting, and channel-related activities, and less to their traditional advertising and media-related activities.[6] A product manager at a medical equipment company provided a succinct summary of the job for both consumer and industrial product managers: "The central role is to shepherd a product through development to introduction. This means working with R&D, engineering, and manufacturing on product definition, and with sales and service on the marketing plan for the product."

FIELD SALES MANAGEMENT

While product management is primarily a twentieth-century phenomenon, selling and sales management have an ancient lineage. Homer wrote of Phoenician traders selling from door-to-door. Other evidence documents what we would recognize as a sales manager with a field sales force working for a daily wage and commissions tied to sales volume. Sea-faring traders in Greece and Rome were typically organized as groups, with a chief merchant in charge of individual peddlers who, on docking in a port, walked through a town and bargained with potential customers.[7]

In its modern organizational form, selling took shape as a distinct function in the last quarter of the nineteenth century, in response to the greatly expanded output of new mass-production industries. Periodic gluts of unsold goods in businesses whose cost structures were now dependent on high rates of throughput, and the consequent need to forecast sales volume with more direct end-user information, prompted manufacturers in many industries to limit their reliance on tiers of wholesalers, concentrate on market share, and develop their own in-house sales forces. By the turn of the century, as Alfred Chandler has documented, modern sales organizations, with offices based in major cities and run by a cadre of professional sales managers, were in place as part of "the integration of mass production with mass distribution."[8]

Today, selling jobs vary greatly, depending on the kind of product or service sold, the number of customers a salesperson is responsible for, and the ancillary requirements (e.g., relative extent of travel, technical knowledge required, number and types of people contacted during sales calls, and the pertinence of customer entertaining). But in most companies where personal selling is an important part of the marketing mix, the salesperson remains at the heart of the company's encounters with customers and so plays a key "boundary role" in the organization.[9] What's important here is not the particular jargon, but the daily reality that it points up. Understanding the issues in boundary roles is vital to managing in the new marketing environment.

Salespeople represent the buying organization to various groups in the seller's organization as well as their company and its capabilities to the customer. As a result, they must respond to the often conflicting rules, procedures, and requirements of both organizations (Exhibit 2-3). Internally, they must interact with sales managers, marketing people (including product managers), production and engineering personnel, credit personnel, service groups pertinent to their products and accounts, and so on. Externally, they must deal with purchasing managers and, depending on the product and buying process, a host of other purchase decision makers and decision influencers. Each of these internal and external groups has its own operating procedures

Exhibit 2-3
Boundary Role Person

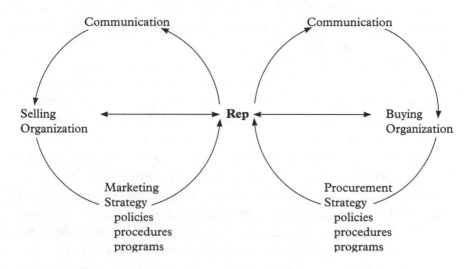

Communication   Communication

Selling ⟷ **Rep** ⟷ Buying
Organization   Organization

Marketing   Procurement
Strategy   Strategy
policies   policies
procedures   procedures
programs   programs

that it considers important. Yet, the essence of most selling jobs is to manage and, in practice, actively *negotiate* the boundary between the vendor and potential customers.

In performing this role, field sales reps are placed in situations that, in turn, help define sales managers' goals, problems, and opportunities. Most sales jobs require travel, some "cold calls" (calling on prospects who do not know the salesperson), time spent in nonselling activities with customer personnel, and providing information on accounts. Sales managers are paid to monitor, improve, and optimize the focus, quality, and expense of these activities.

Moreover, if a company has a marketing strategy (as opposed to a mere abstract set of goals), it should have policies, procedures, and programs that execute that strategy consistently. Otherwise, the selling company runs the risk of trying to be "all things to all people," which is a sure-fire recipe for marketing problems. But this means that the company's salespeople, most of whom are usually responsible for multiple accounts, must deal with a variety of buying policies, procedures, and programs through a single selling policy. The result is some tension between the needs of individual customers (the right side of Exhibit 2-3) and the requirements for efficiency in one or more aspects of the seller's organization (the left side of Exhibit 2-3). Note that the factors discussed in Chapter 1 have increased the diversity of customer requirements in many industries. Hence, this boundary role is becoming more complex, tougher to manage, and more susceptible to costly delays and lag effects.

For all these reasons, the salesperson is often the focus of conflict and controversy within the selling company, and is likely to feel a certain psychological as well as physical distance from the firm. Studies of boundary-role personnel have highlighted the internal organizational conflicts and stresses inherent in these positions, and some have even argued that many firms' sales policies and procedures can be seen as attempts to "keep the sales rep under control."[10]

More generally, the view of selling outlined here emphasizes that the objectives of sales management are to aid, focus, and evaluate the effective performance of a boundary role. It directs attention to how company policies, procedures, and programs do—or do not—encourage the kinds of behavior required for the effective performance of field salespeople, who, in most firms, are the initial and primary contact with potential sources of revenue.

Responsibilities

A key sales responsibility is demand generation which, as with the ancient Phoenician traders, still involves calling on current and prospective customers to stimulate interest in the product with the ultimate sale being made, perhaps, through resellers and/or another entity at the vendor organization. Demand generation can be usefully construed as involving at least five basic types of activities:

1. **Direct customer contact** such as searching out leads, call planning, and making sales presentations;
2. **Working with orders** by expediting shipments or modifying standard order terms and conditions for particular accounts;
3. **Servicing the product and/or account** by supervising installation, managing repairs and maintenance, training customer personnel, helping with inventory or shelf management, or setting up pertinent point-of-purchase materials such as displays;

4. **Working with resellers,** including establishing relationships with distributors or other intermediaries; selling, extending credit, and motivating resellers, and dealing with any conflicts or necessary links between direct and indirect sales channels; and

5. **Information management** in the form of soliciting and receiving feedback from customers and channel intermediaries, providing such information to superiors in the sales area (through call reports) and other areas (product management), and keeping abreast of relevant technical, usage, and competitive developments regarding products and accounts.

The relative amount of time spent on each activity differs among sales forces, depending on the market, the role of personal selling within the company's marketing strategy, and (as noted below) the division of responsibilities between sales and service personnel. Further, some companies divide these activities among different components of the sales force. For example, a key account manager might be responsible for direct customer contact, information management, and some elements of account service at the headquarters level of a trade or industrial customer while salespeople in geographic territories are responsible for these and other activities with buyers at individual stores or plants. Such a division of selling responsibilities is increasingly common as customers become more multilocational (and, multinational) in scope, and raises important coordination issues within the sales function itself (see Chapter 7).

Nonetheless, these five generic types of demand-generation activities are the core of sales responsibilities in most companies. One of the most extensive studies examined 800 firms and found that the frequency and time allocated to each class of activity differed by industry (the biggest differences were in the areas of working with orders and with resellers) but that, in varying degrees, all five types of activities were undertaken by almost all the salespeople surveyed.[11]

Field sales managers are usually responsible for recruiting and training sales personnel, assigning them to accounts or territories, motivating them, and evaluating their performance. Sales managers may also be responsible for direct customer contact and, often, some of the other activities noted above. Earlier in this chapter, I cited the job description of a product manager at a consumer goods firm. The same company described the responsibilities of sales management as follows:

- Track volume and share trends for category and key brands in assigned market areas and at specific retail accounts;
- Develop sales presentations for retail buyers/merchandisers, including business reviews;
- Evaluate field sales performance with regard to:
  Obtaining new item distribution
  Providing merchandising support
  Achieving optimal shelf positioning

Of note in this description is the following. First, while product management's focus is on end-user/consumer behavior in relation to specific brands, sales management's focus is on channel/trade behavior in specific market areas across the brands sold by the company. In this firm, each sales district generated $50–$70 million in business in 1991 (more than the sales volume of many of the company's brands) across hundreds of accounts in a variety of classes of trade. Hence, the consumer-driven plans developed by product managers were constantly being "translated" by sales managers in response to the needs of different trade customers. One result was a tug of war between the two groups. During the 1980s, for example, large multiple-unit grocery chains increasingly demanded that selling be done solely at the head office and that bulk deliveries be made by this manufacturer in specially packaged forms to central warehouses. Meanwhile, smaller retailers wanted deliveries as well as sales calls made to each of their outlets. Each type of retailer also had different perspectives on the role of suppliers' advertising and promotional support. Marketing plans and sales actions often diverged in the face of this customer heterogeneity. The problem was exacerbated when some large accounts wanted this supplier to act as a "partner," sharing the development and warehousing costs of new distribution systems while others looked for "the lowest-cost supplier" in each product category.

Second, whereas product management's compensation and reward structure in this firm has annual brand-profit contribution as the most important measure, sales management has a bonus structure based on unit volume and dollars sold of the firm's total product line. As discussed in the next chapter, differing measurement systems can generate conflicts in the implementation of different aspects of joint tasks.

Third, while product managers work within a hierarchy defined by increasing responsibilities for more products (or, in some firms, "more important" products), sales managers work within a hierarchy organized geographically and with increasing responsibilities for more or bigger accounts. At this consumer goods firm, for instance, the sales force was organized into four regions, each headed by a Regional Sales Director (RSD) responsible for managing both the firm's direct sales force and resellers (in this case, food brokers) and for attaining the region's distribution, merchandising, and volume goals. Reporting to RSDs were National Account Managers and Division Sales Managers (DSMs). DSMs, and the District Managers who reported to them, were responsible for direct and broker sales efforts in their territories and the attainment of annual and quarterly sales objectives. DSMs were also assigned at least one major account as their personal responsibility, and spent much time establishing and maintaining relationships with other key accounts in the division.

In industrial firms, the responsibilities of sales management often differ from this consumer goods example. In general, industrial sales forces have a bigger role in the order management and service dimensions of selling. In addition, while the role of consumer products sales forces has historically been one of facilitating distribution across classes of trade in support of the firm's brand strategies, industrial sales forces are more often specialized by product or customer industry.

For purposes of analyzing important sales tasks, however, the basic similarities outweigh the differences. As one observer aptly noted, "To understand whether a sales rep is functioning in a consumer or industrial sales organization, the central question is, Who is the customer? not, What is being sold?"[12] In the kinds of companies considered here, the sales force deals mostly with institutional customers (retailer, commercial account, or government entity) and, whether the products are consumer goods or industrial equipment or commercial services, is responsible for sales to a variety of accounts in different geographical areas across different classes of trade or vertical market segments.

CUSTOMER SERVICE

"Customer service" involves a variety of pre- and postsale support activities. Presale services aid the buyer in purchasing, and are aimed at closing the sale. Postsale services are designed to keep customers satisfied with the purchase, and are aimed at generating future or ancillary revenue opportunities for the vendor.

Regency Facsimile is a manufacturer and marketer of fax equipment.[13] Its customer service department provides presale support in the form of product demonstrations, trials, and needed technical support; and postsale support in the form of installation, end-user training, warranty repair, telephone support, and other services covered by maintenance contracts. Presale, the service department is often involved in pricing bids for large accounts. As the vice president of customer service explained: "At times we give 20% discounts for existing maintenance contracts to help get new sales of 30–40 machines." Postsale, the service department sells parts and supplies and, through phone support, provides leads to the company's sales reps. These leads typically account for 5–10% of new equipment sales annually.

Now, in more firms several factors make customer service salient in marketing strategies and sales efforts, chief among which are the following:

Product development and differentiation. The changes outlined in Chapter 1—in the nature of product offerings and the rapid diffusion of technical knowledge—make it increasingly difficult to maintain competitive advantage solely on the basis of product features and design. Fewer features are proprietary, and both customers and suppliers focus on service as a key differentiator. In many markets, a vendor's position as preferred supplier is often made or broken on its ability to identify and manage the service elements of product development and fulfillment.

Purchasing criteria. In many product categories, customers make their purchase decisions based, at least in part, on the quality of customer service provided. Perhaps more important, customers make re-purchase decisions based, in large part, on service dimensions. Surveys have found that seven of ten customers that switch from one company to a competitor cite poor service—not price or product quality—as the main reason. Conversely, estimates indicate that a 1% increase in service elements (in such measurable areas as reliability of delivery and time needed to fill orders) can increase sales by the same amount.[14] In many businesses, moreover, service personnel often have more frequent and continuous contact with customers than salespeople or product managers. As one executive noted, "Our service people are constantly on the customers' premises and can be the early-warning system at accounts—a role that becomes more important as replacement orders become a bigger part of spending in our industry."

Selling process. As at Regency Facsimile, customer service often plays a role in pricing proposals and lead generation. Service personnel can also help sales by enlarging and redefining the purchase decision-making unit at accounts. A sales executive at a medical equipment supplier noted that, "Unless accompanied by our technical support personnel, our salespeople would never get past our accounts' purchasing agents to the end users, who are less price-sensitive because they care passionately about the quality, up-time, and support of the equipment they use. This often redefines the sale: from price to the quality of the potential vendor."

Applications development. Service personnel are also often instrumental in identifying new applications for products and responding to product substitutes. During the 1980s, Inland Steel Company established sales service teams to work with customers in the design, development, and prototyping of automobiles, major appliances, and other traditional steel products. The target of these teams is customers' advanced engineering groups, not their manufacturing engineers or purchasing personnel. An Inland executive explained:

> Automobile companies, our largest market, were downsizing their cars, looking to replace steel with substitute materials such as plastics and aluminum, and shopping the world for the lowest cost steel supplies. We wanted to increase our customers' technical knowledge of

the wide variety of steel's potential uses and applications. We also wanted to become part of the new product design process early enough to develop "new" steels to meet performance needs our current products couldn't meet.[15]

Monsanto's nylon fiber division places a similar emphasis on sales service teams for its major customers. An executive noted that "When customers become dependent on your expertise, then you begin to build not on problems but on opportunities."

Cash flow and profits. Service revenues and margins are often more stable than other income statement components. Many products require maintenance in good times and bad. Customers may postpone purchase of a new machine during a recession or budget crunch, but are less likely to postpone service of existing equipment. Hence, as the installed base increases, service revenues increase. By 1990, for example, maintenance fees accounted for $7.4 billion of IBM's revenues and nearly 25% of Digital Equipment Corporation's total sales. In both cases, gross margins on maintenance services were higher than for the firms' increasingly price-pressured hardware lines. Similar economics hold for many telecommunications, office equipment, and machinery suppliers where service contracts have provided (in some cases) more than 50% of the firm's profits.

Customer expectations. Buyers appear to be demanding higher levels of service support in many industrial and consumer product categories. This may be the result of the general emphasis on quality during the past decade as well as the value of fast, reliable service to more dual-earner, time-constrained households. It is also a function of the information now available to both consumers and commercial customers for comparing product features and service performance in many categories.

These factors create the need for more joint activities among service, sales, and product groups. Field salespeople must work more often with service personnel in planning and executing account management activities. Conversely, service personnel need more knowledge about product plans, sales strategies, the formal and informal terms and conditions of the sale, and ongoing account information.

Responsibilities

Common presale service activities include product demonstrations, applications development or customized support, and, perhaps, financing services. Common postsale services include installation, training to enable end-customers or resellers to understand and use the product, field engineering or other product maintenance and repair activities, warranty service, and perhaps shelf or inventory management services. Especially for technically complex products, these pre- and postsale support activities are often divided among different service units—e.g., applications engineers for presale support, field service units for maintenance and repair, and telephone support staff for ongoing inquiries and problem resolution.

A computer firm outlines the responsibilities of its customer services personnel as follows:

1. Installation and deinstallation: the service associated with installation, removal, and relocation of equipment;
2. Maintenance and repair: field maintenance of the installed equipment base;
3. Training: training of operators and users in the operation and application of equipment;
4. Software and procedures support: providing software programs, procedures, and supporting services; and
5. Parts and supplies: providing spare parts and other related assets as well as consumable supplies.

In addition to these primary activities, service personnel at this firm are also involved in the customization and sale of networks, data maintenance centers, and other integrated computer systems.

The industrial salesperson often helps plan and coordinate these services for an account. This can involve working with people in production, distribution, product engineering, and finance as well as with the firm's customer service personnel. For many industrial products, moreover, these service elements must be coordinated with independent distributors as well as between the vendor's own sales and service units.

An example is John Deere's Industrial Equipment Division, which markets earth-moving equipment to contractors through a distribution network of about 400 dealers. Coordinated sales and service to resellers and end-customers are crucial, since a key competitive dimension in this business is minimizing customers' downtime expenses through fast field service and easy availability of spare parts. For contractors, the out-of-pocket costs of a tractor failure can be $500–$1,000 per hour; for a farmer with equipment problems during planting or harvesting seasons, the costs can be even higher. Deere organizes its marketing effort by having its sales managers work with Area Managers for Product Support (AMPS) in its customer service unit. Both sales and service are responsible for customer satisfaction at Deere's dealers, with the AMPS responsible for technical support, product training, repairs, point-of-sale support, and inventory management, including expediting of delivery and other supply chain services. As one Deere manager emphasized, "Our customers' problems and concerns are not usually all technical service or all sales related. So we need close cooperation between the sales rep and the service rep because, to the customer, they're all working for the same company."

Comparable services are important in maintaining shelf space and display support for consumer goods sold through retailers. Here, key service elements involve product merchandising at the point-of-sale. These activities are the responsibility of the firm's sales force and/or merchandising personnel at the vendor or its distributors. Earlier, I cited the job descriptions of brand and sales managers at a consumer goods firm, where developing broad merchandising strategies for each product was the responsibility of brand managers. Implementation of merchandising programs at trade accounts, however, was handled by merchandising personnel in its branch offices and at the independent brokers, who also sell this firm's products. The company's sales manual described their responsibilities as follows:

> Store interest in our products is high because of the strong marketing support that results in high consumer take-away. [But] in our business, the brands merchandised most effectively enjoy the greatest sales. In-store merchandising includes: placing items where consum-

ers can find them easily and be stimulated to buy them; having items available at all the right times and especially during active advertising and promotion periods; having the right quantities to satisfy demand and prevent out-of-stocks; providing promotional support with display and point-of-sale materials.

An important factor affecting interactions between service personnel and the firm's product and sales groups is the service unit's status as a cost or profit center. In some companies, customer service is part of the sales organization at the area or branch level, or it may report to product management through a product/applications engineering group. In such instances, customer service is usually a cost center and considered an expense to be allocated to the individual area, branch, or product unit. Some firms which organize service in this manner use annual performance plans and budgets to staff service groups, but most simply set service budgets on the basis of projected company-wide sales volumes. These service costs are then allocated to user units on a formula basis such as a percentage of direct labor dollars, head-count, or percentage of company sales. In practice, service groups often have an incentive to spend their budgets each year and, during the relevant budgeting cycle, user units pay a fixed amount, regardless of how much they actually utilize the service groups.

In many other businesses, however, scale and scope economies in customer service (especially field repair services) dictate that core service resources be managed at organizational levels broader than the individual product, account, or sales territory. Service is then a separate business unit and often a profit center that may also sell complementary products, supplies, and maintenance contracts. The service unit is expected to recover its operating costs by billing product and sales units directly for services provided. Some firms use this charge-back system for service while offering user units the option of outsourcing for specific product or sales support services. When organized as a profit center, customer service has a dual mission: customer satisfaction *and* profit maximization of the revenue-generating activities it manages.

In both situations, however, efficiencies often require that field service resources be deployed differently than sales resources. In many companies, customer service demands the allocation of three scarce resources: service engineers, parts and supplies, and technical knowledge and data. Further, while selling is usually an activity that occurs throughout the year, the demands on service resources are harder to predict and often come in spurts (e.g., after a new product introduction or following unexpected weather conditions). Thus, efficient utilization of expensive service resources requires a certain critical mass of customers. As a result, while the firm's sales personnel may be dedicated to a select group of accounts, service personnel are often spread over a larger number of accounts.

MARKETING INTERDEPENDENCIES AND MARKET DEVELOPMENTS

Inherent in these product, sales, and service roles are differences and interdependencies that must be managed for marketing effectiveness.

Exhibit 2-4 summarizes the traditional roles and responsibilities of each group. Product management typically operates across geographical territories, with specific brand or program responsibilities. Field sales usually operates within geographical territories or vertical markets, but with specific account assignments. Customer service most often operates within geographical territories, but with responsibilities that cut across multiple product lines and accounts. Given its formal responsibilities, each unit has a different focus on the marketplace: product management tends to view developments in terms of assigned products and end-user markets; sales in terms of its geographic or vertical markets and specific accounts; service in terms of multiple accounts and product lines. Hence, each group has a different window on the world.

Also inherent in these roles is the interlinked nature of their responsibilities, and especially those at the product sales and sales service interfaces. As noted (cf. Exhibit 2-1), each unit is responsible for different aspects of the continuum of activities that impact customers. The need to understand evolving product plans and their place in the firm's marketing strategy makes sales effectiveness dependent on product management's expertise. Conversely, the experience gained by salespeople during their daily interactions with current and pro-

Exhibit 2-4

Traditional Roles and Responsibilities

Product Management	Field Sales	Customer Service
Organization of Roles		
Operates across geographical territories, with specific product responsibilities	Operates within geographical territories, with specific account assignments and responsibilities	Operates within geographical territories, with multiple product and account responsibilities
Allocation of Marketing Responsibilities		

Market Research
Analysis
Strategy
Positioning
End-User/Consumer
  Communications
	Customer Contact
	Order Management
	Account Management
	Channel Management
	Information Feedback
		Applications
		Demonstrations
		Logistics
		Installation
		After-sale
		  Service

Window on the World		
Product / Market	Market / Accounts	Accounts / Products

spective customers is among the most valuable sources of market knowledge available to product management. Service requirements are generated as the output of sales activities while sales success is increasingly tied to the provision of customized service.

Exhibit 2-5 outlines these common interdependencies among product, sales, and service groups and the kinds of synchronous information flows that are important. To do their jobs effectively, product managers need certain kinds of information from salespeople. At a minimum, this includes sales forecasts, customer feedback about product performance and product needs, and ongoing market infor-

Exhibit 2-5

Typical Interdependencies at Sales Interfaces

Product Management   **Field Sales**   **Customer Service**

(From Product Management to Field Sales)   (From Field Sales to Customer Service)

Overall marketing strategies and plans	Overall sales strategies and plans
Product information and training	Account-specific goals and plans
Market research data and analysis	Formal sales terms and conditions
Product positioning	Informal promises made to customer
• vs. competing products	during the selling process
• vs. product substitutes	Account information relevant to
Advertising and promotion goals and schedules	• applications development
Product literature, displays, etc.	• after-sale service
Special pricing analyses and guidelines	
Contracts, proposals, presentation support	
Product customization support and resources	

(From Field Sales to Product Management)   (From Customer Service to Field Sales)

Sales forecasts and results	Presale service support
Customer feedback re	• demonstrations
• current products	• applications
• new products vs. customer needs	• order fulfillment
Applications suggestions	• installation
• buying behavior	
• competitive activity	Postsale service support
Reseller activities, by segment	• customer training and education
Promotion execution and feedback	• maintenance and repair
	• warranty services
	• merchandising support/execution

mation concerning buying behavior and competition. In turn, salespeople need ongoing information concerning marketing strategies and plans, available research data, product literature, and (in most firms) pricing parameters from product management.

At the sales service interface, customer service groups need accurate information about selling strategies and tactics, account-specific goals, and both the formal and informal "promises" made by salespeople during the selling cycle. For their part, salespeople require from customer service information and support in the array of pre- and postsale activities discussed earlier. When this two-way flow is missing or delayed, the results are costly. At a supplier of equipment to the print industry, for example, an analysis of the costs of serving customers revealed that more than a third of service personnel's time was spent attempting to get the installed machinery to do what the salesperson had promised. Conversely, a telecommunications firm in my study lost a major sale to a large chemical company. Of eight people responsible for the customer's purchase decision, only two had contact with the supplier's sales team. Yet, during the selling cycle, the customer was contacted by more than a dozen people from the supplier's service department. But service personnel were unaware that an upgrade of the network was being negotiated, and their own initiatives during routine maintenance tended to subvert the proposal being put forward by the supplier's sales team.

The market developments discussed in Chapter 1 make the timely exchange of this information even more important. But the traditional alignment of roles and responsibilities makes it difficult to achieve the required depth and speed of exchange. Exhibits 2-6 and 2-7 help illustrate why.

Ultimately, companies are in the business of translating their product and service capabilities into solutions to customers' problems and opportunities. Doing this in the traditional organization involves a series of sequential "bucket brigades" (Exhibit 2-6), in which product marketing plans are executed by sales and then by service groups. In this alignment, coordination of these groups is important. But coordination involves a series of sales planning and promotion scheduling efforts aimed at ensuring that the field doers in fact do, some time in the future, what the marketing strategists have planned some time in the past.

This model now often falters because market developments are changing interaction requirements between these groups. There is a domino effect in the market factors discussed in Chapter 1 (Exhibit 2-7). These factors place more emphasis on the firm's ability to customize product service packages for more diverse customer groups. This places more value on the ability to generate and maintain timely segment- and account-specific knowledge throughout the organization. In turn, this places new requirements on field sales and service since, in most firms, this is where responsibility for customer access

Exhibit 2-6

Sequential Bucket Brigades

- Long Lead Times
- Multiple Interpretations
- Features vs. Benefits

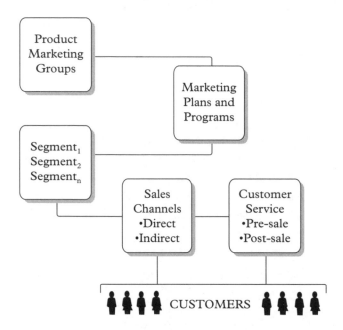

Exhibit 2-7

Impact of New Marketing Requirements on Field Units

- Customized Product-Service Offerings
- Segment-specific/Account-specific Knowledge
- Better Customer Access and Information Exchange

Impact on Field Sales and Service Systems

- New analytical requirements
- New communication requirements
- New implementation tasks

and information exchange primarily lies. These field units have new analytical requirements, because of the need to gather and interpret more information about customers; they have new internal communication requirements because of the need to get this local information back to product and planning groups quickly; and they have new task requirements in their own traditional domains because of the need to take into account broader supply-chain and cost-in-use criteria during the sales and service process.

The result is increasing stress on the traditional bucket-brigade approach to managing product-sales-service linkages. Traditionally, as Exhibit 2-6 illustrates, product management has been the genesis and arbiter of marketing information flows in most companies. Sales and service tasks were highly influenced by product managers' interpretations of market data and their resource allocation negotiations with R&D and manufacturing units in the firm. But in the new marketing environment, local field knowledge from sales and service groups must inform strategy in real time. Their specific knowledge of more diverse and rapidly changing customer needs must be upgraded and then integrated with the broader resource-allocation perspectives of product groups. Also, field units now work in an environment where marketing plans and programs must be adapted to multiple market segments, distributed through multiple channels, and sold as solutions that impact customers *and* their customers' customers.

The traditional alignment of roles generates certain costs in this competitive environment: long lead times in markets where first-mover advantages are more important; multiple interpretations of individual customer needs (and the potential for customer confusion and dissatisfaction) as the marketing process moves along this chain; and, because product features are naturally more tangible and capable of being measured when disagreements arise, an emphasis on product features rather than the broader benefits in the product-service-information package increasingly demanded by customers.

CONCLUSION: THE MARKETING GEARBOX

This chapter's discussion of common formal roles and responsibilities among product, sales, and service units points to a misfit. Shorter

Figure 2-1
The Marketing Gearbox

Need for "concurrent marketing" as customer value
moves from specific product features to a business
solution based on a product-service-information mix

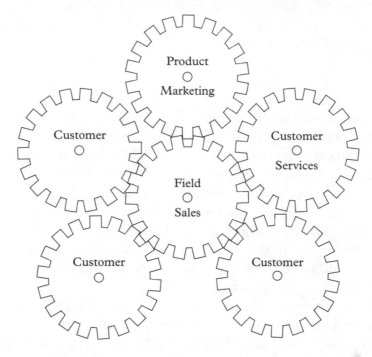

product life cycles and other market factors leave less time for iterations of the sequential process in the traditional alignment of marketing responsibilities. The result is more instances where the bucket-brigade marketing organization reverts to reactive firefighting—developing and executing plans and programs relevant to a previous stage of competition.

More firms now need structures, systems, and processes that encourage better concurrent marketing among the groups that must interact more often, more quickly, and in more depth. For this reason, it is useful to envision the interfaces between these groups as a set of gears (Figure 2-1). This metaphor underscores both the coordination and integration requirements of firms in the new marketing environment. It emphasizes the mutual dependencies among product, sales, and service units and how their joint activities are now central to most customer contact efforts. It also directs attention to organizational factors, beyond formal roles and responsibilities, that affect the behavior of people who must manage these interdependencies. Those wider organizational factors are the focus of the next chapter.

3

Marketing Dialects

■

A few years ago, a division of a medical products firm held an off-site meeting to discuss strategy and implementation in a changing health-care environment. Senior sales and marketing managers were present, as was an outside facilitator who led a discussion of ways to improve organizational effectiveness. The facilitator encouraged participants to list their perceptions of key issues facing the division. The blackboard was soon filled with two lists.

Salespeople say:

- "Marketing people do not spend enough time in the field. They don't take specific customer complaints seriously enough. Marketing needs to establish a system for better field communications."

Marketing people say:

- "Salespeople are always asking for information that they have already received. We spend much effort gathering and writing up product and competitive information, send out that information, and reps call a week later for the same information. . . . This takes time away from other important tasks we have."

- "Marketing should be more demanding with R&D and manufacturing to alter product designs and production schedules."

- "Biggest frustration to our sales reps is lack of timely information."

- "Sales reps' compensation should not be penalized for price erosion . . . that's a product issue out of our control."

- "We are underresourced: too many sales chiefs and not enough implementation people."

- "Our success depends on fulfilling customer expectations for tomorrow, not just today."

- "Sales is happy to criticize, rather than accept responsibility and suggest constructive improvements."

In an increasingly competitive environment, some of these comments were undoubtedly a by-product of a working relationship between headquarters product-marketing managers (each with profit-and-loss responsibility for assigned products) and geographically organized sales managers whose bonuses (about 30% of their total compensation) were primarily tied to regional sales volume. But the comments also reflect the changing nature of their tasks. Salespeople in this firm need more information, more often, from more marketing managers as their tasks involve more semicustomized product-service packages. Conversely, marketing's complaints about "too many chiefs and not enough implementation people" reflect a situation where marketing programs require product managers to interact with more functional areas (especially field sales and service), even as cost-reduction pressures put a lid on staff support resources. Also, while sales generates more customized orders and complains about marketing's seeming inability to alter product designs and production schedules in a "timely" manner, marketing managers respond that "our division now has highly automated manufacturing operations, making design or other product changes a complex and expensive process." Hence, the marketing department in this company rightly evaluated these requests with more than sales' account-specific requirements in mind.

Chapter 2 indicated how formal roles and responsibilities distinguish product, sales, and service units in many firms. This chapter moves beyond formal organization to consider other factors that affect the daily interactions between these groups:

- differences in orientation and time horizons that affect each unit's alignment of priorities or *hierarchies of attention;*
- *measurement systems* that help enforce these priorities; and
- *information flows* that affect the types and roles of data tracked by each unit, and the measurements that influence each unit's priorities and definition of "success."

This chapter discusses how these factors often result in "marketing dialects"—differences in how each unit hears, interprets, and articulates the voice of the customer.

These factors also expand the image of the marketing gearbox introduced in Chapter 2. Gears have two main uses: to increase the power of an engine and/or to increase its speed. In electromechanical terminology, "work" is the amount of weight moved times the distance and speed the weight is moved. In organizations, efficiency within product, sales, and service units—the power of each gear—requires internal coherence among the factors discussed here. But their interaction across these units often impedes effective implementation of marketing programs—the drive or speed of the gearbox—because the consequent grinding can lead to vicious circles or "competency traps"—increased spinning of each unit's particular procedures, rather than mutually reinforcing coherence at the customer interface.

It would be a mistake, however, to assume (as many current approaches to teamwork do) that the goal is to eliminate these specialties. These differences in part reflect the necessary expertise for increasingly complex, and specialized, marketing tasks. Some group in the organization must develop and maintain the in-depth knowledge required to bring a product through development to introduction. Moreover, as the product becomes a customized product-service-information mix, the knowledge required becomes even more specialized. Similarly, one person, or group, must know everything about buying processes, competitive developments, and decision makers at specific accounts. Further, this account knowledge must be kept up-to-date and reflect evolving field realities. Both are full-time jobs that require different types of accumulated expertise. But in an effort to make "everybody responsible for customer satisfaction," too many companies are unwittingly diluting the specialized knowledge needed to compete in a faster-changing, information-intensive marketplace.

HIERARCHIES OF ATTENTION

Most companies serve multiple market segments and pursue a range of product market strategies. One of their key concerns is the need to balance operating efficiencies against market focus. Operating requirements and the need to gain scale economies in product development, advertising, selling, and service generate pressures to group product programs and market segments for planning and management purposes. But to the extent that such groupings overlook (or treat as secondary) differences among these segments, the firm is less likely to be responsive to specific customers and segment opportunities. The challenge in organizing marketing efforts is to "develop and execute different strategies without losing sharpness of focus in each of its markets."[1]

The common allocation of responsibilities discussed in Chapter 2 reflects these multiple requirements, with product marketing focused on product programs (and perhaps applications programs aimed at expanding the market(s) for assigned products), field sales on accounts in geographical or vertical markets, and customer service on accounts and products necessitating pre- and postsale efforts. But as Exhibit 3-1 indicates, these marketing groups differ in terms of time horizons, key performance criteria, and information flows.

The differences are, in themselves, neither good nor bad. Especially in fast-changing markets, the differences can provide a valuable peripheral view for the firm as well as information on multidimensional customer realities. But problems often arise because of conflicting priorities, particularly in terms of (1) the orientation of each

Exhibit 3-1
Typical Differences between Marketing Groups

Product Management	Field Sales	Customer Service
Roles and Responsibilities		
Operates across geographical territories with specific product responsibilities	Operates within geographical territories, with specific account assignments	Operates within geographical territories, with multiple product/account assignments
Time Horizons Driven by		
• Product development and introduction cycles • Internal planning and budgeting processes	• Selling cycles at multiple accounts • External buying processes	• Product installation/ maintenance cycles • Field service processes
Key Performance Criteria		
Measures based on profit-and-loss and market share metrics	Measures based primarily on annual, quarterly, or monthly sales volume	Measures vary, but typically include "customer satisfaction" and cost efficiencies
Information Flows		
Data priorities Aggregate data about products and markets (defined in terms of user segments)	**Data priorities** Dissaggregated data about geographical markets, specific accounts, and resellers	**Data priorities** Dissaggregated data about product usage at accounts
Key data role Makes compatibility with internal planning and budgeting categories a criterion of useful information	**Key data role** Makes compatibility with external buyers' categories important; "timely" data as a function of varied selling cycles at assigned accounts	**Key data role** Makes compatibility with relevant technical vocabularies a criterion of useful information
Information systems Often incompatible with sales and service systems	**Information systems** Often incompatible with product and service systems	**Information systems** Often incompatible with product and sales systems

group's attention and effort, and (2) the time frames and resource allocation patterns that flow from these priorities.

We can consider these issues as differences in each unit's hierarchy of attention. By this, I mean differences in what each group considers as fundamental to "good marketing," what it takes for granted as part of its daily work versus what it considers as discretionary in allocating its limited attention and effort.[2]

Differences in Orientation and Time Horizons

Consider the situation I encountered at a telecommunications firm.

One product group ran an introductory blitz to generate field enthusiasm for its line, and was successful in exceeding target goals. But another product manager noted that, because of this campaign, "I just can't compete for our field sales reps' attention." She therefore redirected her efforts toward telemarketing and reseller channels—distribution components which were not part of her original business plan and where channel support required expensive redesign of many product features. Meanwhile, even though acknowledging the positive impact of the blitz campaign on their reps' efforts, branch managers were worried about its impact on their ability to make the targets on the other products they sold. Similarly, service managers found that the blitz had motivated reps to sell the product to a wider variety of accounts—generating many unexpected service demands.

This example illustrates a common situation at companies: product managers' concern for the well-being of their assigned products versus sales' and service's responsibilities for multiple products at multiple accounts. The difference is exacerbated in many firms by a managerial tradition that encourages interbrand competition for sales attention and resources. The result is often explicit conflict between the groups, in part about what constitutes "success." At one level, everyone may agree that success is ultimately defined by "the customer." But "the" customer is perceived differently by different marketing groups. Hence, various customer-contact activities, which must be coordinated, are accorded different priorities and resources by each group.

In consumer goods markets, an example is the role and evaluation of product promotions. During the 1980s at package goods firms, trade promotion spending increased steadily, claiming about 52 cents of the typical company's marketing dollar by 1990.[3] The usual budgeting process in these firms designates this expenditure by brand group. For product managers, the role of trade promotions is to increase or maintain shelf space and merchandising support in retail channels versus that of competing brands. Success depends on the sales force's ability to sell the deal to retailers as well as manage promised shelf and merchandising support. But as a sales manager at one firm candidly told me, "The reality is that, with more of our brands and competing brands running promotions, we can only really execute and monitor a few significant promotions in any given quarter. I view success as effective delivery of two-out-of-three promotions." In most cases, the promotions receiving field attention were those for the firm's biggest and well-established brands, at the expense of newer, smaller brands.

Product, sales, and service units also differ in terms of time horizons. An industrial product manager explained the time horizons relevant to her core responsibilities: "In our business, crucial product decisions must be made years before introduction, and the consequences of those decisions linger for years afterward. But customers rarely look beyond a one- to three-year time horizon in assessing their needs; their budgeting procedures won't allow them to think longer term. So, customer surveys and sales force feedback are limited means for making key decisions about product requirements." In her firm, however, short-term, account-specific product requirements drive field sales behavior. The difference is the source of common complaints by salespeople that "product management is unresponsive . . . not customer-oriented" and equally common complaints by product managers that salespeople "want us to be everything to everybody and so destroy the coherence of our marketing strategy."

In consumer goods firms, there are analogous differences in time horizons between brand and sales managers. An executive at a package goods firm explained these differences in terms of "clocks":

> Marketing implementation in our business means trying to synchronize different clocks. Retail buyers meet weekly for product and promotion evaluations, and our sales managers get monthly results by

region and district. For brand managers, prominent clocks are the annual promotion calendar for their brands (based on plans established 6 to 12 months ago), year-end results, and a one-year forecast of sales and earnings. For our product group managers, a key performance measure is return-on-net-assets over a three-year period.

In part, different time horizons reflect the local organizational context in each area which, as Chapter 6 discusses in more detail, often has its own career path and personnel policies that reinforce contrasting hierarchies of attention. Each group therefore approaches joint activities with different time lines in mind. A brand manager noted that "You want to make your mark during your limited time with a brand, and that requires getting your 'fair share' of sales attention." A district manager at the same firm described the sales perspective: "I've learned over the years that *all* brand managers believe their particular programs are *always* 'strategically crucial' and they're looking to make an impact immediately. But I can't sell all their initiatives to my field reps or to trade customers. Also, what you do now affects what you can do later with accounts. So, you cherry pick among brand's many programs because you'll see that customer again next year with another new product, promotion, or other initiative."

The groups' time horizons also differ along another important marketing dimension: where in the product life cycle each group concentrates. Especially in industrial firms, product management usually focuses on product development and each product group competes with others for the firm's limited R&D and engineering resources. A product manager at a telecommunications firm outlined a typical situation:

I compete with other product managers for shared Development resources. So, much of my time is spent with Business Analysis [a Finance function] rationalizing my list of needs and trying to place my list higher on Development's list of priorities. A key company asset is the shared network, and that means Development must look at the interrelationships implicated by each product introduction or product modification. And, the complexity of this increases as software-based services become a bigger part of the products we offer to customers.

My perception is that, in practice, Development looks at one chunk of products at a time. As a product manager, it's great when you get the attention and very frustrating when you don't. In the latter situation, you try to solicit more input and support from divisional managers [in the field] concerning needed features in order to make your case with Business Analysis.

In this situation, individual product managers have an incentive to "stretch" a proposed product's applicability across multiple segments in order to justify budget requests and drive development resources in their direction. Their most common method is to use information selectively: crafting segmentation schemes that highlight current or potential product leadership (emphasizing a particular aspect of product features or technology), choosing particular time periods for analysis or forecasts, or simply focusing on data favorable to product proposals and omitting less favorable data. My research uncovered numerous such examples *and,* in many companies, a feeling that such behavior was expected—findings consistent with some previous studies of product management and marketing budgeting procedures.[4]

Meanwhile, with their focus on specific accounts, sales and service managers find the differences in product requirements among customers salient. Hence, even as product managers strive to stretch a product's applicability *across* customer groups, sales and service managers try to specify product requirements more narrowly *within* a particular segment or account. The result can be time-consuming and customer-confusing conflicts that impede what the previous chapters have indicated is necessary: concurrent marketing among the groups responsible for customer satisfaction.

In off-site meetings, it is customary to ascribe these conflicts to organizational politics, with the implication that good citizens in a company act in ways that transcend narrow, local self-interests. This perspective ignores certain realities, especially when it comes to the constantly changing, time-constrained activities of marketing. As Joseph Bower has aptly observed, "politics" in firms is not simply "a pathology, it is a fact of large organization. . . . Ignoring the impact on planning and investment [is] a sure way of generating serious problems."[5] Many teamwork and change initiatives are basically attempts to wish away this fact by invoking the greater good. They too often focus on abstractions like culture, not on the work itself. But individual behavior is powerfully shaped by the organizational roles that people play. Any attempt to rechannel and manage these processes productively must understand its roots. Most managers in a company may indeed be good citizens who recognize that products *and* markets *and* accounts are all important and mutually interdependent. Yet, the aggregate impact of their daily behavior will still impede customer satisfaction.

MEASUREMENT SYSTEMS

"What gets measured gets attention," particularly when measures are tied to compensation and promotion. Differences in time horizons and orientation also reflect reward systems which, in turn, reflect a firm's need to focus on and maintain accountability—the scarcest resource in most companies and a perennially endangered species in complex organizations.

In the setting of quotas, performance appraisals, and bonuses, the focus of sales metrics in most firms is primarily on sales volume, rather than profit contribution or activities/tasks performed.[6] Product management measures are more varied, but profit responsibility, or forms of return-on-assets measures, is usually more prominent. Customer service metrics also vary, but typically involve cost efficiencies in the provision of services and (in recent years) "customer satisfaction" indices based on customer surveys and/or customer retention measures.

These measurements can generate conflicts in the implementation of joint tasks, and companies sometimes try to eradicate these differences through common metrics. Indeed, instituting "goal congruence" through common metrics is probably the most frequent advice proffered to managers interested in improving cross-functional efforts. But companies encounter many constraints and unintended consequences when they try to follow this advice. Therefore, for reasons discussed below, the practical need in most instances is to manage interactions among product, sales, and service personnel in the context of different measurement systems.

Common Conflicts

At companies I studied, managers tended to adopt one of two theories-in-use[7] about measurements of marketing groups: a checks-and-balance or goal-congruence approach. Further, oscillation between these approaches over time, within the same organization, is not uncommon.

One approach views differing metrics among product, sales, and service units as fostering "constructive conflict": a check on each group's tendency to insulate itself from other business concerns that are another unit's formal responsibility. In theory, profit/margin-measured product management will have an incentive to monitor closely sales' execution of its product programs. In turn, volume-oriented salespeople will challenge and modify product plans with timely information from the field about requirements at specific sources of sales volume. Service personnel, concerned with cost-efficient provision of longer-term customer satisfaction, will want to ensure that sales personnel don't "give away the store" and that product management doesn't neglect important pre- or postsale services that influence margin realization.

In practice, however, this checks-and-balance system often works according to squeaky-wheel principles. Particularly aggressive field managers, or the bigger product groups, receive the lion's share of sales, service, or product support. For example, in department stores—where headquarters merchandise buyers usually have profit or margin responsibilities and store department sales managers (DSMs) volume responsibilities—one study found that merchandise was most often allocated by a "goods to the aggressive" method in which "the branch DSM that yells the loudest gets the most goods." Further, since field executives had volume but (at the time of the study) no profit responsibilities, "only the most conscientious tried to balance their desire for more sales-supporting inventory with adequate concern for overstocks."[8]

A more elaborate but fundamentally similar dynamic occurs in industrial firms. An example is IBM where, throughout the 1980s, profit and pricing responsibility resided with each product group while sales reps earned credit toward quotas and bonuses through a point system based on sales of a product at list price. For software and services, points were based on monthly leasing or maintenance revenues. Under this system, each fall point allocations were set during sessions between field sales managers from around the world and senior managers from each product group. An executive familiar with these sessions described the process:

> Product managers essentially lobbied [sales] to place more points on their product line in the annual sales compensation plan. A product manager's negotiating skills could influence this process significantly and, since field reps earned points based on list price, the negotiations usually centered on the allowable price discounts. Since the larger, better established lines had more room to move in this regard, the tendency was to place disproportionate emphasis on established hardware products and less on newer products, especially software and services.

Over time, this system left IBM increasingly vulnerable as its own product line (primarily mainframe products and peripherals until the 1980s) expanded because of maturing demand for mainframe products, new users in a variety of niche segments, and multiplying competitors. Low-end, entry-level products became more important, but the interplay of product and sales measurement systems continued to focus on higher-end products. This same executive added: "The point system had a 50-year history at IBM. But we knew something was wrong when, for three years running, 75% of field reps made their point targets while the corporation missed its annual growth, revenue, and profit goals."

Hence, these marketing metrics influence behavior in many ways that, regardless of what formal plans may *say* about goals, affect company strategy and implementation. In my experience, the most common negative impacts of these measurement systems are:

• Competition between product units for field sales attention;
• Coordination and opportunity costs at major accounts; and
• Long-term subversion of product policies and service requirements.

Interproduct competition for sales attention. In four firms I studied, multiple product groups went to market with a pooled sales force. During the marketing planning process, selling expenses were apportioned annually (usually on the basis of the previous year's percentage of sales) to individual product units. A product manager explained: "The tendency for P&L-measured product managers is to view the apportionment as a fixed cost [during the relevant budgeting cycle], and then to push for as much sales attention as possible to their particular product line."

This internal competition has important consequences. At IBM for many years, it favored the established product lines, such as mainframe computers, at a time when demand patterns were moving swiftly toward smaller computers and services. At another firm, interproduct competition for sales attention affected channel strategy and, over time, distribution capabilities. As in many companies, a large portion of product expenses at this firm reflected development costs; once developed, a product's variable manufacturing expenses were relatively small and, after investments in highly automated production facilities during the 1980s, a decreasing proportion of the firm's total product costs. Product managers' measurement systems, in terms of how selling attention and expenses were allocated, affected interactions between the groups. As an executive noted,

> Investments that improve a product's manufacturability show up as variable cost reductions on the product manager's P&L sheet. But with apportioned marketing expenses treated as a "fixed cost" for product units, there is an incentive for those managers to add product features that might increase the size of the potential market, but little incentive for each to invest in sales support that improves field-marketing productivity.

Account management. A related issue concerns the impact on account management tasks. Every company in my sample had established a key-account program to stimulate more cross-selling at important customers. These customers were important not only because of the current volume they represented, but also because of their strategic significance. These were the accounts that often bought across a vendor's product line and, in some industries, set standards or precedents that affected marketing efforts at other accounts.

However, prevailing metrics often made it difficult for account managers to orchestrate coherently the vendor's product and pricing package. Especially in the face of lower-priced competition, cross-product initiatives concerning delivery, merchandising, or product customization are often necessary. But, as one manager commented:

> A customer might be interested in a package of products from us, but the product units aren't particularly interested in systems selling or the best package. Each is primarily interested in its particular product line and resistant to altering price, features, or terms and conditions for the sake of the package. This is a problem because customers are looking for productivity and cost improvements [and], as a vendor, you provide those improvements with a system, not individual product components.

Over time, moreover, the lack of coordinated product-service packages at such accounts can result in a price-sensitive "averaging" of a multiproduct firm's capabilities. At a medical equipment supplier facing increased concentration in its customer base, an executive noted that "Traditionally, we categorized customers by products and amounts bought from various product divisions. That's the way we think and measure, but not the way markets act. [Competitive developments] now require us to tailor a product package to select accounts, or risk averaging our capabilities."

Impact on product and service policies. Conversely, the predominant weighting of sales volume in sales force metrics affects longer-term product development initiatives and service requirements. The marketwide perspective of product managers may reveal evolving market changes that must be addressed. But the quarter-by-quarter need to fuel sales attention and current volume can drive product development and service resources in directions that subvert the longer-term strategy.

In a package goods firm, for example, sales policy dictates that one division's products all be placed in one core location in the supermarket snack aisle. But as the category matured, product managers naturally sought to introduce new products, packaging concepts, and line extensions. These initiatives generally required new aisle locations, merchandising efforts, and contacts with different store buyers. These initiatives also ran counter to the quarterly volume metrics that formed the basis of sales compensation and evaluation criteria. Eventually, the division's competitive position suffered as product managers, trying to make a measureable impact on their short-term P&L performance, were reluctant to champion product ideas which involved different selling requirements unlikely to meet with short-term sales support. The result was a gradual but steady decline in market share and the company's influence with powerful trade buyers. This, in turn, only fueled the downward spiral of short-term promotions aimed at bolstering this quarter's sales and merchandising efforts for established products.

Together, these measurement dynamics have companywide implications. In the past decade, many companies have embarked on ambitious merger and acquisition strategies. These investments are typically based on the alleged "synergies" involved in pooling development resources across a wider product line, improving channel efficiencies and throughput by common sales and service efforts, and eventually cross-selling more products to (and thus solidifying relationships with) bigger and more powerful key accounts. But these investment strategies often don't work out because of the issues embedded in the metrics of front-line marketing managers.

Common Constraints

In order to enhance synergy, companies often adopt the goal-congruence approach to marketing metrics. Their reasoning is straightforward and follows traditional economic theory concerning incentives and organizational behavior: without congruent metrics, locally optimizing behavior is likely among resourceful, self-interested individuals in different organizational units.[9] In general, the objective is to craft a measurement system that minimizes what economists call moral hazard—lack of agent effort on behalf of the principal because of inadequate, or countervailing, incentives.

The conditions facing marketing practitioners, however, are complex and make the application of this theory fraught with difficulties in many firms.

Consider the issue of how to pay the sales force, which generates the stream of orders and product and service requirements that flow from orders and installed-base customers. Faced with the conflicts outlined in the previous section, managers often attempt to make profit responsibility—instead of, or in addition to, volume metrics—a key component of the measurement and reward system for field sales personnel as well as product management. In 1989, for example, IBM made field marketing units profit centers responsible for sales and service of all products. But a 1991 reorganization again moved product and pricing responsibility to product groups. Similarly, a major package goods firm restructured sales compensation in 1990 to include product profitability: under a new incentive plan, salespeople received bonuses based on different products' profitability. But two years later, the company reinstituted the previous system in which sales' key metrics were volume and merchandising goals while profit responsibility remained with individual product groups.

Why did these changes not work? What are the constraints or unintended consequences of adopting common measurements for product, sales, and service units?

One reason, underscored by my research, is often simply the lack of information systems required to generate the new measurement data (see Chapter 5 for more on this topic).

Another reason is the unintended impact of a sales profitability metric on different products of a multiproduct firm. At the package goods firm, for instance, the short-lived case incentive value plan indeed focused sales force efforts on higher-margin items. But it had a very negative impact on the firm's many lower-margin items that require high volume to maintain purchasing economies and the manufacturing throughput levels essential for cost/price competitiveness. Similarly, many industrial firms sell commodity and specialty items that differ significantly in terms of their profit margins, but that also have important interrelationships up-stream in the firm's value chain in terms of purchasing, product development, and manufacturing economies. Often, high-volume sales on the commodities are necessary to maintain the cost structure (and higher margins) of the specialties.

A third reason is that, even within a single product group, the relative importance of margin and volume tends to change in the face of competitive threats and opportunities more rapidly than managers can (or, are willing to) change the relevant measurement systems. Frequent changes in sales compensation can send mixed signals and all too easily engender a cynical "this, too, shall pass" attitude on the part of sales personnel.

More generally, most businesses need to concentrate simultaneously on volume *and* margins. A consumer goods executive described a common situation:

> We purchase tons of agricultural commodities and sheer volume drives our purchasing discounts as well as manufacturing and physical distribution efficiencies. If there's not a certain level of volume and trade deals, our retail customers won't stay with our line or buy into the next merchandising program. Therefore, we have profit responsibility in product marketing and primarily volume responsibility in sales, and both objectives are fundamental. . . . We must guard against clever and profitable marketing programs that can't be sold in sufficient volume, and volume-driven sales requests that aren't profitable.

Manufacturing value-added is typically higher for industrial products than consumer goods. But for more industrial products, a larger portion of product expenses is R&D and fixed manufacturing costs as newer, capital-intensive production systems are adopted. Managing these costs is essential to profitability, and product managers must understand and respond to the P&L implications of design changes. At the same time, as Bela Gold points out, computer-aided manufacturing "requires substantial investments not only in computer and related communication facilities, but also in appropriate production machinery, tooling and transfer equipment, and in related instrumentation and controls. As a result, the ratio of fixed costs to total costs is raised, increasing the penalties of fluctuations in capacity utilization rates."[10] Managing these costs is also essential, and requires the concentrated efforts of account managers and other sales personnel charged with maintaining a stream of orders.

A final reason why companies often abandon (or, are reluctant to adopt) shared profit responsibility among product, sales, and service units is its perceived impact on decision making. Because of the daily and visible pressures from customers and competitors, sales' interactions with product and service units are among the more time-constrained nodes of interfunctional activity in most companies. One executive echoed others in comments about his firm's experiment with giving profit responsibility to sales as well as product management:

> We decided sales should focus on selling, not on how to run the business. With dual profit responsibility, it took us much longer to make and implement marketing decisions—a big cost in our marketplace where first-mover advantages are now very important. Also, each group has a bigger incentive to get involved in the details of the other group's planning process, but less expertise and responsibility to manage the outcome. The result was a lot of finger pointing when a product's sales didn't meet forecasts.

For all these reasons, then, metrics vary. But the constraints in aligning incentives do not mean that measurement systems are irrelevant or can be ignored. Sales behavior, in particular, responds to the measures in place, and Chapter 8 discusses sales compensation in more detail. Rather, the complexities noted here indicate the ongoing need to find ways of creating fruitful complementary relationships in the metrics that apply to product, sales, and service units. What product managers in many firms now often view as sales' "inertia" in the face of changing market conditions, salespeople might well call "the best use of my limited time in order to maximize income."

Further, the difficulties in instituting shared profit responsibilities among these groups indicate that—contrary to economic theory and the wishes of many managers—achieving goal congruence is easier said than done and, even when done, not a magic bullet. If common incentives were the total solution—rather than an important element of a solution—companies would have solved their coordination problems long ago. The challenge is managing these multiple customer-contact activities in a context where each group necessarily focuses on different components of overall business performance.

INFORMATION FLOWS

These marketing units also differ in terms of (1) information priorities and, hence, the type of data tracked by each unit, and (2) the role and use of the data that are tracked. These differences can result in a modern marketing version of the legend concerning the blind men and the elephant. Because each has contact with a certain part of the whole, each disagrees vigorously about the nature of the animal—or, more specifically, about the nature of the external marketplace that all must deal with.

Priorities

Implicit in the contrasting hierarchies of attention described earlier are differing information priorities. Product managers view data about assigned products and pertinent markets (usually defined in terms of consumer segments or product applications across geographical boundaries) as their highest information priority. Sales managers view timely information about geographically defined markets, specific accounts within those markets, and the activities of resellers or other business partners at those accounts as priority data. Service managers need information about both products and accounts, but in different terms. An executive at a market research firm described common differences in this way:

> Product managers tend to synthesize the information they receive; they're looking for commonalities across the data because they naturally think in terms of segments, or what seems common to aggregate groups of customers. Sales managers tend to disaggregate the information they receive, and look for exceptions—why account X differs from account Y—because they sell to specific customers, not "segments." Service most often feels a lack of pertinent information, and wants data about products or sales in terms of its delivery, installation, or maintenance implications—information rarely contained in the product literature, call reports, or other data that service typically receives from other groups.

In the companies I studied—as in most firms—accounting systems tracked costs primarily by product categories, rather than customer or channel categories.[11] Also, market research reported through the product marketing organization, and research funds came from product managers' budgets. Hence, as Chapter 5 explains, it is product management's priorities that usually define the kinds of data and research available to sales and service units. The result is often a gap between the aggregate data most meaningful to product-planning activities and the disaggregated data meaningful to account- or region-specific selling and service activities.

In many firms, these differing information priorities become visible when marketing programs require product-bundling strategies and field sales and service integration at important accounts. Different product groups have commissioned research—or otherwise gathered and categorized data—with different segmentation schemes, making it difficult to identify and evaluate cross-product sales opportunities. An executive at a medical products company described a representative situation:

> Traditionally, distributors and hospitals have dealt with our individual product divisions, and so [encounter] a wide variety of pricing, billing, and order-entry procedures. As the channel and end-user markets in this industry consolidate, however, we find it hard to leverage the collective volume we represent across our product lines at key accounts. One reason is that the different procedures have meant different ways of collecting customer data. It's not easy, and sometimes not possible, to compare these figures and know how much we actually sell to specific accounts.

Among other things, these differing information flows mean that product, sales, and service managers often meet to discuss customer-related issues on a reactive, rather than proactive, basis. Furthermore, each group arrives at such meetings with ideas based on different data sources and with different assumptions about who "the customer" is. In practice, it is difficult to achieve integration under such circumstances.

Uses

The role and use of data differ among the three marketing units. In politics, an historian has noted, the fox knows something about many things while the hedgehog knows a lot about one important thing. In many ways, product and service units are fox-like in their information uses, whereas the role of information in sales is to provide hedgehog-like focus at accounts.

Product managers need data relevant to product development, costing, and pricing decisions. More than sales or service managers, product managers often work through formal presentations as part of their firms' market planning process. Hence, compatibility with the *selling* firm's budgeting vocabulary is an important criterion of useful data.

Sales managers need data relevant to the concerns of different accounts. Compatibility with multiple *buying* vocabularies is more important to them. In addition, the varied, less-formal, and often time-constrained contexts of sales calls make "a few key points" the criteria of useful information for salespeople. A market researcher at a consumer goods company, for example, noted that "Our brand managers want detailed data; they're trained to use such data for strategic brand planning and as tools in seeking more resources. By contrast, our reps must sell quickly to buyers or store managers as they're walking through the store or checking inventory."

Service personnel often deal with customer personnel on a wider basis than do their product or sales colleagues. Especially in industrial firms, service's field maintenance and installation responsibilities make detailed data about product specifications and delivery requirements important. But, in contrast to the data uses of product or sales units, compatibility with relevant technical and/or logistical vocabularies of customers is a key criterion of useful service information.

These differing roles of data often create "transmission problems." Recall the meeting described at the beginning of this chapter, in which sales managers complained about the lack of timely information, and product managers about salespeople asking for information they already had. These complaints reflect fundamentally different information usage cycles. Product managers must gather and present data to and from a variety of functional areas. At one company, charting a product's competitive price and share for annual planning purposes meant soliciting data from more than 20 countries as well as finance, warehousing, and sales departments. Further, these data are often assembled for the company's capital budgeting process which, in many firms, adheres to a fairly rigid schedule. At packaged goods firms, for example, the process takes months, during which time brand managers are often fully occupied and therefore less responsive to field requests for information. By contrast, the timing of sales' and service's information needs is irregular, less capable of being scheduled, and generated (in many salespeople's eyes at least) by an "urgent" customer need.

In addition, it is easy for individual product managers to lose sight of the sheer volume of information that can overwhelm salespeople in many firms. A graphic illustration of this occurred during my field research. For three days at the start of one week, I interviewed product managers at a computer firm. In the midst of a major product introduction, one product group walked me through the announcement process, including the detailed and seemingly sensible means taken to distribute relevant product literature to branch offices. On Friday of that week, I interviewed a branch manager. When I mentioned the product introduction and the apparent care taken to arm the sales force with relevant information, he escorted me to a fair-sized conference room known as "the archives." In stacks sometimes as high as six feet or more were numerous pamphlets, books, binders, videotapes, and other materials. "This is literature that we've received from product groups in just the past quarter," he explained. "It's impossible for salespeople to read all this. What they don't read angers a particular product group. But if they actually spent the time to go through this material, they'd have no time to sell. And that would [annoy] *all* our product managers."

Addressing these information-usage situations becomes more important as short-cycle times, first-mover advantages, and other factors discussed in Chapter 1 become larger aspects of competitive strategy.

COMPETENCY TRAPS

The differences among marketing groups, summarized in Exhibit 3-1, in part reflect the task requirements in each unit. Their differing priorities, time horizons, measurement systems, and information flows are ultimately generated by the need to develop and maintain discrete types of expertise along a continuum of value creation and value delivery functions.

For this reason, some conflict among the groups may be inevitable, and can even be healthy: it can provide a blunt but potentially effective means of disrupting, and so potentially up-dating, established hierarchies of attention in each unit. Indeed, some have postulated an inherent Catch-22 in firms' teamwork and coordination efforts. As integration among internal units occurs, differences diminish, and behaviors across groups tend to converge. The result is that the organization may exhibit greater reliability in performing current activities, but the diversity of beliefs and behaviors necessary for further adaptation is eliminated.[12] This danger is especially pertinent to marketing which, owing to the necessity of getting and keeping customers in a dynamic marketplace, should be a prime instigator of adaptation and change throughout the company.

At the same time, market developments make faster, better coordination among these units more important. Specialized expertise is important for the achievement of in-depth knowledge, learning-curve effects, and many daily efficiencies in the management of product programs, sales efforts, and service tasks. But, collaboration among these specialized units—the integration of discrete value-creation and value-delivery activities in a coherent marketing effort—is also essential. As a classic statement of this tension noted:

> As organizations deal with their external environments, they become segmented into units, each dealing with a part of the conditions outside the firm. This is a result of the fact that any one group of managers has a limited span of surveillance. . . . [But] these parts of the system also have to be linked together toward the accomplishment of the organization's overall purpose. This [leads] to a state of differentiation and integration within any organization.[13]

Hence, the relationship among the factors discussed in this chapter is perhaps better captured by expanding the image of the marketing gearbox introduced in Chapter 2. As Figure 3-1 indicates, these mar-

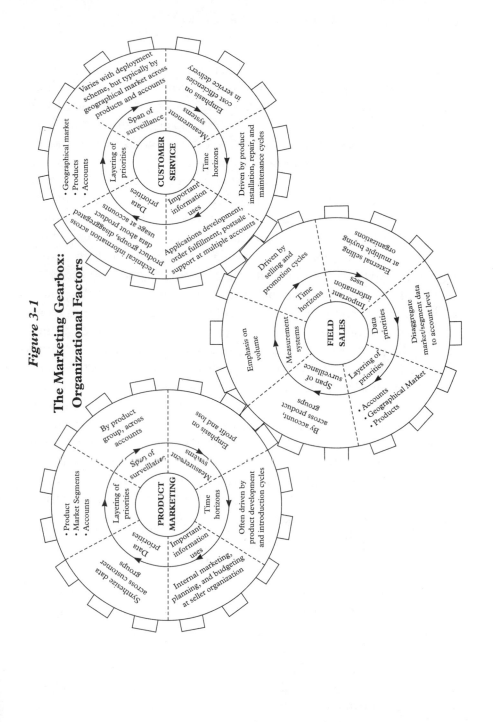

Figure 3-1

**The Marketing Gearbox:
Organizational Factors**

keting units must synchronize their activities in a context in which each unit's span of surveillance on the external environment, its metrics and time horizons, and its information flows and priorities differ. They differ because over time each unit adopts routines that accelerate the performance of its subset of customer contact responsibilities. This division of labor is necessary, and may in fact be increasingly necessary, as more work becomes "knowledge work" driven by groups of specialists rather than all-purpose generalists—a fact sometimes overlooked by those who advocate the abolition of functional departments and the proliferation of short-term, ad hoc project teams as a panacea for organizational problems.[14] Provided these routines support procedures with the highest potential for customer satisfaction and firm performance, moreover, this specialization is economically advantageous.

But in most busy organizations, and especially in the time-constrained environment of selling and marketing, the routines themselves soon become part of the accepted "way we do things around here." The result, for the organization as a whole, is too often a series of competency traps.[15] Each unit's familiarity and accumulated expertise with established procedures provide efficiencies within its own domain. But these same established routines and interactions between groups keep the firm from gaining experience with procedures more relevant to changing market conditions. Other alignments among product, sales, and service units may be more appropriate. But competency, confidence, and unit performance are associated with the information flows that support the metrics that complement the current priorities in each marketing group.

CONCLUSION

How can companies avoid competency traps and maintain the benefits of specialization? How can organizations effectively manage the issues that affect the daily give-and-take between marketing units with mutual dependencies yet distinct roles in customer contact efforts?

Examining in some detail the differences among these marketing groups helps clarify the challenge firms face. The key issue in achieving concurrent marketing capabilities is *not* to eradicate these differences. Expertise in the performance of specialized marketing activi-

Exhibit 3-2
Market Orientation Implies Developing and Executing Customer Solutions across Internal Product, Sales, and Service Units

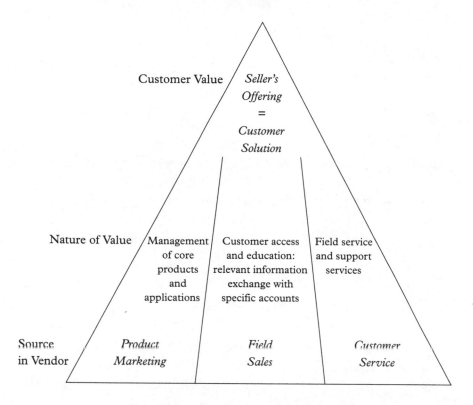

ties, as well as accountability and speed to market, are aided by the differences outlined here. Nor is the goal to somehow make "everybody responsible for the customer." Multiple efforts from different groups in the organization do indeed influence customer satisfaction. But in most busy organizations, what everyone is responsible for in theory, nobody is responsible for in practice.

Rather, the key issue is how to link efficiently and effectively the knowledge, capabilities, and operations necessarily located in different areas and marketing dialects in most firms. Without appropriate linkages, the differences discussed in this chapter generate two costs for the firm.

Exhibit 3-3
**But Differentiating Factors among Product, Sales, and
Service Can Result in Fragmented Solution with
Limited Customer Value**

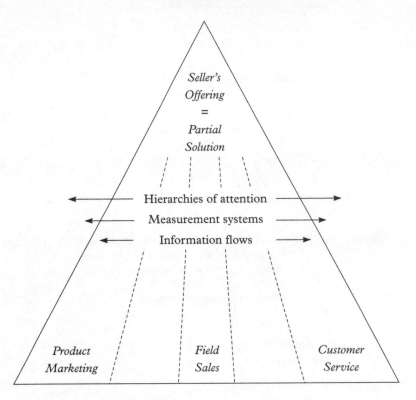

One cost is fragmentation at the customer interface. Being market-oriented means developing and executing customer solutions across internal product, sales, and service units (Exhibit 3-2). Each has a role to play in delivering value to customers. Product groups must manage the core products and applications that customers value. Sales groups must develop and maintain the customer access and information exchange required to identify and keep relevant the firm's product offering. Customer service groups provide the pre- and postsales support that plays a more prominent role in the seller's package. Together, each unit in the vendor is an integral part of the solution that customers buy.

But, as Exhibit 3-3 indicates, the differences discussed here tend to direct funding, attention, and efforts within, rather than across, these units. A fragmentation occurs in what should be, from the customer's perspective, a seamless flow of value creation and delivery. The result is a partial solution, with limited customer value and usually negative competitive consequences.

The other cost is more subtle. These differences rarely mean paralysis in interactions among these units. Managers needing to "get product out the door" will forge ad hoc agreements sooner or later. But the nature of these agreements is unlikely to be optimal and the process itself can be harmful. One executive, commenting on interactions between product and sales managers in her company, expressed it well: "We spend so much time bargaining, and the result is that we often unintentionally reward managers for their internal negotiating skills, not for problem solving or customer-oriented performance."

Part II considers what some companies are doing to build concurrent marketing capabilities and avoid the economic and organizational costs of fragmentation.

II
BUILDING LINKS

■

4

Structural Linkages

■

PART I concerned the challenges facing firms in a marketplace characterized by changing bases of customer value, increased segmentation, supply chain developments, and shorter product life cycles. In this environment, many companies are grappling with the organizational issues analyzed in Chapter 2 as they try to avoid the competency traps discussed at the end of Chapter 3.

What are firms doing to manage new marketing requirements? At the companies I studied, major initiatives fell into three categories: an emphasis on structural devices such as formal liaison units; changes in research and information systems utilized by product, sales, and service units; and alterations in broader management processes and other aspects of the human resource infrastructure, especially new career paths and training programs.

This categorization is neither exhaustive nor mutually exclusive. Many firms utilize a variety of linkage devices among (and, in addition to) those noted above. Moreover, as Exhibit 4-1 suggests, these initiatives are themselves interdependent. New structures without supporting information systems, or new information systems without the appropriate people and organizational processes have limited impact. But these initiatives are the most widely used, and each often represents the platform on which management can build complementary mechanisms for improving product-sales-service coordination. Fur-

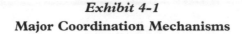

Exhibit 4-1
Major Coordination Mechanisms

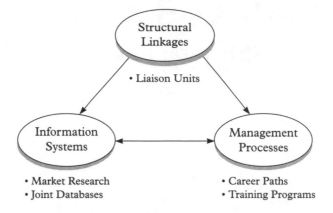

ther, the emphasis on each initiative tends to differ for companies in different business settings.

Part II evaluates the benefits, vulnerabilities, and marketing environments associated with each linkage device. This chapter considers a key tension in organizing marketing activities and, with IBM's experience as a running example, focuses on a structural device for integrating sales, product management, and customer service activities. Chapter 5 takes up the issues involved in making research and information systems more responsive to new marketing demands. Chapter 6 focuses on changes in career paths and training programs.

Today's challenges are compelling companies to make expensive, time-consuming, and sometimes irreversible choices about where and how to attempt linkages along the continuum of marketing tasks. Together, Chapters 4 through 6 outline a coherent way of assessing the costs, benefits, and general management requirements of the major coordination options. Part III considers the account management, sales compensation, and service systems required for ongoing field implementation of these concurrent marketing capabilities.

MARKETING ORGANIZATION: ORTHOGONAL REQUIREMENTS

Despite intense interest in organizations, formal organizational structure has not been a popular topic in recent years. Indeed, in tones reminiscent of 1960s generalizations about how "small is beautiful," structure is now usually depicted as "part of the problem, not the solution." More than a decade ago, *In Search of Excellence* stressed that "Excellent companies are a vast network of informal, open communications. . . . Small is productive."[1] Since then, many books, articles, workshops, and business school courses have preached the virtues of "skunk works," "dynamic networks," "the virtual corporation," "chaos" (in the physicist's sense of the term), and the "fall of hierarchy" as organizing principles.

Yet, while management theorists now downplay the importance of formal structure, companies continue to reorganize frequently and managers study closely any revisions to their companies' organizational charts. Why?

One reason is that these charts are abstract but important signs of influence and current concerns. The facts of formal structure—the creation and staffing of specific positions—are vital in understanding how tasks do (or don't) get accomplished. Over time, the way a company organizes its marketing activities, in particular, determines the kinds of customer contact skills that are developed. This, in turn, affects the strategies realistically available to the firm. Further, as Alfred Chandler, Jr. has persuasively documented, the "keep it small" advice fails to address the need to develop the economies of scale and scope that shape much of the competition in a global marketplace.[2]

Another reason concerns the dual requirements at the heart of marketing organizational decisions. Marketing is about getting and keeping customers. Its primary responsibilities are managing the company-customer interface. Internally marketing managers must keep the firm's strategy aligned with changing buyer behavior, the various distribution channels used to reach important segments, and threats and opportunities posed by the competition. Externally marketing managers must execute current strategies effectively while

Exhibit 4-2
Marketing and Boundary Spanning

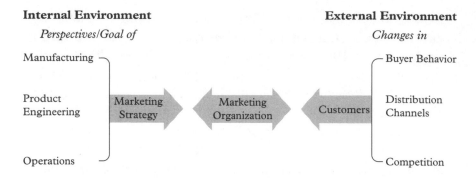

coordinating product, sales, and service inputs to that strategy in a dynamic marketplace.

Thus, as Exhibit 4-2 emphasizes, the essence of the marketing job is to manage a series of internal as well as external boundaries. Marketing helps interpret for the organization the ambiguous mosaic of information that *is* the external environment (or "market") of a firm, and it tries to keep the firm in tune with changing market realities by acting as the voice of the customer within the firm. More than in most other areas of the firm, marketing managers must move beyond the boundaries of their official job descriptions and formal authority to get their jobs done.

One result is that, in organizing customer contact activities, most companies have two requirements which, while not mutually exclusive, do pull marketing managers and resources in different directions. One concerns what's necessary to maintain the skills, attention, and motivation needed to compete for current sources of revenues; the other concerns the skills and capabilities which must be developed to compete in new markets. We can think of these dual marketing imperatives as orthogonal requirements.[3] (In geometry, "orthogonal" lines meet at right angles.) Exhibit 4-3 outlines these requirements.

Be predictable and consistent. Because capacity planning, production scheduling, operating cash-flow estimates, bank borrowing requirements, and hiring patterns throughout the firm are contingent

Exhibit 4-3
Marketing's Orthogonal Requirements

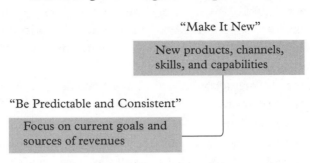

"Make It New"

New products, channels, skills, and capabilities

"Be Predictable and Consistent"

Focus on current goals and sources of revenues

on annual sales targets, the marketing organization is under constant pressure to "make the numbers." This is especially true as technology becomes a bigger part of product and service efforts: large fixed-asset investments must often be made years before the actual introduction of products and the generation of sales revenues. Thus, an effective marketing organization must focus its personnel (especially field sales personnel) on current goals and sources of revenues. In turn, consistency and predictability in marketing operations are valued by other functions in the firm.

Make it new. At the same time, however, marketing management needs to generate new sources of revenue through new products, new channels, and new applications. This is especially true as more fragmented markets and shorter product life cycles make multiple niche strategies and leapfrogging in price/performance characteristics key aspects of competition. Thus, marketing must develop new skills and capabilities—with minimal disruption to its efforts to maintain current sources of revenue.

Marketing managers often refer facetiously to these dual requirements as the "monkey law of marketing"—that is, in making its way through a competitive jungle, the smart monkey never lets go of one branch (an established means of generating revenues) until its other hand is securely fastened to the next branch. The problem is that this view of change is often a prescription for inertia rather than innovation. As Chapter 3 indicated, the very rules and procedures that optimize current revenue generation in each marketing unit also inhibit

the development and execution of new skills and strategies. The result
at most companies is that the imperatives of the first goal (Be predictable and make quota) overshadow the longer-term and necessarily
risky demands of the second (Make it new), which leads to marketing
myopia[4]—a business definition that ignores product substitutes and
new ways of serving customer needs.

In the more formal terminology of the behavioral sciences, this is
a problem in "requisite variety." When the complexity or variety
that exists in the environment to be managed exceeds the variety or
information-processing capabilities of the people who must manage
it, stasis or mistakes are usually the result. As Karl Weick noted:

> When people have less variety to cope with the system, they miss im-
> portant information, their diagnoses are incomplete, and their reme-
> dies can magnify rather than reduce a problem. . . . A better match
> can occur basically in one of two ways: either the system becomes less
> complex or the human more complex.[5]

During the past decade, organizational theorists and consultants
have emphasized the latter: making managers more complex by initiating efforts whose goal is a "cultural revolution" that allegedly
broadens their knowledge of the totality of an organization's environment and their ability to influence cross-functional activities. By contrast, the structural linkages discussed in this chapter emphasize the
former: making each component of a system less complex by creating
boundary positions whose occupants manage the interfaces between
units with minimal disruption to the functional expertise still required
in each unit to manage current revenue streams.

A key assumption of the structural approach is based on the street-
smart aphorism that "all politics is local." This approach assumes that
most people in complex companies do—and should—focus on meeting local objectives because demonstrating one's value to a functional
area is easier than demonstrating one's value to the organization as a
whole or to an abstract goal (being "customer-oriented"). A related
assumption is that, especially in time-constrained marketing activities,
most managers do not (and cannot) make decisions about the broad,
cross-functional aspects of integrated product-sales-service pro-

grams. A separate and explicit structure is required to do this efficiently and effectively.

IBM's response to increased coordination requirements in its marketplace illustrates the benefits, and costs, of emphasizing structural linkages.

A TALE OF TWO PRODUCT INTRODUCTIONS

In 1986, IBM was finalizing plans to release a new mainframe computer, the System 9370.[6] Introduction had been scheduled for 1987. But, concerned that an impatient market was seeking competitive alternatives, product managers wanted to release the computer in the fall of 1986. Sales managers argued that the company should not release a major product in the fourth quarter. "Product transitions are critical," one manager noted. "Once an announcement is made, many customers stop buying the current product generation while they evaluate the new technology. The result can be stalled sales and quota-crushing delays for sales reps."

The conflict was escalated to IBM's Management Committee (MC), which agreed with the product managers and rescheduled the introduction for October 1986. However, the decision was not without costs. Established sales plans had to be revised. The order fulfillment process in place in customer service units at the time of introduction could accept only a limited number of product options. And, as one manager explained, "When the product was introduced, some field managers were still angry about the decision while many salespeople, working hard in the fourth quarter to make their annual numbers, did not attend the necessary training classes for the new product." The sales results for the 9370 were significantly less than anticipated in the original business plan.

Reflecting on the 9370 experience, one IBM executive commented:

We have close relations with installed-base customers and processes for determining product requirements. The problem was implementation. The product, sales, and service groups responsible for execution had conflicting priorities and opinions, and the company had few

mechanisms to resolve disagreements short of a last-minute interven-
tion by the MC. As a result, with the 9370, we were trying to sell
hardware without the total solution in place.

Other executives mentioned additional factors, some of which reflected organizational history, others the forces of industry evolution.

A turning point in IBM's history was the development of the Sys-
tem/360 series of computers in the 1960s. With the S/360, IBM
offered upward compatibility over a wide product line, a variety of
common input/output devices across the line, and a single general-
purpose line of equipment for a variety of data-processing applications. Management decided to introduce all S/360 products simultaneously so that customers would perceive the full impact of the new
line. This meant that multiple labs and manufacturing plants in
different product units had to coordinate more closely than ever to
meet a rigorous schedule for product development.

The S/360 eventually consolidated IBM's position in general-
purpose mainframe systems. But it required a tumultuous series of
internal efforts. Introductions were repeatedly delayed because of the
fragmented nature of multiple product development responsibilities;
customer needs expanded during the delays and slowdowns; cost
overruns ballooned so much that, according to one study of the project,[7] the programming costs alone nearly tripled beyond original estimates in two years; cash flow was affected—the company had to issue
unprecedented amounts of debt, and its heretofore stellar performance on Wall Street was threatened.

After an internal review, management instituted changes. "After
the 360 experience," an executive explained, "the notion of functional
excellence and start-to-finish responsibility for a product became a
guiding philosophy at IBM. And since P&L responsibility was lodged
in the product units, the System Manager became accountable. In
turn, this accountability encouraged [product managers] to want
maximum control over their own resources and priorities."

IBM also instituted a new Phase Process for reviewing product
plans from concept development through specifications, production
scheduling, announcement, and introduction. At each phase, the relevant groups involved were required to assent, dissent, and commit

resources to plans that were typically based on three- to five-year fore-casts. Another executive noted:

> The Phase Process was part of our contention management system where the basic assumption was that, by forcing "yes" or "no" positions at each phase, the best decision would emerge. However, the result was a tug of war between product and channel groups, and this conflict escalated as our business grew, as new product lines were introduced, and as customers' emphasis on total solutions increased interdependencies among these units.

Until the 1980s, when IBM changed its pricing strategy, most customers leased IBM equipment and software. Under these rental agreements, customers could return equipment and cease payments with 30 days' notice. As its business grew, rental agreements required enormous working capital investments. By 1981, for example, the capital required to fund rentals was $4.6 billion, or more than twice as much as IBM's total investment in plant and property in that year. In addition, as one executive explained, "Product life cycles became shorter. You couldn't design a machine, put a rental price on it, and maintain that price for three to five years. Competitors came out with comparable machines, and it became very difficult to implement price decreases with all that rental inventory out there." Another reason was that, as more mid-range and low-end products were introduced, the equipment itself became less expensive and so more amenable to up-front purchase.

These related changes in buying behavior and pricing policies affected both sales and product requirements. In the leasing environment, IBM's sales force had focused on growing the installed base and understanding current customers' needs. Salespeople became proficient at selling additional capacity for existing applications. New users were a secondary priority. But as buying moves to purchase, the field must sell to a broader range of buyers with a complete solution, rather than an incremental sale that builds on the technology infrastructure already in place at an account. Software and services become a bigger part of the purchase, which requires multiple distribution channels and better market information.

By the late 1980s, all of these factors were converging and accelerating in IBM's marketplace.

Shortly after the 9370 introduction, IBM was preparing another
major release: the mid-range AS/400 line. For some years, IBM had
been losing market share in this segment to minicomputer firms while
a maturing mainframe market made mid-range systems increasingly
important. One executive recalled:

> As we looked at this product introduction, we asked, "What did we
> learn from the 9370 experience and what should we do differently?"
> We decided we needed one group responsible for orchestrating the
> introduction among the developers, the marketing managers in head-
> quarters, field salespeople, and the industry specialists who have
> knowledge of required applications and important indirect channels
> of distribution.

In response, the MC appointed (one year before the planned introduction date) William Grabe (a senior executive with significant sales
and product management experience) as project manager for the
AS/400 release. He established a team of 15 people, and assigned
members to manage various interfaces important to the introduction,
including systems managers in the product unit, industry specialists
at headquarters, and sales and service personnel in field organizations.
Executives from these units met monthly to discuss coordination issues concerning the AS/400. One manager involved described the
meetings as follows:

> With the MC's backing, Bill could insist on having key executives (no
> substitutes) from relevant functions attend these meetings. Each
> month, we filled a room with about 40 people for an all-day shootout
> in which issues were surfaced and eventually resolved. These meetings
> were contentious, but communications improved dramatically. After
> the first meeting, moreover, executives brought implementation man-
> agers from their units. So, there was also more ability to develop spe-
> cific action plans.
>
> The result is that we were able to focus a number of different
> groups on core success factors for the AS/400 line: providing a good

migration path for our installed base of mid-range users; providing a variety of relevant applications at the time of introduction, not some time afterward; and providing salespeople with literature, training, and other forms of support for specific applications and target markets.

The integration of effort paid off. During its first year on the market, the AS/400 increased IBM's share in the mid-range segment from 18% to 29%. A survey found that, of accounts purchasing an AS/400, 57% were not replacing existing systems, indicating that the product had opened up new segments for IBM as well as traded up installed-base customers. Two years after introduction, an industry journal commented:

> When IBM announced the AS/400 line of mid-range computers, it met with some skepticism. But, to everyone's surprise, the AS/400 has turned into one of Big Blue's hottest-selling products. . . . Estimates [put] the total market for the AS/400 and related products at more than $10 billion annually. If this revenue belonged to a separate company, those numbers would make it the third largest information systems supplier in the United States.[8]

Using the AS/400 as an example, IBM's management created a position, the Assistant General Manager of Marketing (AGMM), formally charged with coordinating product-sales-service needs within each major product unit or line of business (LOB). "With six to ten major product introductions annually," an executive explained, "something like the AS/400 team had to be institutionalized and not formed on an ad hoc basis." Those appointed AGMMs were (like Bill Grabe) all senior managers with years of experience and responsibility in a variety of functions.

Exhibit 4-4 outlines the formal responsibilities of AGMMs. Each reported directly to the General Manager of his or her line of business, and each was measured on worldwide revenues and profits of that LOB's product. In explaining the purpose of the position, an executive at IBM emphasized that "AGMMs occupy a crossroads position between the field sales and service organizations, the applications and industry specialists at headquarters, and the product management or-

Exhibit 4-4
Overview of AGMM Responsibilities

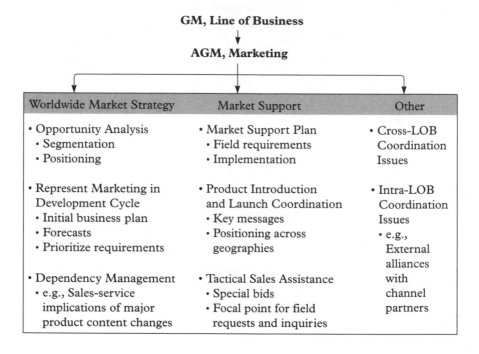

GM, Line of Business

↓

AGM, Marketing

Worldwide Market Strategy	Market Support	Other

• Opportunity Analysis
  • Segmentation
  • Positioning
	• Market Support Plan
	  • Field requirements
	  • Implementation
		• Cross-LOB Coordination Issues

• Represent Marketing in Development Cycle
  • Initial business plan
  • Forecasts
  • Prioritize requirements
	• Product Introduction and Launch Coordination
	  • Key messages
	  • Positioning across geographies
		• Intra-LOB Coordination Issues
		  • e.g., External alliances with channel partners

• Dependency Management
  • e.g., Sales-service implications of major product content changes
	• Tactical Sales Assistance
	  • Special bids
	  • Focal point for field requests and inquiries	

ganization. Their challenge is to facilitate the convergence of these groups."

THE UNDERLYING ISSUES AT IBM

I have described at some length these contrasting product introductions for two reasons: (1) The problems illustrate underlying market, organizational, and historical factors that affect product-sales-service interfaces in many other companies and industries; and (2) IBM's response—the creation of a formal liaison unit charged with aligning market and resource groups—illustrates many of the issues involved in a common structural response to these factors.

The 9370 experience is an example of how uncoordinated product, sales, and service efforts result in internal conflicts, poor implementation, and a failed attempt "to sell hardware without the total solution in place." By contrast, the AS/400 release was managed by one group explicitly responsible for orchestrating the introduction among the developers, industry specialists at headquarters, and marketing managers in the field. The result was a very successful product launch which, only two years after introduction, represented a major business for IBM.

These immediate origins of the AGMM position are important. But the unit is also an attempt to deal with wider forces reshaping marketing requirements in IBM's business and, conversely, the organizational heritage that evolved at IBM with the S/360 product line. Three aspects of this history are noteworthy.

First, note the value of start-to-finish responsibility for a product in IBM's business—and many other businesses. Product development is often the locus of the most expensive investments in a business, especially in a rapidly changing technological environment. Some process for encouraging "functional excellence" in this activity is required, as the S/360 experience indicates. Organizational theorists are quick to ridicule managers for their narrow, "stovepiped" functional concerns. But managers who have gone through the delays, slowdowns, broken promises to important customers, escalating cost overruns, and financial pressures of a major product introduction intuitively understand IBM's response to this episode.

Second, the Phase Process was a serial procedure where disagreements were surfaced and managed through a contention system that allowed escalation up to the corporate Management Committee. In this process, headquarters product units, not the field sales units, clearly wielded the most organizational power.

Third, it is useful to consider when such a contention system is, and is not, appropriate. As the IBM history suggests, the system can work when:

1. Technological uncertainty is high (thus, increasing the value of the options bought by having multiple product development programs), while market uncertainty is manageable (e.g., customers face switching costs from their installed software on a vendor's proprietary system);

2. Extended product life cycles provide the time frames required to

manage interactions and disagreements between marketing
groups by escalation up the hierarchy; and

3.   It's possible to have a central organizational arbitrator like the
     MC break deadlocks, without being overwhelmed by the sheer
     number of umpire calls generated by the market.

These conditions held for some time after the introduction of the
S/360. But the market conditions for the 9370 and AS/400 introductions in the late 1980s were characterized by shorter product life
cycles, more emphasis on time-to-market and first-mover advantages,
a move toward open systems (reducing switching costs for customers), a variety of specialized niche competitors, and increasing demand for integrated solutions across product, sales, and service units.
An executive at IBM provided a useful distillation of these changes
that, during the past decade, have turned IBM from a synonym for
excellence and market power to a handy metaphor for "stumbling
giant":

> IBM's original genius was to allay big customers' fears of computing
> by assuming responsibility for proprietary, general-purpose products.
> For years, few vendors could duplicate our abilities. But today, differ-
> ent parts of the computer industry's value chain are each served by
> many specialized firms. There is less value placed on a vendor's hard-
> ware, and more on the ability to take on the risks of developing and
> implementing customized solutions. Yet, no one company can assume
> these risks for all types of customers. Market selection becomes more
> important.

In the aggregate, these changes represent an evolution from a
general-purpose to a solutions marketplace. The impact on effective
marketing is profound. Exhibit 4-5 outlines this change and the implications for a firm's cost structure, product policy, and organizational
requirements. In this exhibit, I have described this contrast in the vocabulary of the computer business. But many other companies are
grappling with similar changes. Consumer goods firms face analogous
market developments: from mass marketing to micromarketing where
increased segmentation and trade-oriented solutions are more im-

Exhibit 4-5

Impact of Market Changes on Business Drivers

	General Purpose	**Solutions Market**
Cost Structure	Scale-Sensitive Hardware as major element of vendor's cost-of-goods-sold	Applications-Sensitive Software as major element of vendor's cost-of-goods-sold
Value Chain	Vertical Integration From silicon to customer via a single vendor	Vertical-Markets Focus Multiple components via a solutions integrator
Manufacturing	Long lead times and world-scale capacity within a product line	Flexible, segment-responsive capacity and need to accelerate cycle time
Product Policy	Proprietary Systems Emphasis on cost-effective hardware and compatibility with installed-base software	Emerging "Open" Systems Emphasis on high value-in-use systems for target segments
Product Life Cycles	Like the Old Auto Business Five-year model changes	Like a Fashion Business Time-to-market pressures
Market Segmentation	Aim for the common denominator among customer groups	Aim for complete, tailored solutions to selected segments
Key Sales Tasks	Focus on high-end line extensions and aggregate market developments primarily via direct sales channels	Sell more new products and segment-specific requirements via a combination of direct and indirect channels
Organization	"Functional excellence" with strong centralized product units assuming start-to-finish responsibility; coordination via the contention system	"Market-driven" project management that requires locally responsive coordination among multiple sales, service, and product units

portant. And many service companies need to move from offering general-purpose services to segmented value-added services. In each case, the nature of marketing tasks is altered, and the IBM experience indicates both the scope and the difficulty of the challenges.

For years, IBM grew and prospered in the general-purpose environment. In this marketplace, product groups had to perform two important tasks: (1) understand the needs of the average customer as an input to cost-effective product development, and (2) motivate a quota-driven sales force to devote attention and training to their particular product line. The first task was performed by strong, centralized system managers with start-to-finish responsibility for their products—what we would now call "heavyweight product managers" who have broad responsibility and clout for their projects within a functional organization.[9] The second task was performed by annual negotiating sessions between product and sales units.

In the solutions market, however, marketing requirements are more decentralized and place more emphasis on: (1) providing customized product-service packages to different customer groups, and (2) picking the optimum customer segments relative to the investments in hardware, software, applications development, services, and direct and indirect channels needed for each segment. Expertise in product development remains crucial in this environment. But ongoing input from, and interaction with, multiple field groups in different geographies are also crucial, making the traditional organizational structure for managing these interfaces increasingly costly, time-consuming, and inefficient.

The unsuccessful 9370 introduction was a symptom of the organization's failure to deal with these new requirements while the successful AS/400 introduction indicates one potential mechanism for addressing the challenges of the new solutions. With shorter product life cycles, moreover, the firm must accelerate development cycles and introduce more products more often. Hence, "something like the AS/400 team had to be institutionalized," and IBM's response was the AGMM structure.

In the terms of the earlier discussion in this chapter, the AGMM tries to help manage the orthogonal needs of companies in rapidly changing environments. It operates at the interface between each product unit (responsible for R&D, product planning, and manufacturing of its product) and field marketing units in each geographic area (responsible for sales and service of all product lines). Reporting to the general manager of its product group and measured on worldwide revenues and profits of that product line, the AGMM tries to influence both product development in its unit and field marketing in the geographies, so that the two are integrated.

What are the management issues associated with this approach?

FORMAL LIAISON UNITS

Many companies have created or expanded positions whose purpose is to coordinate marketing interfaces. As with the AGMM positions at IBM, these liaison units are usually located at headquarters and tend to focus on upstream interactions between product, sales, and service groups in the development of products and marketing plans and in the introductory phase of product programs. Hence, these units are often part of the organizational structure at companies where product development requires technical expertise and sales/customer input far in advance of introduction (high-tech firms), or where the marketing planning process and field implementation demand not only concentrated attention to the distinct positioning of individual products with end-users, but also coordination of multiple products that flow through common distribution channels to these customer groups (branded package goods).

In these business settings, coordinative mechanisms address a situation where product, sales, and service units must work together on different aspects of marketing planning and implementation while maintaining expertise in ongoing product development and account management tasks. The goal is to get local market input taken into account earlier in the product- and marketing-planning processes. In turn, these liaison units often act as the voice of the field with product managers and, conversely, as product merchandisers with field sales and service groups.

In consumer goods firms, a structural linkage analogous to that of the AGMM is the position known as sales planning at many companies. These units are generally responsible for activities outlined in the

position description from a major international marketer of packaged
food products:

> The Sales Planning group is responsible for the design, implementa-
> tion, and coordination of all promotional activity, both national and
> local. Manages the Marketing Department's timely and accurate sub-
> mission of promotional and product source documents. Deals with
> Distribution and Manufacturing to accommodate Sales' needs. Man-
> ages the Merchandising and Materials interface to ensure spending
> is kept to annual budget. Also responsible for the development and
> coordination of Sales Force incentive programs, and effective roll-out
> of new products.

The head of Sales Planning at the firm explained that "this means
our mission is to plan the work and work the plan":

> We are a primary interface between Sales and Marketing during all
> phases of business development. We review local programs developed
> by Sales and provide direction to ensure these programs accord with
> Brand strategies. We also seek to ensure that volume and contribution
> goals are achieved in all trade classes. We evaluate field promotional
> funding requests to determine their cost effectiveness, and communi-
> cate the relevant brand group's response as well as any necessary
> follow-up. We are a liaison between Sales, Marketing, Distribution,
> and Manufacturing. In large part, this means translating other func-
> tions' requirements into effective field communications and programs.

In other industries, similar responsibilities are often lodged with
sales support or product planning units. At Microsoft, the Sales Operations Group is responsible for coordinating product managers' plans
with field sales activities. Similarly, many industrial firms have planning managers within their product divisions, charged with liaison activities that span both product development and introduction efforts.
Product-planning managers at a manufacturer of capital equipment
are responsible for:

- Developing the product line by soliciting ideas and requests from
  field personnel and working with development managers;

Exhibit 4-6
Typical Context for Use of Marketing Liaison Units

Focus	Facilitate product-sales-service interactions in developing product marketing plans and during introduction phase of product life cycle
Most Common Marketing Environment	Product: complex, fast-changing technology; long lead times between product development and actual introduction
	Market: multiple products flowing through common channels of distribution to diverse end-user groups
Management Issues	Costs, credibility, and staffing

- Estimating market potential for proposed product-line additions;
- Coordinating production and delivery schedules;
- Preparing instructional and training materials;
- Conducting product seminars [for salespeople as well as customers]; and
- Working with sales personnel on problems of selling and servicing equipment.

Faced with market changes that increase coordination requirements, the response of many companies is to establish such a unit or to devote more resources and decision-making scope to traditional product planning or sales operations activities. Exhibit 4-6 summarizes the typical focus, marketing environment, and key management issues of these liaison units. The following sections discuss in more detail their benefits and vulnerabilities.

Benefits

Establishing a formal liaison unit recognizes certain daily organizational realities. First, such units can legitimize product-sales-service collaboration in companies (like IBM) where these activities have long resided in separate areas, each steeped in its own well-engrained standard operating procedures. These positions are a visible means for specifying required two-way information flows and capturing learning about joint activities—important benefits when companies need to introduce more products faster to more customer groups. Equally important, they are a specific decision-making mechanism in an environment where important trade-offs and timely information now exist at the interface between marketing groups, rather than primarily within each area.

Without a formal structure in place, informal methods of managing these linkages are often too time-consuming, treated as a distant "secondary priority" by each group, or are simply ineffective because attempts by managers in one area to get involved in another group's plans are viewed as infringements. In my research, I found this to be true at smaller as well as larger firms and whether or not the company was a turf-conscious bureaucracy.

Second, these units are both conduits and circuit breakers in firms where product groups compete for field attention. As conduits, they provide a single point of contact for product managers or salespeople needing answers to questions or information updates, and minimize multiple individual communications between the groups. At a division of a consumer goods firm, sales planning is the information clearing house between a dozen brand managers and three sales forces through which their brands go to market. Without such units, communications between product and field groups would be more time-consuming and, as one liaison manager noted, "more susceptible to multiple interpretations that can make our field activities and product positioning inconsistent across branches and countries."

These units also function as circuit breakers whose role is to prevent product groups from overwhelming sales and service with uncoordinated promotions, contests, and other means of gaining field attention. Recall the situation, described in Chapter 3, of the branch sales manager who consigned the voluminous amounts of product literature he received to the "archives" because, if his salespeople actually read the material, "they'd have no time to sell." Similarly, every liaison unit in my research emphasized that its role was, in part, to "shield the field" from the sheer volume of literature and information requests developed by product groups utilizing a common sales channel.

At a telecommunications firm where product introductions have accelerated dramatically in recent years, the liaison unit between headquarters product managers and field sales managers developed an explicit system for routing information. Each piece of information is assigned a status code: "Hotline" (time-sensitive information such as pricing or rate changes, sent to each branch within four hours); "Direct Line" (important but not time-sensitive information, distributed every two weeks); "FYI" (distributed at branch managers' discretion); or "Heads Up" (information about general industry developments or upcoming activities, distributed monthly). The manager of the unit noted that "Every product group is vying for field attention, and views all information about its line as crucial. But part of my job is to protect the field from information overload, and this system helps establish necessary priorities."

Third, when staffed by a mix of sales, service, and product personnel, these liaison units help shape product programs with field implementation requirements in mind. At a consumer goods firm, sales planning holds two-day quarterly meetings with sales managers in each region. Also in attendance are brand personnel who, in successive one-hour sessions, present up-coming product and promotional plans. At one meeting I attended, field feedback included the following:

- "This plan isn't relevant to food wholesalers, who are important in my region. We need to take into account the following aspects of their operations."
- "My experience with last year's couponing event indicates . . ."
- "After all I've heard today, I'm afraid we're overloading promotional events in that quarter and dissipating their impact in the field."

Such feedback concerns topics that were vital to implementing product managers' plans and were conveyed easily and candidly.

Finally, liaison units can also help make dispersed customer re-

quirements salient earlier, and of higher priority, in the planning process. Some managers stress the analogy with quality initiatives in their
companies. These units, as one executive commented, help "make
visible issues that cut across product and sales groups, just as quality
circles helped build our awareness of the cross-functional requirements of quality management." In an industrial products company,
a product-planning manager explained that "My role is to inject
industry- or other vertical-market applications criteria into what otherwise would be investment decisions guided mainly by established
product categories." Similarly, a sales-planning manager at a consumer products company noted that, at meetings with brand executives, "My role is to constantly remind brand management that we
sell to consumers through different classes of trade, and these channel
requirements now affect all elements of the marketing mix. It's better
to deal with these requirements proactively in brand strategies, rather
than reactively via more trade deals."

When the liaison unit has its own dedicated resources for product
or promotional activities, moreover, the impact on traditional resource
allocation priorities can be substantial. At IBM, one AGMM unit had
a limited budget to fund development initiatives. Based on its experience with sales and service groups, the AGMM believed a new low-
end product would be an important addition to the line. The AGMM
informed the relevant product manager that her group could have $x
million and a certain time frame to develop this product. She re-
sponded with a figure of $2x million and a longer development sched-
ule. "Our response," noted the head of the AGMM unit, "was to indicate that we would take our funds to another product group to get the
work done. And her reaction was, 'We'll look again at our assumptions
and get back to you.'" They finally compromised on the time and
money involved, and the project was launched.

Vulnerabilities

The vulnerabilities of this linkage mechanism involve costs, credibility, and staffing requirements.

Liaison units represent another management layer with attendant
costs in salaries, support systems, and overhead. At IBM, the AS/400
project team involved 15 people. But, as Exhibit 4-4 indicates, the

responsibilities of the AGMM units went beyond the product introduction tasks of the AS/400 team to include product development
input, worldwide strategy coordination, and ongoing tactical sales
support. As a result, within two years and despite corporate pressures
for cost reductions and downsizing, each AGMM unit had a staff of
25 to 50 people focused on areas such as market research, product
planning, and sales support activities.

These staffing levels are often necessary for conducting the liaison
tasks. But it requires a critical mass in the firm's product portfolio and
sales base to be economically viable. Hence, liaison units tend to be
established in larger companies where the additional management
layer can be a mixed blessing for marketing decision making that, already, involves multiple review levels. At one company I studied, a
liaison unit, originally established to speed interactions between product and sales groups, was soon perceived by both groups as yet another checkpoint, stalling the firm's response time to a fast-changing
market. "It's like a government program," said one manager. "Once
established, it just grows and moves into areas not part of its original
charter or expertise." As discussed below, this is a perennial danger
and an issue that senior executives must monitor and manage.

Even when liaison units stay lean and focused, they face a constant
challenge from line managers in product, sales, and service areas who
view them as interlopers, rather than integrators. This conflict may
be inevitable because liaison units must balance consistent product
strategies with customized channel requirements—or, as the head of
sales planning at one firm put it: "If either Marketing or Sales is en-
tirely happy with us, something's wrong. We must guard against clever
marketing programs that can't be sold to the trade and against volume-
driven sales requests that aren't profitable." Hence, liaison managers
are often in the unenviable position of providing each group with less
than it asked for, and so tend to be the focus of many contentious
negotiations.

In my interviews at consumer goods firms, for example, brand
managers consistently referred to sales-planning managers (who formally reported through the brand management hierarchy at these
firms) as "salespeople" while sales executives referred to them as
"brand planners." Similarly, an AGMM manager emphasizes that

"The nature of the job means that we are seen as the 'outsider' by both camps: to be a marketing person in a product development organization is to be perceived as opting for resource commitments based on transitory or account-specific evidence; to represent product developers to field sales is to be perceived as providing 'too little/too late' help with urgent account requirements."

Further, liaison units rarely have line authority over the groups they deal with. They are like matrix managers who have responsibility (but not commensurate authority) for various aspects of decision making. They must therefore develop informal sources of influence with their peers. One liaison manager noted, "The fact is that we sit in the middle between product development and manufacturing units, on the one hand, and sales and service units, on the other. And we don't 'own' many resources on either side. So, information, personal relations, and judicious use of the escalation process [to senior executive levels] become key management tools in this job."

To develop the necessary credibility and organizational influence, these units require managers with a good track record and updated knowledge of changing product and field realities. Experienced product, sales, or service managers are, however, often reluctant to accept a position that has no line authority. And, to keep knowledge of R&D or sales developments current, these units must rotate personnel in and out of headquarters every few years. At IBM, the head of an AGMM unit noted that, "In staffing, you need a balance between short timers and long termers":

> We have rotating 12- to 18-month assignments in this unit for field managers in order to keep our contacts and information current. But we also have much longer assignments for those who deal primarily with product development issues because it takes time to understand the technical and other issues involved in a multiyear development project. My staff is about 80% short timers and 20% long termers, and I think that's about the right mix.

The danger with this level of staff turnover, however, is that some members of the liaison unit are always seen by other groups in the company as "still learning what their job is."

The head of sales planning at a consumer goods company outlined the staffing requirements in her liaison unit:

It's not easy to get good salespeople to join Sales Planning, despite the opportunity we offer to learn about the whole business. Salespeople have freedom in the field, a company car, and incentive pay, and see corporate headquarters as "claustrophobic." It also takes time and continuity to understand the various brand strategies we support, develop contacts and trust in the brand groups, and master the subtleties of the marketing planning process. Staffing this unit is a difficult balancing act.

But unless this balance is achieved these units will be viewed as gatekeepers who, as one brand manager complained to me, "generate meetings where minutes are kept and hours are wasted."

KEY DIAGNOSTIC QUESTIONS

Given the mix of costs and benefits in this approach, the following questions are useful in diagnosing the management issues associated with liaison units.

* Who are the managers selected for such units and do they possess the organizational credibility and personal skills required?

These units are highly dependent on the personal stature and influence of their members. In my research, successful liaison units were staffed with managers seen as "going places" in the firm; unsuccessful liaison units were seen, justly or unjustly, as staffed primarily by those who "couldn't cut it" in core product, sales, or service positions. Attracting managers with visible track records of accomplishment, and providing a career path that takes into account the necessary turnover in these positions, are crucial prerequisites for effective liaison units.

Even when staffed by credible personnel, these units require a blend of managerial skills. At least three skills are fundamental:

Analysis. Liaison managers must create a useful model of market opportunities that is relevant to the managers they must influence.

Developing this model requires an appetite for data analysis and the ability to "speak the languages" of multiple groups.

Operations. This skill involves translating market concepts into operating budgets, plans, and schedules. Probably the biggest complaint I heard about these units was that, while they improved coordination, they also slowed decision making. Precisely because they work at the interface between busy marketing groups, liaison managers must be good implementers.

Communications. This skill is the internal "selling" part of the job. As well as gathering and disseminating information, managers lobby others in a variety of areas and should be able to deal effectively with what are, implicitly or explicitly, negotiations with budget-conscious line managers. This involves interpersonal skills and a tolerance for ambiguity in a position that has little formal authority over the multiple groups that the manager deals with.

- What decision-making rights are lodged with liaison units, and what decisions remain with product, sales, or service groups?

Liaison units necessarily encroach on decisions that were once made solely by product, sales, or service managers. The traditional balance of power is disrupted, with resulting conflicts. Arguments can introduce a useful market tension in the organization and help readjust the balance in areas where one unit has, in the name of functional excellence, been indifferent to other important issues. But these turf battles take time, affect decision making, and can subvert the initial goal in establishing the unit: better responsiveness to increased coordination requirements.

Addressing this issue involves clarifying what aspects of joint tasks are the primary responsibility of each functional group and what aspects are those of the liaison unit. The head of sales planning at a consumer goods firm commented: "A few months after this unit began, it became apparent that we needed a better job description. So, with top executives in Brand and Sales, we outlined those areas where my unit has either the final say, veto power, or recommendation responsibilities. This narrowed our scope, and not everything happens the way I want it to happen. But it's also improved our ability to do what *is* in our domain."

- Over time, how does the liaison unit tend to operate: as forum for the exchange and resolution of different perspectives, or as convenient proxy for customer contact?

As noted, liaison units are simultaneously conduits and circuit breakers. The danger is that, over time, these units unwittingly become another barrier between the product, sales, and service groups—primarily a circuit breaker rather than a logistically efficient conduit. It is top management's responsibility to monitor this process and ensure that these units are not allowed to build empires or be used by the groups they deal with as a convenient proxy for actual feedback from customers and channel partners.

CONCLUSION

Organization charts don't make decisions; people do. But, when managed effectively, structural linkages such as liaison units can play a valuable role. In busy organizations, they are a means for capturing learning about joint activities, and for combining one group's product/ technology perspectives with another group's channel/account expertise.

Central to the liaison role, however, is the ability to help gather and disseminate efficiently product, market, and customer information relevant to different marketing groups. The topic of effective marketing information systems in a changing competitive environment is the subject of the next chapter.

5

Market Research and Information Systems

■

IN marketing, the value of information is tied to its use in influencing buyer-seller exchange. But as Chapter 3 indicated, different
marketing groups have different information needs, even as market
developments generate more interactions between these groups. The
result in many firms is suggested by a chief financial officer at an industrial products company:

> New data sources in our industry and information systems [IS] in our
> company provide capabilities that were impossible five years ago. In
> an environment where time is money, we also have a big incentive to
> substitute data for dollars in areas like order entry, inventory manage-
> ment, and both pre- and postsale services. But we actually make mini-
> mal use of these capabilities, despite steadily growing budgets in market
> research and information technology. This is expensive and a big op-
> portunity cost because the marginal utility of unaccessed data is zero.

Accessing data points to an important dimension of coordination
and, as this chapter shows, is a key role for market researchers working
with IS managers. "More communication" through more teams or
task force meetings is a frequent prescription for cross-functional collaboration. But without a relevant and accessible information infrastructure these meetings can simply be more opportunities for finger
pointing, not joint problem solving.

This chapter focuses on the issues involved in making research and information systems more responsive to new marketing requirements. It first discusses why a linking of research and information systems has become competitively significant and why the role of traditional market research needs redefining. Then, using the experience of Packaged Products Company (PPCo) as an example, the chapter considers the benefits, costs, and management challenges of re-aligning research and information systems that affect product, sales, and service groups.

INFORMATION SYSTEMS AND BUYER POWER

Managers in every industry I examined mentioned that, during the past decade, customers' knowledge about exchange dimensions has increased significantly, with commensurate impacts on buyer power. Information technology allows purchasing personnel in many multi-location accounts to coordinate more closely than ever their negotiations with vendors.

Among the trends affecting health care businesses is the growth of group purchasing organizations (GPOs). In 1980, only a minority of health care sites were enrolled in GPOs. By 1990, the majority of hospitals and clinics were members of multiple GPOs. In these arrangements, individual hospitals submit their purchase preferences while price and delivery are negotiated centrally. The GPO has the information systems to compare terms and conditions among its members, and bargains with vendors for the best "street price" available at a particular point in time. One impact of this system is that primary purchasing authority for many medical products has shifted from end-user departments in health care sites to more centralized GPO purchasing agents. These buyers make demands that cut across the vendor's product lines, sales regions, and service units. A manager at a medical products vendor commented:

> These customers structure negotiations on the premise that they can deliver so many thousands of beds to the manufacturer with the best terms. What was a technical sale to a lab manager now involves dealing

with professional purchasing people who come armed with computer
print-outs of *every* item purchased by *every* member hospital from *every* supplier they deal with. With the volumes at stake, you soon learn
what the sports announcers mean when they talk about "the thrill of
victory and the agony of defeat."

In telecommunications, technology introduced during the past decade allows commercial customers to track more precisely their telcom usage patterns. These customers receive monthly reports that
summarize call activity in great detail: how much is voice, fax, or data;
how much is through each vendor's service offering and at what rates;
how much is domestic (and over what distance); how much is international (and to which countries); and how much has been generated
by each plant site, sales branch, or functional department within the
customer's organization. With this data, telcom managers can identify
cost savings or value-added applications for different groups of users
within their firms. This knowledge, in turn, generates more account-
specific requirements that span product and sales groups at the
vendor.

The consumer package-goods business represents a dramatic instance of information technology's impact on buyer power. As one
experienced market researcher noted: "Through the late 1970s, the
technologies available to the consumer marketing-research industry
had been basically unchanged since the inception of the field in the
early 1930s when pioneers like Gallup, Nielsen, and Starch set up
shop. Technologies used in the 1970s were the same ones available in
the 1930s—telephone surveys, door-to-door personal interviews, di-
ary panels, store audits, response meters, story boards, and so forth."[1]
Throughout this period, there were improvements in research sam-
pling and statistical techniques. But unlike the electronic technologies
developed in the 1980s, these improvements did not change the char-
acter of consumer marketing or power relationships in the distribution channel.

Consider the impact of scanner systems at retail check-out count-
ers. By 1992, most food stores had such systems and other classes of
trade were rapidly installing them. Scanner data give retailers a new
basis for making product stocking and merchandising decisions.

Trade buyers can use the data to test, in their regions or stores, manufacturers' claims about the impact of advertising or promotions on product movement. Further, technology allows retailers to tie this data to their handling costs, warehousing expenses, and shelf space allocations in order to calculate the direct product profit (DPP)—the profit contribution of an item after all trade allowances are added to gross margin and after all shipping, warehousing, and other handling costs attributable to the item are deducted. High DPP contributors are given more support; low contributors are discontinued. An executive at a consumer products manufacturer explained the marketing consequences:

> It used to be that manufacturers knew what was going on in most useful detail, and would tell the store managers. Now it's the other way around. The problem came home to many of us when, in a meeting with the CEO of one of the largest retailers in the United States, he said, "I know exactly how many dollars and units of your company's products each of my stores sells. But I bet you don't know how much you sell through my stores." We spent weeks trying to find that data only to discover he was right; our information systems weren't set up to provide that kind of data.

Further, information developments in some consumer markets may be a precursor of developments in other industries during the coming decade. Real-time data concerning product movement is a technical reality for a number of retailers (and some industrial distributors) in the United States, Canada, and Europe. This development places even more pressure on their vendors to customize and synchronize their own information-gathering procedures by account.

INFORMATION SYSTEMS AND MARKETING FRAGMENTATION

For these reasons, most companies I studied were in the midst of what their managers viewed as a disruptive but necessary overhaul of systems used to disseminate marketing-related information. The necessity was clear. Over time, information systems in their product, sales, and service units had become fragmented and often technically incompatible with one another. One executive described these separate systems and databases as "information silos" from which units "launch data missiles at each other," with minimal impact on coordination efforts. Meanwhile, developments at buyers require sellers to assimilate market data faster and at more granular levels of detail.

In telecommunications, commercial customers' greater ability to track usage patterns means that competition among vendors increasingly focuses on specialized applications. Selling such applications can raise customer loyalty in a business with more alternatives and fewer switching costs, but requires significant sales time, service resources, and software development. Also, these specialized applications tend to lack mass-market appeal. One telcom vendor found that more than 70% of its sales of such services came from less than 30% of its customer base, underscoring the importance of shared customization criteria to guide cost-effective product development and field sales and service efforts.

Two major vendors I studied found themselves in the following situation: their product, sales, and service units each used different and incompatible information systems, resulting in inconsistent and money-losing bids for commercial business. One manager referred to the "morning-after syndrome," in which "we first congratulate ourselves on winning a big contract, then find out that sales has underestimated product configuration costs and product managers have not factored in postsale service issues. We have sometimes literally implemented the old joke about losing money on each unit while trying to make it up in volume!" This set off equally dysfunctional "correction" behavior in future bids: to protect themselves, managers in each unit then consciously *over*estimated the costs of fulfilling a proposed contract. The vendor priced itself out of the running at important accounts, leaving the door open to competitors with better means of aggregating product, sales, and service information.

In consumer goods, the information systems now available to retail buyers have often created a mismatch in manufacturer-trade negotiations. A buyer at a major U.K. grocery retailer commented:

Off the record . . . of the salespeople I see, only 20% have any decent information and only 10% are up to the standards of our buyers. Some of them have still not stepped out of the 1950s and simply don't understand the category economics of the products they are selling. . . . There is no way they will negotiate the best deal.

This mismatch in information sources is often revealed in terms of trade promotions. By the late 1980s, at U.S. consumer goods manufacturers, spending on trade promotions surpassed advertising expenditures as a percentage of the marketing budget. For many firms, such spending has reached hundreds of millions of dollars annually. In some years, according to one estimate, the average U.S. grocery retailer is reportedly offered nearly 20 times as many manufacturer trade promotions as can be accommodated within the available instore display space.[2] But at a number of the consumer goods firms I studied, trade spending is captured by three incompatible information systems lodged in brand, sales, and logistics units, and can only be aggregated at the national level across product groups. For these firms, specifying promotional paybacks in terms of class of trade or account often is impossible or requires time frames far in excess of the relevant selling cycles. Yet, as one manager emphasized, "These data are crucial if sales is to generate profitable volume. As the trade changes, the field will have more control over local promotional expenditures and must understand the ROI implications."

In addition, these technology issues can unwittingly exacerbate conflicts. With the advent of laptop computers, companies have devoted much money to sales automation in an effort to increase the sales force's call capacity and productivity.[3] But the lack of a common information infrastructure among marketing groups often makes the returns on these investments elusive, and can generate unintended negative consequences in the organization. As one executive commented about the impact of his firm's multimillion-dollar investment in user-friendly sales automation: "Now, when product and sales managers meet, disagreements are aired with print-outs from different spreadsheets, people start referring to 'the facts,' and the tone often becomes sarcastic and accusatory on each side."

A striking example of the problem is a consumer goods firm in my research. Sales used "tagged distribution," monthly audits of company and wholesaler warehouses to track the percentage of items already "tagged" or bar coded, and so ready for distribution to stores.

Product managers used "percentage store selling," data indicating the percentage of retail outlets that had actually sold at least one item of a product during a time period. The former measure overreports distribution compared to the latter, but it formed the basis of sales' internal reporting system and was enshrined in the software salespeople used with their new computers. The differences in tracking distribution fueled vigorous arguments, especially during new product introductions and promotional campaigns. One executive explained: "New brand assistants, who monitor roll-out, were unaware of the different reporting systems. They often came away from one of their first important interactions with field managers believing that salespeople were lying about implementation results or deliberately obfuscating the data."

A shared information infrastructure is therefore vital to managing marketing effectively in the new environment. It helps provide a needed common language about market realities—even if disagreement persists about the appropriate response to these realities. Moreover, the information itself becomes both a means and motivation for cross-functional efforts, affecting what people can and will do when interactions with other organizational units are essential for customer satisfaction.

MARKETING VERSUS MARKET RESEARCH

In theory, the market research function—charged with understanding customer needs—should help integrate these information flows. In practice, this was not the case at most companies I examined. One reason is that "market research" in these firms really means "marketing research," with research staffs largely serving the information priorities of product marketing managers.[4] Their output often has little relevance to the daily concerns of sales and service managers.

The traditional alignment of market research at consumer goods firms, for example, is outlined in Exhibit 5-1. Market research reports to, and is usually funded by, the product marketing department. In obtaining and facilitating use of syndicated data, research plays a screening and support role for product managers. In conducting studies of advertising copy, consumer behavior in product categories, industry

Exhibit 5-1

Traditional Alignment of Research Responsibilities:
Consumer Goods Firms

Marketing

Product Managers	Research Managers	Sales Managers
Decisions	Support	Decisions
• Product development	• Syndicated research	• Gain distribution
• Packaging	• Market analysis	• In-store presence
• Pricing	• Consumer research	• Merchandising
• Advertising	• Industry forecasts	• Execution of trade
• Promotion development	• Industry data analysis	promotions

Consumer Focus   *Trade Focus*

trends, and competition, research plays an analytical role for product groups. And, in preparing forecasts and market analyses for top management, research plays a role in the marketing planning process while, as a centralized headquarters function, helping ensure comparability of product market data across business units and over time.

Each role is valuable and important. But they all tend to support the traditional alignment of product management responsibilities outlined in Chapter 2: cross-geography, product-specific responsibilities, with a strategic focus on consumer pull tools and techniques.

By contrast, market research departments in these companies have traditionally had much less to say to those groups that deal with the implementation of brand strategies through the distribution channel. An executive at one of the world's leading suppliers of scanner data emphasized: "Most people in corporate market research departments have little contact with channel issues and a poor grasp of sales force needs, in particular. Their training and experience are primarily in analyzing consumer attitudinal data, not the shopping behavior data now flooding the market." Just how limited this contact can be is suggested by the allocation of the market research budget at one major consumer-goods manufacturer in my study. As recently as 1992, this company spent more than $40 million on consumer research, but allocated only four people (and less than $1 million) to studies of its top 200 trade accounts—the buyers and channels for more than 80% of the firm's sales volume.

Technology is highlighting the gap between traditional research and research relevant to new marketing requirements. Reliance on attitudinal data grew because, for decades, behavioral data about consumers were unavailable or prohibitively expensive to gather. As a result, those trained in market research techniques since World War II have been operating largely in a U.S. social science paradigm of samplings, surveys, polls, and controlled "laboratory" experiments. The inputs are what consumers *say* they did, or will do, in their purchasing decisions. But there is now growing evidence that indicates big differences between how people respond in surveys and polls and how they really behave in the marketplace.[5] Meanwhile, scanner data, direct response, and interactive media technologies, among others, make information about what people actually *do* with their money at the point of purchase more accessible.

Effective management of marketing interfaces requires both types of information: data about actual purchase behavior and attitudinal data that can help explain and predict that behavior. Hence, a realignment of research roles and responsibilities is under way at many companies. The evolving alignment in consumer goods companies is outlined in Exhibit 5-2. It differs from the traditional alignment in three important ways: (1) market research has close contact with the company's information systems managers (and may report through the IS, rather than product marketing, organization) because more research data are driven by technology developments at research suppliers and trade channels; (2) research resources are often allocated to decentralized market teams, rather than centrally to headquarters product groups; and (3) the role of research is explicitly that of a cross-functional facilitator, rather than primarily a support/analytical resource for product management strategies.

In this alignment, the research budget may come from various groups, including sales, service, and IS as well as product management. In addition, research that was performed centrally by the market research department is now often done by other groups. Some

Exhibit 5-2
Evolving Alignment of Market Research Responsibilities

Marketing	Research/IS	Field Sales
Product Managers	Research Managers	Sales Managers
Decisions	Facilitate	Decisions
• Product development, packaging, positioning by user/market segment • Pricing • Advertising • Consumer promotions • Supply chain impact	• Syndicated research • Consumer research • Account reviews • Joint databases • Decision support systems • Supply chain data • Systems/data integrity	• Gain distribution • Space management • Merchandising • Promotion design and delivery by market and class of trade • Account management
(Consumer/Market Focus)	Translate/Support	(Trade/Market Focus)

shifts to external research suppliers; some is done by sales and service units via decision-support tools purchased and actively supported by the research function. As research budgets and personnel are assigned to these groups, moreover, their role often becomes one of information exchange among the units that research now interacts with. The goal, as one manager explained, is "to involve research more directly with decisions and implementation tasks that require interaction between different parts of the company. Research should provide a shared understanding of the impact of each function's decisions on other units involved."

The experience of Packaged Products Company[6] illustrates the kinds of changes involved in trying to achieve this goal as well as the management issues raised by these changes in research and information systems.

PACKAGED PRODUCTS COMPANY

Founded early in the twentieth century, Packaged Products Company had, by 1990, more than $1 billion in annual sales from candies, crackers, nuts, potato chips, and other snack foods. Nuts and potato chips are PPCo's largest product lines and, nationally, the firm holds leading market-share positions in these categories. PPCo products are purchased by an estimated 35% of U.S. households through 10,000 customers in several classes of trade, including supermarkets, drug stores, convenience stores, mass merchandisers such as K mart and Wal-Mart, and smaller independent grocery stores. Together, supermarkets, mass merchandisers, and convenience stores accounted for about 80% of PPCo's dollar volume in 1990, with the latter two classes of trade growing faster than the former in recent years.

In most product categories, PPCo competes with other national brands as well as private label and regional brands. The national brands (including PPCo's) are priced 10–20% higher than private label products while regional brands vary widely in price, depending on their strength in a particular area. In its biggest product categories, moreover, PPCo operates in a more mature and competitive marketplace. Many new light low-calorie lines and microwave product forms have proliferated competition for consumer attention and retail shelf space among snack-food suppliers. One result is that, whereas in 1980 nuts and potato chips accounted for about 75% of total salty-snacks volume in the United States, by 1990, they accounted for less than 60%.

Marketing

Marketing at PPCo (as at most consumer goods companies) was organized by product group. Product managers had P&L responsibility for assigned brands. Sales, organized geographically, had regional sales directors (RSDs) responsible for managing both the direct sales force and independent food brokers that also sold some of PPCo's products. RSDs' goals for sales volume and merchandising support were assigned during the annual marketing planning process in which objectives, by brand, were established by product management and sent to sales for allocation across territories. Many of the salespeople had been in their territories for years and, as one manager noted, "had grown up in the business when consumer demographics and the retail landscape looked very different than it does today."

Until 1990, a marketing services department reported through the brand management organization and provided research for product managers. In 1989, Karen Maslin was hired from another consumer goods firm to head the department. Maslin described her role:

From my experience at other firms, I was aware of the barriers which arise between marketing and sales, and I had opinions about what research can do to bridge those differences. My feeling is that research rarely finds or develops unique information. Our major value-added is packaging and disseminating learning among different functional audiences. We look at who would benefit most from certain kinds of information, who can add to it, and how to make the data a catalyst for constructive interaction between the groups that build and sustain our products in the marketplace.

After speaking with managers, Maslin identified three factors as especially important in considering how research should be organized and conducted at PPCo:

- The impact of new information sources on trade-buying criteria;
- Increased competition for in-store merchandising support; and
- The consequent need for more fact-based selling efforts by the sales force.

New information sources. By 1990, most of PPCo's retail accounts had installed point-of-sale scanner systems that gathered sales data at SKU levels of detail. Retailers gave this data to firms such as Nielsen Market Research or Information Resources in return for a local market report and studies of product movement under various selling conditions.

Among other things, the data revealed many differences in the level and types of demand in PPCo's product categories. Per capita consumption of potato chips, popcorn, pretzels, and snacking nuts, for example, varies by 80% or more across regions of the country. Consumers' preferences in product features (with or without salt or butter, honey-roasted versus plain nuts) also vary significantly among different geographical areas and classes of trade. A sales manager noted that "Retailers can now track these differences in a trading area, and expect their suppliers to respond. But our salespeople were working with the national data supplied by marketing services, and were outgunned in their negotiations with store buyers. Those buyers didn't want to hear about our national market share; they were comparing our product movement in their area versus local brands or the retailer's own private label goods."

The data affected the trade's buying criteria in other ways. Because it allowed comparisons across product lines, many retailers had shifted their buying emphases to criteria based on total category profitability. In other words, rather than viewing a vendor as providing more or less gross margin on one brand of peanuts or potato chips versus a competing brand, these accounts were allocating warehouse capacity, shelf space, and merchandising support to maximize overall profitability within a broader category of products (e.g., salty snacks). This placed PPCo in the position of competing not only with its traditional competitors in each product line, but also with many other firms in heretofore unrelated product lines also seeking more space and support in increasingly crowded food aisles. Further, the definitions of "category" varied by account and class of trade. Yet buyers were asking for data that compared PPCo products with alternative uses of their limited store real estate—whether or not these alternatives coincided with brand managers' traditional definitions of competition in their line. A PPCo executive noted:

> Some chains now staff headquarters buying positions with MBAs who are comfortable with these data analyses, give them category responsibility, and have P&L metrics drive their bonus compensation. Our salespeople must understand the stores' marketing programs and how best to optimize our participation in those programs. This differs from traditional sales practice, which emphasizes personal relationships at the store level, a focus on individual products, and a constant flow of trade deals.

Merchandising requirements. Developing broad merchandising strategies for PPCo's products was brand management's responsibility. But in-store implementation was handled by the sales force and brokers. A PPCo executive emphasized that "Store interest in our products is high because of the strong end-user marketing support that results in high consumer take away. But in our product categories, the brands merchandised most effectively enjoy the greatest sales. To sell at their best, our products need to be displayed prominently and in a variety of display types."

Plan-o-grams[7] were the primary vehicles used by salespeople and retail buyers to place products on a shelf or display. At most accounts, the amount of space was traditionally based on the percentage of sales that a vendor's brand contributed to retail sales in that product line. With broader distribution than its direct competitors and a leading market share in many of its product lines, PPCo had historically garnered generous amounts of shelf and display support. Hence, well-engrained "proven" merchandising techniques had evolved at the company. An example was the merchandising of snack nuts. Maslin found that received wisdom called for grouping all PPCo's nuts products in one store location. "The idea," she explained, "was to demonstrate our brand strength in one 'core' location of the store. For years, this was our national merchandising strategy and it drove our plan-o-gram analyses, bargaining for amount and types of display space, and sales force training and bonus systems."

But the broadening definition of snack foods, in conjunction with the move toward category management, was altering the retail trade's merchandising decisions. PPCo now competed for shelf and display space with marketers of soft drinks, cookies, and other items. These firms often muscled their way onto shelves and displays with deep trade promotions and the payment of slotting allowances[8] and other fees. In turn, as an executive commented, PPCo's salespeople were pressured to "justify every foot of shelf space and every display allocated to our products. New software being used by retail buyers allows them to input store data and run plan-o-gram analyses on a more decentralized basis. They're impatient with one-size-fits-all approaches to product merchandising where there are different consumer-buying patterns in poor versus affluent neighborhoods, or in grocery versus convenience outlets. But our merchandising policies weren't making these distinctions."

Fact-based selling. This term refers to the aggregate impact of information developments on sales requirements. PPCo's sales force had dealt primarily with store and regional managers at accounts. Many salespeople had called on the same accounts for years, developing strong relationships with local managers. As one rep commented, "In many outlets, the store manager would let me fill out the order form and arrange the snack food shelves."

But, especially at larger chains, buying and stocking decisions for many products were now made by headquarters personnel. These buyers demanded specific data, formal analyses, and delivery terms for which PPCo's salespeople were unprepared. Relationships at the store level remained important but, in the absence of pertinent data, much less persuasive than the promotional monies a vendor was willing to spend. The trade classes where volume was growing the fastest, moreover, were also those where these information demands were highest.

Maslin saw this as symptomatic of a series of "disconnects" in PPCo's gathering and dissemination of marketing information. To emphasize the gaps and to raise awareness of them with PPCo's top management, she used the inversely related listing of priorities depicted in Exhibit 5-3. While more volume in PPCo's major product categories was moving through mass-merchandiser and convenience store channels, PPCo's sales information and selling capabilities were still aimed primarily at supermarkets and independent grocery stores. Although category management perspectives altered trade buyers' criteria for evaluating and supporting products and vendors at many accounts, PPCo's marketing information systems still focused on individual brands. Salespeople needed more market and supply chain information in their negotiations with buyers, and brand managers needed more field input to accommodate now-visible regional and channel differences in consumer behavior, but the marketing services department had little contact with sales and distribution groups in the company.

BRIDGING THE GAP AT PPCo

In 1990, marketing services became the Research & Analysis (R&A) unit, a name change that, according to Maslin, "signals recognition of our changing role in the organization." The responsibilities of R&A were expanded to include sales forecasting and promotion evaluation studies. In 1991, R&A was moved from the product marketing organization to a new department which also included information systems and physical distribution services. Research funds that had come solely from individual brand groups were now supplied from IS, sales, and logistics as well as brand management. For product managers,

Exhibit 5-3
Disconnects in Marketing Information Needs at PPCo

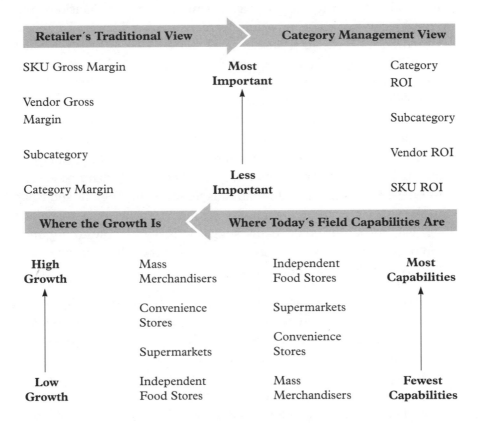

Retailer's Traditional View		Category Management View
SKU Gross Margin	**Most Important**	Category ROI
Vendor Gross Margin		Subcategory
Subcategory		Vendor ROI
Category Margin	**Less Important**	SKU ROI

Where the Growth Is		Where Today's Field Capabilities Are	
High Growth	Mass Merchandisers	Independent Food Stores	**Most Capabilities**
	Convenience Stores	Supermarkets	
	Supermarkets	Convenience Stores	
Low Growth	Independent Food Stores	Mass Merchandisers	**Fewest Capabilities**

R&A continues to provide consumer research, brand-specific studies, and ongoing reports about market developments and competition. For sales and distribution groups in the company, R&A supplies a variety of information services that help link their activities with product marketing efforts.

The development of these services and their impact on marketing interfaces are relevant beyond consumer goods contexts. At PPCo, new information flows revealed interdependencies that, in turn, generated new uses of existing marketing and sales information as well as changes in training, career paths, and the focus of IS investments.

Until 1990, PPCo relied on warehouse withdrawal data for tracking a product's sales. One of Maslin's first initiatives was to establish scanner data as the common basis for sales forecasts, market analyses, and marketing-planning information. She noted that "Retailers were using this data to make stocking and merchandising decisions, but our sales and marketing programs were speaking a different language. Moreover, internally this data created an exchange between product and sales managers that increased the perceived need in each group for more information from the other."

This data underscored the need to alter heretofore national product marketing programs for different regions and retail channels. As a result, R&A was asked to provide field offices with the information services required to access this data, and so improve their ability to analyze local demand patterns and better tailor sales programs to their accounts. In 1990, use of this data was tested in one region, and R&A managers met with salespeople for feedback. Salespeople welcomed the data and contributed many suggestions about how to augment and package the data for use in sales presentations. But, Maslin noted, "It was also clear that they required training and support":

> Much of our sales volume is through busy brokers that deal with many other suppliers, and to retail buyers who allocate 20 to 30 minutes for a vendor's sales rep to make her case. When you factor in the socializing and inevitable interruptions, there is simply not much time available.
>
> Ideally, our reps emphasized, they wanted a presentation they could use at their customers. Format and a few key points were important to them. This was different from our interactions with brand managers, whose training and formal planning presentations encouraged them to be active analysts of the data they receive.

This led to another R&A initiative: the development of account reviews on request of sales personnel (which, Maslin noted, "They are more apt to do since now sales is paying for research and influencing its focus"). These reviews analyzed specific category issues at an account, utilized data relevant to the account's trading area, and provided recommendations. An R&A manager described the process:

> The requests are initiated by an account manager or rep who sees an opportunity or threat at a customer. My role is to gather data from a

variety of internal and external sources in order to provide a customized profile of the account and the place of our products in the relevant category. Then, with sales and brand managers, we provide competitive analyses, category overviews, and recommendations down to
plan-o-gram levels of detail.

Sales' role is to understand the key issues at the account, and how
relevant buyers perceive and define the category. When salespeople
have cultivated good relationships, they have also created a climate in
which customers will truly listen to our data, appreciate its relevance,
and act on strategic recommendations.

In turn, these account reviews helped educate brand personnel
about developments at increasingly powerful trade customers, instill-
ing a more proactive awareness of in-store requirements in their packaging and promotion plans. By revealing the true extent of PPCo's
spending on trade promotions, the reviews also triggered a focus on
promotion analysis. Maslin commented: "Promotion data had been
spread across multiple departments whose different record-keeping
procedures made trade deal execution very complex, and made it
difficult to answer some basic questions. How is trade deal money
being spent? What promotion events are more, or less, effective? What
types of in-store merchandising support do we really get for the
money?" Working with brand, sales, IS, and distribution areas, R&A
developed a promotion-reporting system that integrated this data with
manufacturing and shipment data on the one hand, and product sales
data by region and account on the other. Working with external software vendors, R&A provided tools for analyzing what specific types of
promotions mean for product movement, "forward buying" at retail
accounts, and sales over multiple time periods.

A finance executive at PPCo emphasized that this information
"helps foster accountability for the biggest item in our marketing budget." This accountability motivated initiatives in other areas of the
business. As was common throughout the industry in the 1980s,
PPCo's promotions encouraged trade buyers to engage in forward
buying. That is, buyers stocked up on products currently promoted
and then often canceled purchase orders for these products later in the
season. This system played havoc with manufacturing and logistics

efficiencies at PPCo's plants and warehouses. Further, salespeople, measured in terms of case volume, were rewarded by forward buying, regardless of the actual impact on PPCo's cash flow and profits. As one rep candidly explained, "We sold the deals; and if that caused problems in other areas of the business, so be it."

The promotion analyses caused a re-evaluation of these practices. PPCo set a goal of decreasing working-inventory levels by 10% over a two-year period. An executive noted: "To achieve required order fill rates, we were manufacturing products 30 to 60 days before shipment. But when sales and product managers better coordinate forecasting and promotion planning across brand groups, you can have a major impact on working capital requirements in this business."

This information exchange also led to a new view of merchandising requirements. R&A's studies found that prominent in-store displays were indeed key marketing vehicles for PPCo's product line. But the effectiveness of different types of display varied across product category and trade channel. Maslin explained:

> In convenience stores, consumers often eat our products shortly after purchase and, within limits, price point is irrelevant. But space is very limited in these stores, and so being at the counter is crucial. There's a different merchandising dynamic in supermarkets, where aisle placement and shelf arrangement are more important. In mass merchandisers, the dynamic differs yet again: price is important and many of our products are viewed as traffic builders by store management. But we were approaching all these accounts with essentially the same merchandising strategy.

New information flows between brand and sales groups were the impetus for changing the traditional merchandising strategy based on a single core location in the store. This, in turn, altered the frequency and type of trade promotions offered: the core location had usually been obtained through deep deals, whereas the more differentiated merchandising strategy required less promotion to gather trade support. Further, analyses indicated that, with the appropriate feature display, a price discount on PPCo products typically increased sales and turns by greater percentages than the same combination of price and feature for many other snack foods. A sales executive noted that "This was contrary to received wisdom among buyers, and it's very useful and eye-opening information when you're selling mature products whose shelf space is under siege at accounts." With IS managers, R&A helped customize software that allowed PPCo reps to perform these analyses and redesign plan-o-grams at accounts. The new merchandising approach soon became a part of sales training programs.

Finally, these initiatives spurred changes in both the sales and product marketing organizations. Salespeople had been responsible for selling and service activities at their accounts. But as information exchange with other areas of the company increased, selling required more fact-based preparations while merchandising activities became more differentiated. This situation led to a redeployment of the sales force and the addition of part-time merchandisers for in-store service tasks. A sales executive explained that "Many reps were initially reluctant to surrender these duties. But they soon found that the part-time personnel, if managed properly, free up time for higher value-added activities. Meanwhile, we found that we could hire three part-time merchandisers for the fully burdened cost of one full-time salesperson, thus improving our service capabilities without increases in selling expenses." One result was better profit margins for PPCo as its costs of serving trade customers decreased while the time available for actual selling activities increased.

In product marketing, new information systems motivated the creation of a market analyst position, located in regional offices and staffed by people with brand management experience. The goal was to place in major market areas a person with the skills and perspective required to deal with all the new information and to work with other functional areas to customize profitable marketing programs in that area. Another goal, as an HRM executive explained, was to "establish a cadre of people with experience in both headquarters and field marketing positions. We talked for years about 'local marketing' but, like most firms in the industry, limited this to promotional programs. Now we have the data required to localize in depth. The market analyst positions also provide a career path that institutionalizes the flow of this information across product and sales groups."

Managers at PPCo eventually came to refer to R&A as "the Swit-

zerland of the organization": neutral territory and a means for exchange among brand, sales, R&D, manufacturing, distribution, and
finance units. Maslin emphasized that "Most of these initiatives essentially involve making visible data traditionally gathered in separate
areas, consolidating that data through new information systems, and
then disseminating the information in forms appropriate to each area.
But I don't see R&A as a substitute for functional efforts. We're more
a conduit for increasingly necessary cross-functional exchange."

REALIGNING MARKET RESEARCH AND
MARKETING INFORMATION SYSTEMS

The activities of the R&A unit at Packaged Products Company set
off a chain reaction that improved information flows and concurrent
marketing capabilities in the firm. As Exhibit 5-4 suggests, this chain
reaction was initially driven by a realignment of the traditional roles
and priorities of market research. This crucial information-gathering
and dissemination function was moved from its reporting structure
within the product management organization and joined more closely
to the firm's IS capabilities. In conjunction with new technological
capabilities and Maslin's leadership, revised research and information
systems soon became a catalyst for more and better exchange among
product, sales, and service (i.e., merchandising) groups. These exchanges helped build a common language about fast-moving market
developments among geographically and organizationally dispersed
marketing managers. The result was a shared vision of trade customers
and end-consumers, and eventually specific initiatives ranging from
promotion planning and working capital goals to in-store merchandising strategy and the organization of sales and product management. In
turn, these actions aided and motivated even more information exchange and cross-functional collaboration between these groups.

There are analogous developments in the role and conduct of market research in other industries, as companies find that their existing
marketing information systems inadequately address new marketing
requirements. As at PPCo, these changes can provide substantial benefits. But they also raise conflicts and issues that must be managed in
order to derive those benefits.

Exhibit 5-4

Impact of Revised Market Research and Information Systems at PPCo

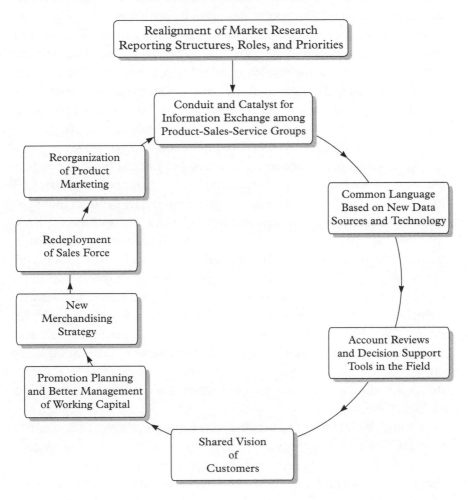

Benefits

These initiatives can help bridge marketing dialects, develop databases relevant to concurrent marketing activities, and increase the effectiveness of the formal liaison units discussed in the previous chapter.

First, as one executive observed, "Product marketing often builds an information system for its purposes while depending on sales and service for inputs. Salespeople, who receive few direct benefits from the system, tend to ignore it. Ironically, the system then denies product managers access to important market information." A realignment of research procedures can help break this vicious circle. At a medical products company, research is now conducted by teams of individuals from R&D, manufacturing, IS, product management, sales, service, and market research. Sales identifies accounts relevant to a particular threat or opportunity and manages access to buyers and end-users. The team then visits customers to examine issues ranging from new products to modifications of existing products and services.

Previously, suggestions in these areas had filtered back to product managers from patchy sales force call reports. After being interpreted by a product group, survey research was initiated by product management, conducted by headquarters market research, and passed back into manufacturing, sales, service, and other areas affected by product plans. The head of research referred to this traditional process as "start-stop" research in which interdependencies among the units only became apparent over time and usually *after* substantial investments had been made by one group. But in research's current role, he noted, "We can discuss the implications after the customer visit and with implementation units present. Market research facilitates the exchange of information and, over time, acts as the organizational memory and conductor of more formal studies relevant to issues surfaced in these discussions."

Second, by aligning market research more closely with IS, companies also create technologically driven opportunities for useful data exchange. A key role for research managers at some firms has become the development and maintenance of joint marketing-sales-service databases. At the card division of American Express, for example, market research and IS functions have been melded. The result has been improved account management. Prior to the reorganization, reviewing an account required an average of 22 queries. Multiply this by the number of accounts to be reviewed in order to make segmentation decisions, and one begins to understand American Express's relative inertia during the 1980s in the face of more competition in the credit card market. Now, thanks to the Knowledge Highway (a centralized marketing information system), this data can be obtained from a single source. Problem accounts can be identified and dealt with more quickly (aiding customer retention), data accuracy has improved (as has the ability of marketing managers to identify and introduce services that are valued by different customer groups), and the cost of processing a query has fallen (effectively reducing SG&A costs in a high-fixed-cost service business).

Similar opportunities are now available to industrial firms. At an industrial products firm which goes to market through more than a thousand distributors, a database managed by market research allows for on-line interaction between product and sales units concerning price discounts, product mix, and promotion programs. This streamlining improves the speed and consistency of response in an environment where bids are common and distributors monitor terms and conditions closely. In another manufacturing company, a computerized expert system provides sales representatives with analyses that help in profitably customizing product service packages for their accounts. A market research manager explained that the benefits of the system simultaneously depend on, and encourage, this interunit exchange: "Product and sales groups have ongoing access to different types of information and experience. Product managers understand the cost and strategic implications of different packages we might offer. But the dynamics of buying behavior among customers are especially important in assembling product service packages, and here sales often has the requisite knowledge."

A company making especially effective use of technology at marketing interfaces is Sea-Land Service, a provider of transportation services.[9] Sea-Land has developed a database known as SMART (Strategic Mapping and Revenue Tracking) which, under the direction of its information resources department (an amalgam of IS and market research), combines data from internal groups with external sources such as government import declarations. Constantly updated and electronically disseminated, SMART provides product, sales, and service groups with easy access to common information about customers, competitors, and current capacity constraints. Marketing uses SMART to track revenue and profits by region, country, market segment, salesperson, and account. Sales and service reps have on-line access to SMART's directory of transit times and schedules for each Sea-Land vessel, market share information, and sales performance by segment.

The database improves coordination at very actionable levels: sales forecasting, scheduling, and identification of priority segments. The interactive nature of the database allows sales and service to provide real-time information to product managers (who set prices, container configurations, and other arrangements for Sea-Land vessels) about the services most important to various customer groups. A grocer shipper might require a container that can accommodate both fresh and frozen foods; for footwear shippers, just-in-time delivery is crucial; apparel customers require garment packing by size and color. In turn, Sea-Land's ability to provide these differentiated services cost effectively, and so increase sales and profits in a "commodity" business, is tied to this database. SMART helps product managers clarify what drives each segment and how best to configure product and pricing variables; it helps sales sort prospects according to potential financial return and so do a better job of targeting high-margin prospects in a business where profitability is closely related to the amount and types of cargo that move on the firm's shipping assets; and it helps service managers deploy these assets more efficiently. A Sea-Land executive noted that SMART is altering relations among these units and describes the company as evolving toward "an information network, on which we hang transportation assets such as ships, trucks, trains, warehouses, depots, and offices."

Third, these realignments of information flows complement the role of formal liaison units in the organization. As Chapter 4 indicated, timely information is crucial to the operation of this structural linkage. But because many companies have gathered and interpreted information according to a limited marketing research paradigm, liaison units often lack the data they need. Conversely, cross-functional research initiatives can help maximize the benefits and minimize the vulnerabilities of these units.

At PPCo, for instance, one impact of R&A initiatives was the reorganization of the sales-planning group into a trade-marketing unit. The change is more than semantic. As one executive explained: "Sales

Planning had a focus on helping individual brands develop sales attention. Input into brand planning was negligible. Trade Marketing focuses on the entire category and works with product, finance, manufacturing, and sales units." The change became possible when R&A, by building information bridges, also provided the liaison unit with the ability to work credibly across these organizational boundaries. Similarly, liaison managers at a computer company work with a new IS/research group to generate cross-product data about applications and vertical markets, in addition to traditional research concerning the price/performance features of competing products. A liaison manager commented: "Our role relies on information relevant to both the product and sales groups we interact with. In the past, however, we were good at getting information *from* product *to* sales but not the other way 'round."

Conflicts and Vulnerabilities

For many companies, however, these initiatives in market research and information systems raise issues concerning costs, availability and use of new information sources, and data integrity.

First, the costs of realigning research in this manner can be considerable. A major development effort, with new technology investments, is often necessary. At Kao, the leading Japanese consumer packaged-goods company, all marketing and sales managers have access to a joint database containing shipment, point-of-sale, market share, and product cost information as well as current consumer feedback from Kao's 800 number. This database provides a crucial link and cross-functional coordinating mechanism in this company. But Kao also regularly spends about 3% of its revenues on a joint research/IS function, compared to an industry average of about 1%.

Direct expenditures on these capabilities, moreover, are usually only the tip of the iceberg for many firms. As an executive at a prominent systems consulting firm explained to me: "Our common rule-of-thumb is that hardware and software account for only 40% of the total cost of implementing a marketing-sales information system. For example, incorporating shipment and account order information—data with high sales interest—usually involves developing compatible protocols with many other processes throughout the company."

Other costs involve technology upgrades, software customization, ongoing maintenance of the data, and end-user training. Note that at PPCo new information flows had to be accompanied by new sales training. The head of R&A recalled that "Sales had historically not utilized much data in their selling activities, and many reps were overwhelmed by the data now available to them. Their common theme was, help me translate this stuff into actionable business applications. This required basic training in the meaning and use of the data."

Second, companies encounter other obstacles in generating and disseminating information across product, sales, and service units. Customized, often account-specific research, is usually more expensive to conduct and keep up-to-date than the broader market and product performance surveys associated with traditional market research at many firms. In consumer goods markets, scanner data sold by syndicated research firms make this information increasingly available. But in many industrial markets, this information is not available from a single external source, and must be patched together from multiple sources.

Even when the data are available, other issues often inhibit its use. As noted, many research personnel lack training in the analysis of the behavioral data now available in consumer markets, or in the conduct of the customer visits and cross-functional studies that are relevant at industrial firms.[10] For their part, sales managers often view research expenditures as money taken from their promotion budgets, or money that might otherwise be used for hiring another salesperson or other means of increasing call frequency. Hence, even as sales personnel clamor for more information, sales management is often reluctant to make the investments required to provide it.

Third, while joint databases can improve marketing coordination, they also raise growing concerns about privacy issues. Linking customer data from multiple external and internal sources has proven effective in many industries. Witness, for example, the benefits some firms have reaped by linking credit card usage with airline frequent-flyer rolls or by purchasing lists that help target their marketing efforts. Several services have emerged that match customer records across companies' databases, providing a more holistic picture of customer buying behavior. For example, Ogilvy & Mather's Dataconsult business unit uses consumer sales data to model the expected value of a customer. Initially developed for direct mail organizations in business markets, this approach combines customized research with records of consumer transactions to adjust both the frequency and nature of marketing communications to the expected lifetime value of various customer groups.

Arguably, such data services increase consumer choice, improve the efficiency of marketing efforts, and, by enabling firms to target customer groups more precisely, ultimately decrease the number of intrusive communications to customers not interested in a product or service. But the mere existence of such databases, and the exchange of customer information among organizations, aggravate growing concerns about data privacy. Such concerns are at the heart of controversies and lawsuits surrounding the use of credit information. Furthermore, it is not clear which kinds of database marketing efforts will elicit criticism. In the United States and Europe, the legal precedents for such use of data are in flux because regulations did not anticipate the current technological capabilities. In practice, companies utilizing these databases essentially created their own guidelines before the law (or customer feedback) defined the parameters of appropriate action. Hence, as consumers, the media, and legislators sift through the issues raised by these marketing practices, companies like Blockbuster Video, Lotus Development Corporation, TRW, and others have found themselves on the defensive. The result has been a number of costly, embarrassing, and potentially precedent-setting reversals.[11]

Finally, established cost-accounting systems at many companies can render problematic these initiatives concerning marketing information systems. Joint product-sales databases, for example, can simply accelerate the flow of information based on accounting-driven (versus market-driven) designations. As one executive emphasized, "Without better activity-cost and product-profitability measures, reconfiguring information systems is of limited use and, in practice, old procedures will prevail."

KEY DIAGNOSTIC QUESTIONS

In managing information systems that affect concurrent marketing capabilities, important diagnostic questions include the following:

- To what extent is the firm or unit conducting market research relevant to the multiple groups involved at the customer interface, or is marketing research primarily relevant to product managers?

This chapter emphasized the differences between market and marketing research. The former is required for effective information management in the new marketing environment. A major reason for the disconnects in information needs at PPCo was that, for decades, the brand management organization established priorities in the firm's gathering, analysis, and dissemination of market data. These priorities, which focused information flows primarily on individual brands, evolved when a few mass-media outlets provided effective access to most consumer groups and when smaller, independent food retailers were the main trade accounts serviced by the firm's sales force. By the late 1980s, however, communications media had proliferated and fragmented while less than 100 trade customers accounted for more than 80% of the firm's sales volume. Yet, the marketing services function continued to gather and process data according to the old paradigm.

The result was a paucity of information about growing channels and, in the field, difficulties in developing sales and service capabilities for the new environment. The move to Research and Analysis was the catalyst for a new way of viewing the marketplace and interpreting data. In effect, R&A helped realign established hierarchies of attention in brand, sales, and service groups, and led to combinations of information more relevant to changing trade and consumer behavior. It also spawned initiatives that institutionalized ongoing exchange among brand, channel, and account perspectives in an environment where information needs are dispersed throughout the supply chain and distribution channels.

Reflecting on the pre-R&A organization of marketing information systems at PPCo, an executive commented: "Product management was at the center of information flows. They received the data, analyzed it with certain goals in mind, and then doled it out to other functions. But in the current environment, that process, even when conducted rigorously and with a minimum of politicking, bottlenecks required market information." PPCo's situation is representative. For many companies, a first step in managing marketing information should be a review of their current funding, reporting, and staffing policies for market research.

- Does a joint product-sales-service database exist? If not, what are the opportunities for creating one? If yes, what are the necessary inputs to the database and how does the firm monitor the quality and integrity of those inputs?

Another lesson of the changes discussed here concerns the potential and power of joint databases. The potential lies in the rapidly increasing capacity of computer hardware and the development of software-based modeling techniques that can give marketers access to, and useful analyses of, unprecedented amounts of customer data. In many firms, moreover, product, sales, and service units already gather data pertinent to their separate marketing dialects. Hence, the technological means for joint databases exist and, in many cases, the data has already been gathered. But most firms lack a managerial mechanism to consolidate and disseminate this data across marketing groups.

Power lies in the impact such databases can have. A common database is both a means and motivation for cross-functional efforts. At the same time, a useful database requires more than simply assembling data from different groups. As the PPCo example also indicates, effective use of this information requires translation, ongoing support, and monitoring of the inputs.

This last point bears emphasizing. As in many other firms dealing with an increasingly diverse set of channel and end-user customers, a key goal for PPCo was to make local field data more prominent in marketing decision making. But without a dedicated monitoring mechanism, the quality of the inputs can be suspect. In the case of scanner data, important items in a firm's product line may not be scanned, and there are class-of-trade biases because of the store samples used by the major providers of such data. In industrial firms, the input of salespeople is usually crucial to revised marketing information systems. But sales force call-reporting procedures in many firms are inadequate, and sales managers are often reluctant to press the sales force to use them because "this takes time away from selling." Conversely, there are questions about the ability and motivation of salespeople to provide accurate information. Trained and compensated to "get the order," salespeople often overestimate the level of product performance desired by customers and the likelihood of actual purchase.[12] This is especially a danger for new or radically innovative products and services. AT&T, in developing a product that combines the features of telephones, fax machines, computers, and electronic blackboards, found that its sales force was considerably more optimistic about sales volumes and exhibited very different preferences in product features and design than customers.[13]

Hence, a mechanism for monitoring inputs is also required in making these changes in research and information systems.

- Do measurement systems help, or hinder, the use of new marketing information systems?

Reward systems often lag the introduction of new marketing information systems, inhibiting, or even distorting, productive use of the information. PPCo again provides a telling example. When scanner data initially became the basis for integrating sales forecasts with brand planning, sales bonuses continued to be based on territory sales volume as measured by warehouse withdrawals. A sales executive recalled: "Despite the availability of better measures of sales performance at accounts, reps kept asking for and using the old numbers since those were the numbers discussed in their performance evaluations." The subsequent initiatives described in this chapter required a realignment of marketing metrics as well as market research activities.

More generally, the experiences of the firms I studied in implementing new information systems should make managers skeptical about widespread claims that information technologies mean the elimination of hierarchy and the ascendance of flat, networked organizations. For one thing, a management mechanism for translating and prioritizing the growing volumes of data is necessary. For another, as these information systems become the medium for reallocating resources in companies, we should not expect managers to use the systems without local interests in mind. As an acute analysis of recent IS developments put it: "No amount of data modeling, no number of relational databases, and no mere invocation of 'the information-based organization' will bring about a new political order of information. . . . If information is truly to become [a] valued commodity in the businesses of the future, we cannot expect to acquire it without an occasional struggle."[14]

As at PPCo, changes in information exchange can alert managers to the impact of current metrics on other parts of the business. But without changes in measurement systems, especially sales compensation systems (see Chapter 8), they are unlikely to have lasting impact on behavior.

CONCLUSION

As firms face increased coordination requirements, market research has the potential to become more than a window on external customer needs. When managed in conjunction with the new technologies available, it can also be the locus of important internal integration efforts among marketing groups.

A relevant research and information system, however, is finally a necessary but not sufficient cause of effective marketing. These systems are used by people in the context of broader human-resource management processes in the organization. Two of these processes, career paths and training programs, are the subject of the next chapter.

6

Career Paths and Training Programs

■

CHANGES in structure and information systems provide enabling means for developing concurrent marketing capabilities. But in dealing with new marketing requirements, attention must extend beyond these dimensions. The required capabilities are finally built on a foundation of understanding and commitment among the individuals whose varied activities compose customer-contact efforts.

Many companies I studied encountered problems in establishing such a foundation because of the limited perspectives of managers in their product, sales, and service units. The situation was described by one executive:

> Most managers in a company may be "good citizens" who want to do what's right for the firm, not just their area. But they're often unaware of the impact of their decisions on other areas of an interdependent business system. Our goal is to develop and disseminate systems savvy throughout the organization.

A key to building this systems savvy are human resource initiatives that broaden perspectives, build interunit experience, and establish relationships that encourage and support appropriate behavior. Some companies have revised HRM policies with these aims in mind. They have found that their initiatives do not simply adapt to structural and information links. Rather, two aspects of HRM policy—career paths and training and development—are especially important in determining whether and how these links are used and kept up-to-date.

This chapter first discusses the connection between individual and organizational learning when market factors increase required coordination among marketing groups and decrease the time available for utilizing formal coordination mechanisms. It then considers the issues raised by traditional marketing career paths in many firms as well as initiatives in this area and in management development programs. Finally, the chapter discusses the benefits and vulnerabilities of these initiatives, and provides diagnostic questions useful in clarifying the focus of career pathing and development programs for marketing personnel.

INDIVIDUAL AND ORGANIZATIONAL LEARNING

The notion of organizational learning has attracted much attention in recent years.[1] Theorists now recognize that companies develop repertoires of capabilities which enable and constrain their responses to changing environments. There has been a stream of seminars, retreats, and mission statements aimed at promoting "organizational change" or shifts in "corporate culture."

But how does an *organization* learn and adapt? In fact, companies learn and change through the behavior of their individual members. Behavior is shaped by the formal roles and responsibilities of managers, but roles and responsibilities are also defined and interpreted by individuals with accrued skills and attitudes. The importance of individual learning for organizational learning is, as Daniel Kim observed, at once "obvious and subtle—obvious because all organizations are composed of individuals; subtle because organizations can learn independent of any specific individual but not independent of all individuals."[2] This link is especially close in fast-changing market environments and especially crucial in marketing activities, where the impact of the environment is most keenly felt and where much of the nitty-gritty of strategy implementation resides.[3]

A useful way to think about the role of individual learning in man-

Exhibit 6-1
Market Characteristics and Coordination Mechanisms

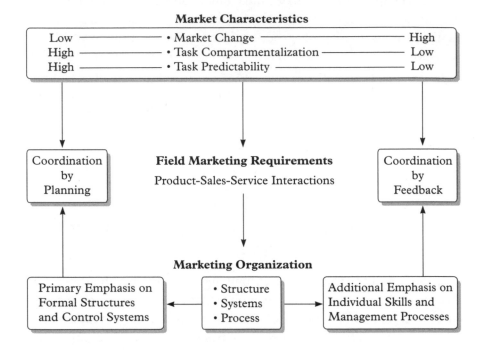

Market Characteristics

Low	— • Market Change —	High
High	— • Task Compartmentalization —	Low
High	— • Task Predictability —	Low

Coordination by Planning

Field Marketing Requirements

Product-Sales-Service Interactions

Coordination by Feedback

Marketing Organization

Primary Emphasis on Formal Structures and Control Systems

• Structure
• Systems
• Process

Additional Emphasis on Individual Skills and Management Processes

aging marketing interfaces is by way of Exhibit 6-1.[4] This framework distinguishes between two different, but not mutually exclusive, approaches to organizational coordination. "Coordination by planning" refers to the formal "programmed interaction of tasks, [where] interaction is clearly defined by rules. . . . Coordination by feedback, on the other hand, refers to negotiated alterations in the nature or sequence of tasks performed by different units."[5]

In this framework, field marketing requirements include those activities that involve interactions among product, sales, and service units during the process of demand generation and demand fulfillment. These requirements are determined by the market. Among the more important market factors to consider are: the amount of market change (e.g., the pace of product life cycles or new entrants); the compartmentalization of marketing tasks (i.e., the extent to which these tasks can be segregated in different units versus the extent to which customers' buying processes require ongoing coordination across the seller's product lines, sales units, and service resources); and the relative predictability of those tasks (e.g., capable of being standardized across segments or, at the other extreme, customized by account or order).

In turn, a primary purpose of any marketing organization is to implement strategy by aligning the firm's resources and capabilities with field marketing requirements. Implementation means monitoring at least three aspects of organization: (1) structure (reporting relationships and formal linkage mechanisms among product, sales, and service units); (2) systems (measurement and control systems as well as research and information systems utilized by marketing personnel); and (3) process (the kinds of interactions that occur between individuals in different units and the kinds of skills that are, and are not, developed by managers in the organization).

When market change is low, when marketing tasks can be substantially compartmentalized, and when those tasks are predictable and therefore capable of being routinized, relying primarily on formal structures and systems for managing marketing interfaces can be successful. Key goals in this environment are to focus on purchases and rebuys of discrete products or services (rather than a bundling of multiple products and services), optimize scale economies (rather than economies of scope), and develop expertise solely within each area of the organization. Field marketing tasks require less information, and/ or lots of the same types of standardized information, to be dispersed and understood across each unit.

But when market change is high, when marketing tasks require much interaction across units, and when those tasks are increasingly customized and therefore less predictable, reliance on formal structures and systems is inadequate. Key goals in this marketplace are to allocate resources efficiently but flexibly, optimize economies of scope, and develop expertise that spans different parts of the organization because customer contact tasks require that more information (and more different types of information) be spread across units. Field implementation in this environment is more dependent on internal communication and coordination among individuals, since these customized, nonroutine tasks necessarily involve many decentralized alterations to generic plans and strategies. An industrial sales executive commented on account management tasks in his business: "At most accounts, we now have many different people involved with different pieces of the business and varying opinions about what the customer 'really' wants. To get things done, you work more closely with people that you've worked with before and trust."

In this sort of marketplace, relying solely on formal coordination mechanisms can be counterproductive. Without the lubricant of appropriate individual skills and perspectives, formal structures and systems can unwittingly stovepipe interactions, inhibit needed cross-functional efforts, and bring the marketing gearbox to a grinding halt. "Coordination by feedback" becomes more important because customer contact tasks involve many negotiated alterations in the nature and sequence of interdependent marketing activities. The skills required to do the job include people's knowledge of, and relationships with, other units of their firm as well as their ability to analyze and respond to problems at their accounts. Indeed, these internal relationships are a *prerequisite* for external responsiveness to customers.

The market factors discussed in Part I are moving more companies in more industries toward the right side of the spectrum in Exhibit 6-1. As an example, consider the role of individual learning and cross-functional relationships in managing marketing tasks in a changing health care environment.

BECTON DICKINSON DIVISION

Becton Dickinson (BD), a diversified medical products firm, is organized into autonomous divisions. Becton Dickinson Division (BDD),[6] the largest in terms of sales volume, sells hypodermic needles and syringes to hospitals, clinics, and other health care institutions. In 1990, Gary Cohen, BDD's new vice president of marketing, described the situation facing the division:

> Like most medical products manufacturers, we are facing price pressures associated with tighter health-care reimbursement procedures as well as many new requirements in our traditional markets. So, it's important that we keep our marketing efforts aligned with current cus-

tomers' evolving needs and continue to provide superior value in our division's core product areas.

At the same time, new products and services mean developing new marketing skills, programs, and partnerships not currently a big part of our activities. How do we organize to handle effectively our existing business while building the capabilities required for new business developments?

This is an example of the orthogonal requirements that, as explained in Chapter 4, typically confront a marketing organization. In addressing these challenges in a rapidly changing environment, Cohen found that changes in career paths and training programs were at least as important as structural changes in the organization.

More than 50% of BDD sales are to hospitals, where its products are used by nurses, physicians, and other medical personnel in many departments. Salespeople traditionally called on the director of nursing, the head of a hospital lab, or another end-user department to get BDD products specified. Then they negotiated terms for orders with the hospital's purchasing department. For years, BDD enjoyed an enviable position: the market share leader *and* premium-priced player in its product category. During 1985–1990, however, several forces realigned marketing tasks.

Pressures to Realign Marketing

Cost containment. In 1984, new government reimbursement procedures for Medicare patients (40% of all hospital patient days at the time) mandated payment based on national and regional costs for each "diagnosis-related group," not on the individual hospital's costs. Also, these average costs were continually updated so that, as hospitals improved their performance, they were subject to stricter payment limits. During the latter half of the 1980s, hospital admissions fell and the average length of a patient's hospital stay declined. This affected BDD in several ways.

First, customers pressured manufacturers to lower prices and reduce their inventory-carrying costs. In hospitals, medical supplies account for 10–15% of operating costs while the order processing and logistical expenses of sourcing supplies are another 10–15%. The av-

erage number of weeks of supplies inventory at hospitals fell 25% between 1985 and 1990 and, as one BDD salesperson noted, "just-in-
time delivery became real for materials managers. Hospitals order
hypodermics frequently, and most now have a standing weekly order
for needles and syringes."

Second, cost containment increased the power of the purchasing
department at health care institutions. End-users were more concerned with quality than price. But purchasing personnel, Cohen explained, "often view hypodermics as commodities because they're not
familiar with the specific needs and applications in each department
or with the many medical devices that hypodermics must be compatible with. Therefore, an important marketing task is identifying and
developing those applications that sustain our value versus lower-
priced competitors."

Third, group buying organizations often made sourcing of BDD
products a multihospital purchase handled by decision makers at
levels beyond the individual hospital. This placed new demands on
BDD's sales programs and, because groups often bundled purchases
across product categories, on the ability to coordinate with other BD
divisions.

New product-service packages. Customers' emphasis on inventory
reductions made a vendor's distribution and supply chain services
more important. Meanwhile, the increase in the number of AIDS patients heightened medical personnel's concerns about safety, especially
about skin punctures. A related development concerned medical
waste disposal. In 1990, U.S. hospitals generated more than 2 million
tons of waste, 10% of which was considered potentially infectious
by the Environmental Protection Agency. For many supply items,
hospital disposal costs often far exceeded acquisition costs. Cohen
noted:

> The opportunity and threat is that the nature of the purchase is being
> redefined. Inventory, safety, and disposal costs make customers more
> conscious of total cost-in-use. Because of our broad line and distribu-
> tor network, we have the potential to offer innovative product/service
> packages. But this requires different kinds of internal and external co-
> ordination.

Competition. BDD's competitors included Sherwood Medical and Terumo, a Japanese firm that entered the U.S. market in the 1980s. Sherwood and Terumo were also divisions of diversified medical products firms, but each had lower market shares in hypodermics than BDD. As hospital purchasing consolidated, both competitors saw an opportunity to increase their presence in an important category by offering hypodermics as part of a product package. Terumo emphasized lower prices and Sherwood emphasized new features. The result was fierce competition for large-volume accounts in a business where volume, production scale economies, and a vendor's cost position are intimately connected.

Corporate financial pressures. A slower-growth, more price-sensitive market inevitably placed financial pressures on BD. Further, the need to continue funding R&D aggressively in a technologically dynamic industry meant that manufacturing and, especially, marketing expenses were the items most closely scrutinized. BD initiated cost reduction programs in each area and, as the largest division, BDD was a prime target for cost-cutting moves. Hence, while marketing tasks were more complex, financial constraints made "adding more people" an infeasible response for BDD's marketing organization.

Exhibit 6-2 outlines the changes occurring in BDD's marketplace during these years and the consequent pressures on the division's marketing organization. During this time, BDD repeatedly reorganized marketing in an attempt to deal with new requirements. In 1985, marketing was structured along product management lines. But it was increasingly difficult to manage adequately across markets as buying groups became more prominent, new alternative care sites proliferated, and hospitals' purchasing strategies became more heterogeneous. "We needed programs tailored to different segments," an executive explained, "but lacked the focus to do this." Thus, in 1987 marketing was reorganized into a market management structure. This improved applications development. But, without dedicated product managers with start-to-finish accountability, product introductions were too often late and over budget in an environment where speed-to-market and cost control were also important. Therefore, in 1989 marketing was reorganized into a combined product/program structure. Marketing managers again had specific product responsibilities,

Exhibit 6-2
Influences on BDD's Marketing Organization

BDD Corporate Context
- Slow Growth
- More Capital Investments
- Cost Reduction Pressures

Customers
- Price Pressures
- New Purchase Criteria
- Changing Decision-making Unit
- Group Buying Organizations
- JIT Delivery

BDD Marketing Organization
- Premium-priced Player
- Impact on Established Account Relationships
- Need to Reach New Buyers
- Need to Develop New Product-Service Packages

Competition
- Lower Prices (Terumo)
- New Features (Sherwood)
- Bundled Product Offerings
- Distribution Pressures

- Impact on Sales Tasks and Channels of Distribution

but also program assignments that cut across products and markets. For example, a product manager might also be responsible for developing programs for nonhospital sites or for safety or waste disposal services.

Despite these structural changes, however, BDD's market share and margins declined. Further, the division's sales force was demoralized both by poor sales results and the number of organizational changes in marketing. Historically, sales and marketing at BDD were separate tracks. Yet, forces in the health care environment made sales more reliant on marketing and vice versa. Account management now required more marketing attention because customers required specialized product-service programs that salespeople could identify but often lacked the expertise to deal with. Product management needed sales to provide access to more decision makers and influencers in order to develop increasingly customized products and services.

Cohen had been a product, market, and then program manager in each marketing reorganization. He believed that "All these dimensions are important. But the issue is *who* performs these responsibilities and whether they have the connections with other parts of the organization that are now required to develop and implement marketing programs." When he became head of marketing, Cohen began to stress organizational dimensions besides structure. In particular, he began recruiting some sales personnel for marketing positions, and redesigned training programs to emphasize joint marketing-sales participation. In subtle but important ways, these initiatives made a difference in the division's product, sales, and service programs.

One new recruit was Bob Short, who had been in sales with BD for 19 years before becoming a product manager with additional responsibilities for managing product development and in-service training for hospital customers. In the past five years, BDD had in fact introduced many new products, all of which received high-quality ratings. But these products had mixed success. Small changes in a needle or syringe often had big implications for BDD's manufacturing costs, postsale service at customers, and stock-keeping needs of distributors. "Product managers did excellent end-user research," Short noted. "But they were removed from important field realities. The result was often poor support for a new product that, in the eyes of many salespeople, complicated their lives at important accounts and distributors."

Product development became part of a multifunctional team with representatives from inventory control, manufacturing, R&D, and product management. "My role," Short explained, "is to make sure that sales and service needs are considered up-front, and here my previous experience is useful. I'll get several calls weekly from reps who have identified an opportunity such as a syringe with a special plunger for infant applications. Conversely, I have credibility with sales managers when these requests are denied because, while producing this product may get the order at one account, it will damage our costs across other parts of the business."

Similarly, Short's previous experience had an impact on service. A key task for sales reps was conducting in-service training when a health-care facility adopted a BDD product. Reps gave product demonstrations and educated end-users on proper usage. A sales manager explained that "A syringe is so fundamental to what a nurse or doctor does in many departments that it becomes part of them, like a watch or wedding ring, and they're resistant to changing habits. Because of a heightened awareness of the potential costs of an accidental needle stick, in-service must be handled patiently with each department."

Because of his field experience, Short realized that good in-service helps build relationships and brand equity, but that BDD's in-service programs differed by sales district. With former sales colleagues, Short developed standards and tools for in-service training across regions, disseminated best practice, and (with other product managers) established processes for making in-service a visible part of product planning. "Bob knows what details are important in the field," noted Cohen. "On the other side, in-service efficiencies provide an important marketing advantage. Despite higher product prices that reflect our quality, we can now often quote lower total costs to accounts for product and training as a package."

Another new marketing manager was Peggy Ferro, who had been in sales for five years before becoming a product manager with additional responsibility for working with BDD's Key Account Managers (KAMs). As buying groups became more influential, sales tasks changed. "I saw this happening in my territory," Ferro explained. "Purchasing becomes a more formal process that requires you to get more information about many matters in addition to price and product. Yet, account managers often lack the experience and time to gather this information, and then rely on price to get the order or renew a contract."

With the KAMs, Ferro instituted quarterly reviews of BDD's top 30 accounts. Equally important, her reviews and joint calls with KAMs became a means for getting product management access to decision makers at key accounts. "Product managers have the information and perspective to identify and develop cost-effective service programs in areas like inventory management, waste disposal, and safety. These programs lower our total cost-in-use versus competitors," Ferro noted. "But KAMs acted as gatekeepers who were reluctant to let these personnel deal with their customers. Despite our wide product line and array of services, cross-selling was not happening."

As in many other firms, BDD's key-account managers are veteran salespeople. "They have long-standing, valuable contacts at these accounts," Ferro explained, "and rightly feel that their efforts are an important reason why we have a leading share in our product category. Also, KAMs hear about any problems or promises at their accounts, must accommodate the customers' perceptions of vendor performance, and their incentive compensation is tied to sales results at specific accounts." One KAM was blunt about his attitude toward past "help" from marketing: "I spend years sweating for business in an increasingly tough marketplace. Then, somebody from product marketing, with a particular product to push and less at stake than I have at that customer, wants influence over my activities and contacts. No way."

In this situation, it was essential that someone with visible sales experience build links between product marketing and KAMs. In theory, BDD already had a mechanism for doing this: a call-reporting system and database provided information about product usage at customers while each restructuring of marketing had included a key-account support function. But in practice, Cohen commented, "We were organized to monitor but not to innovate and act. The systems were inert until people like Peggy and Bob helped build the trust and learning needed to make the systems work." Moreover, the relevant learning worked in two directions. Ferro and Short made marketing more responsive to changing field realities. But they also made sales more responsive to longer-term marketing initiatives that, in the past, would have been dismissed as "A nice idea that doesn't help with this year's quota."

In the next few years, joint training for marketing and sales evolved into integral parts of the division's planning process, and career pathing between the two became common and desirable. During this time, BDD implemented a series of innovative product, service, and account management programs that relied on product-sales-service coordination throughout its distribution channel. New safety products and waste disposal services have helped transform a no-growth division into one now growing at double-digit rates. A joint venture with a producer and distributor of intravenous products yielded a new needleless IV product that, in turn, minimized the danger of needle sticks and costly litigation. Even though this new product costs nearly twice as much as traditional syringes, hospitals still save money and, in 1994, BDD's sales revenue on this line alone was nearly equal to its traditional needle sales. At higher prices and with the cost efficiencies of volume production, margins on the new line are much higher than for traditional needles. "What might have been viewed simply as a threat of product obsolescence to be resisted by price cuts at big accounts," noted Cohen (now the division president), "was transformed by joint product-sales efforts into a successful new business."

By 1994, BDD had more than recouped the share loss suffered during the 1985–1990 period and net income had improved substantially despite even tougher cost controls in health care. A major reason, according to Cohen, is that "While our competitors sell product and price, we redesigned our business to focus on total cost-in-use. And our ability to do this depends on the learning we've accrued in both product marketing and sales."

CAREER PATH MANAGEMENT

The situation Gary Cohen initially faced at BDD is common. Individuals are recruited for specific areas within firms and acquire successive levels of expertise along one area's career path. This develops a certain kind of learning, but also reinforces the hierarchies of attention discussed in Chapter 3.

For decades at most consumer goods firms, career paths for successful brand and sales managers have had the characteristics outlined in Exhibit 6-3. Brand assistants are recruited from MBA programs while sales reps are usually recruited from college or military service. In each area, time horizons and promotion policies differ. At one firm, the head of human resources explained, 80% of new salespeople are expected to be "career hires" (i.e., salespeople throughout their tenure with the firm) and 20% are "developmental hires" (i.e., potential managers within and perhaps beyond the sales function). By contrast, nearly all brand hires are treated as developmental hires within an up-or-out promotion philosophy which puts a premium on their performance during their initial years with the firm and which involves frequent rotation among product groups. To advance from brand assistant to brand manager generally takes three to five years. But with at least six associates vying for each brand management position, many

Exhibit 6-3
Traditional Product Management vs. Sales Career Paths: Consumer Goods Firms

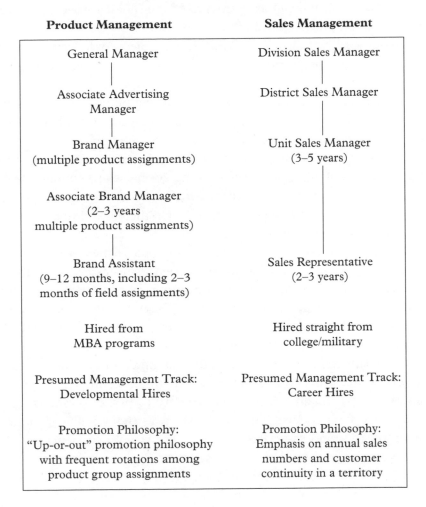

Product Management	**Sales Management**
General Manager	Division Sales Manager
Associate Advertising Manager	District Sales Manager
Brand Manager (multiple product assignments)	Unit Sales Manager (3–5 years)
Associate Brand Manager (2–3 years multiple product assignments)	
Brand Assistant (9–12 months, including 2–3 months of field assignments)	Sales Representative (2–3 years)
Hired from MBA programs	Hired straight from college/military
Presumed Management Track: Developmental Hires	Presumed Management Track: Career Hires
Promotion Philosophy: "Up-or-out" promotion philosophy with frequent rotations among product group assignments	Promotion Philosophy: Emphasis on annual sales numbers and customer continuity in a territory

accept other assignments during this period or leave the company. Those who stay change their assignments every year or two, moving from a small brand with few assistants to more senior brands or new product projects. One result, as a marketing manager put it, is that "There's always a biological clock ticking in our brand groups: if you don't move on to bigger assignments every year or two, you know there's something wrong." Meanwhile, promotion from sales rep to district manager takes a decade or more, and does not entail as many of the "switching" assignments of the mobile brand manager. Indeed, in the interests of building account relationships, switching is discouraged by sales executives. Hence, salespeople learn a great deal about their territory, but much less about other aspects of the business.

Similarly, training differs. Training for new brand assistants consists primarily of project assignments in which the individual learns marketing and industry fundamentals, becomes familiar with company procedures and staff groups, and spends a short obligatory stint in a field sales assignment. Sales training covers selling fundamentals and account dynamics. But, except for the encounter with the brand assistant temporarily assigned to the district, there is little exposure to the marketing organization.

These people thus approach work on joint activities with different assumptions and few of the shared experiences necessary to translate and resolve inevitable differences in their marketing dialects. In terms of the gearbox metaphor introduced in Chapter 2, the gear ratio for each group differs, leading to more costly conflicts and misunderstandings in a new marketing environment.

In consumer goods companies, for example, a key product-sales activity is the allocation of promotional funds to different regions. Brand groups usually delegate this activity to brand assistants (less than a year's experience with the firm) or, as the amount of money increases, to brand associates (two to three years' experience) while sales groups are represented by district or division managers, each with 10 or more years' experience with multiple budgeting cycles. A product manager noted that, in these sessions, "The sales force was essentially a 'black box' for the brand personnel. For instance, I didn't know how sales positions were compensated and evaluated. The de facto rule for new brand assistants was, 'Do the same as last year's person did with a few minor changes based on the brand's current share position.' We missed many opportunities and probably wasted lots of money." The process has other costs. A sales executive gave his perspective on these interactions:

As a district manager, I resented negotiating with people younger and less experienced than I. They were essentially reinventing the wheel each year, and your region usually got what it wanted. But you feel like a second-class citizen in the company when these decisions are officially made by someone who really doesn't know as much about in-store dynamics as you do.

In industrial firms, career paths in product and sales units are usually less segregated. Some sales experience is often a prerequisite for a product management position. But, especially in technically complex product categories, similar tensions emerge. Product managers have undergraduate technical degrees, are increasingly recruited from MBA programs, and rotate among product lines as preparation for a general management position. Salespeople have less technical training, and their careers keep them for some time in a territory or a vertical market segment. In many industrial firms careers in sales and service units are the mirror image of the brand-sales situation in consumer companies. Sales is the fast track up the management hierarchy while service personnel accrue "time in territory" with end-users and resellers. Yet, as firms emphasize product service packages, necessary joint activity between these groups increases.

To address this situation, some companies have initiated changes aimed at providing managers with experience in multiple marketing areas. These initiatives include cross-functional assignments, joint performance-evaluation procedures, and new field-marketing positions that provide additional career path options for managers in each area.

Cross-Functional Assignments

Some consumer goods firms have expanded both the length and type of sales experience required for brand personnel. Whereas this experience had been limited to a two to three month tour of duty at the brand assistant level, extended sales assignments are more common for senior as well as junior brand personnel. Conversely, the liaison units described in Chapter 4 are also used to give promising sales personnel extended exposure to brand marketing processes and perspectives.

In some companies, the deployment of multifunctional account teams (discussed in more detail in Chapter 7) is an opportunity for mid-level product and sales managers to work together. At Procter & Gamble, these teams are staffed by salespeople from different P&G divisions as well as brand personnel assigned to a large account. These managers spend one to two years working together at customer sites and, as one brand manager commented, "You come away with an appreciation for what's involved in executing brand programs and who actually does this in our sales channels."

Other companies have established explicit cross-functional career tracks. General Mills, Kraft General Foods, and other consumer goods manufacturers have begun recruiting for sales positions in the same way they recruit for brand personnel: from leading business schools. These recruits spend some years in sales, but are also viewed as candidates for mid-level positions in brand management. An individual who shows high potential and continued good performance can expect to rotate through both functions every few years. The goal, as one HRM executive explained, "is to develop a cadre of future general managers who, after a decade on the job, have a deep acquaintance with both consumer and trade marketing processes. They will have genuine experience, and credibility, with both sides of the business." Similarly, some industrial firms, such as Hewlett-Packard and IBM, have encouraged more movement between sales and service units. The usual direction is from service to sales, in part because the increasing service component of the product means that these personnel are more directly involved in product and account development as well as traditional postsale service activities.

An interesting example of cross-functional career pathing is the telecom firm MCI, where these practices were initially a response to competitive necessities but are now considered part of the firm's competitive advantage. MCI was founded in 1968 and, for more than two decades, waged legal, regulatory, and marketing battles that required (as one executive phrased it) "high leverage and frequent brushes with bankruptcy, a willingness to alter plans repeatedly in the face of new threats and opportunities, and low tolerance for functionally oriented wallflowers." Because of its heritage of constrained financial resources and the need to move fast against much bigger and better-established competitors, MCI has long "put a premium on attracting and developing people who know how to drive and manage change," as its annual reports emphasize. One aspect of this culture is the extent of cross-functional mobility, especially for marketing people who, in a high fixed-cost service business, must work with many groups in developing products, setting prices, and other activities. Movement between corporate product marketing groups, sales assignments in one of MCI's divisions in the United States or abroad, and other functions such as product development and field service, is encouraged. The following verbal vita from an MCI manager is not uncommon: "During my seven years with the company, I've worked in marketing, sales, MIS, finance, and now international operations, and I had offers from legal and product engineering."

In part, this mobility was required and sanctioned by the firm's growth after deregulation of the Bell System in 1984. In the 1980s, MCI's revenues grew at a 25% compounded rate as its share of the U.S. long-distance business went from less than 1% in 1980 to more than 12% by 1990. Many new people were hired and, throughout the decade, the average age of MCI employees was less than 31 years. Hence, they were more able to accept the frequent geographical moves that cross-functional career paths typically require. By the late 1980s, these career paths were consciously encouraged by the firm's chairman, William McGowan. Among other things, MCI developed an internal electronic mail system, which connects every employee and where job openings are posted. Managers in product, sales, and service units can inquire about positions in other areas, and even negotiate employment terms, with E-mail.

The process has its costs. But the company has developed a web of relationships among managers in all functional areas (one manager described MCI to me as "a vast sorority and fraternity network") and a cadre of people whose learning has been shaped by their career paths. One result is that, compared to other telcom firms, MCI is renowned for its rapid product development, and its ability to implement marketing programs swiftly in a rapidly changing industry. An executive pointed to its career path management as an integral part of MCI's strategy, and described the costs and benefits in these terms:

What I both love and hate about MCI is that everybody thinks everything is their job. The positive aspect is that people want to be part of
a perceived problem, not run away from it; and we're able to do things
quickly and responsively in the marketplace. The negative aspect is
the redundancy and long hours that sometimes result from this "all
hands on deck" approach.

Performance Evaluation Procedures

Another aspect of careers is performance evaluation processes. Learning about other areas can be stimulated by such procedures, even in
the absence of explicit cross-functional assignments. Some companies
I studied have initiated joint evaluation processes, especially for sales
and service personnel.

At a medical products firm, sales and technical service representatives receive bonuses based on customer satisfaction ratings. But they
also evaluate each other's contribution with a questionnaire that considers "attitude, professionalism, quick response, and contribution
to customer satisfaction." These questionnaires are also completed
by customers and reviewed by the managers to whom sales and service reps report. Then, account personnel meet biannually to explain
their evaluations of one another. A manager noted that "This procedure generates a discussion between sales and service of specific accounts—a considerable benefit in a business where, for good logistical
reasons, the salesperson is usually dedicated to a select group of accounts, but these accounts are among dozens that clamor for the service rep's attention."

Beyond formal evaluations, informal procedures are also important. In most consumer goods firms in the United States and Europe, product management has long been viewed as the lead function.
Other functions, including sales, have been seen as support groups
whose role is to implement brand marketing's plans. One result is the
second-class citizen perceptions noted above. The situation is different in Japanese consumer-goods companies. Because of the historical
nature of Japanese retail channels and their intensive service requirements, these companies have long demanded close integration between brand marketing and field sales and merchandising efforts.

At Kao Corporation, brand managers are responsible for many of the same activities as their Western counterparts, including brand strategy, product positioning, and liaison with advertising agencies. But, with sales personnel, they are also responsible for market share and volume targets. These targets place Kao brand personnel in frequent contact with sales groups, who have a status above that of support units for brand managers. Indeed, a tradition at Kao requires that brand managers who fail to attain their goals must attend a sales meeting, apologize with an abject bow, and say, "I'm sorry."[7] Such procedures are an informal but powerful form of performance evaluation while communicating vividly the importance of developing marketing plans with early cross-functional input. Similarly, at Honda dealerships in Japan, cars are first washed by dealer sales personnel before being sent to the service bays. This activity is viewed as a sign of respect for the dealer's service personnel—a reversal of the status system that operates between sales and service units in most Western companies.

Field Marketing Specialists

Another initiative involves the creation of field-marketing specialist (FMS) positions—i.e., product, geography, or vertical market specialists. These positions are usually intended to improve the field's ability to sell and service a new product or market, or to facilitate coherent adaptation of headquarters marketing programs to different regions or channels of distribution. These positions also provide an important cross-functional career path option for managers in each area.

Some computer firms have established area product management units, each dedicated to certain products in a country or market segment. Their responsibilities include forecasting, sales support, identifying important applications (and the implications for field service and distribution channels), and coordinating product introductions in that area. Similarly, some consumer products companies have decentralized many core elements of their marketing mix to field-marketing specialists. In the past decade, Campbell Soup has implemented a major reorganization, in which brand sales managers in 22 regions make many decisions formerly handled by headquarters product management. The goal is to secure a competitive advantage by positioning

Campbell as a leader in the development and execution of trade-marketing programs.

Consumer goods marketer Frito-Lay has been even more aggressive, and made this approach a cornerstone of its revised strategy. Through the mid-1980s, Frito-Lay's marketing programs were developed by headquarters brand groups and executed the same way in all areas by the firm's route reps. In 1988, Frito began delegating control to 32 marketing areas, each with P&L responsibility. In this structure, the Zone Marketing Manager (ZMM) changed from a sales support to a marketing position, filled primarily by people with previous headquarters brand experience. ZMMs have two roles. One is administering trade spending, which accounts for the majority of each area's marketing budget. With sales managers, ZMMs set the trade promotion calendar, which (in a departure from past practice) differs by region and class of trade. The ZMM's second major role is coordination with headquarters brand groups, especially for product introductions or line extensions. Brand planning and R&D remain centralized, but (as one executive explained) the ZMM is the primary means for a brand manager to "sell" the field on a new program. Conversely, ZMMs negotiate with brand groups for types and levels of media spending, consumer promotions, and sales incentives. Individuals on each side of these interactions learn about processes and concerns in the other area.

An important benefit of these field-marketing positions is that they are a means for moving managers, information, and analytical capabilities from headquarters (where established administrative support often locates such resources) to pertinent local levels (where customers, and important customization tasks, are located). Further, the relevant learning in customer contacts increasingly involves working across the firm's product groups—an activity that individual product managers often have little incentive to perform and that field sales and service personnel cannot perform easily or in needed depth.

TRAINING AND DEVELOPMENT

The experience afforded by cross-functional career paths is invaluable. But this approach takes time. Meanwhile, marketing activities require a shared perspective in daily interactions among product, sales, and service managers. Companies have found their traditional training and development practices inadequate for this purpose and are supporting new initiatives in this area.

For a company trying to develop and maintain concurrent marketing capabilities, traditional training programs raise several issues.

First, marketing training in most firms is a menu of specialist courses that rarely place product, sales, and service personnel in the same room. Consider the situation at computer firms I studied. Faced with declining hardware margins and the emergence of standardized open systems, these vendors have shifted their strategies to emphasize selling an array of integrated services, including the maintenance of competitors' equipment at customer sites and even managing IS departments for accounts. Based on my research, I do not believe it is an exaggeration to suggest that, in the current environment, the major computer firms could literally swap their strategic plans and there would be no appreciable difference in actual marketplace behavior. Implementation of this common strategy, however, is typically stymied by uncoordinated sales and service activities. At two companies I studied, salespeople stressed the company's desire to "establish long-term relationships by providing integrated solutions to your total data-processing needs." But service personnel balked at repairing competitors' equipment or providing warranty services to a network that included applications developed by an external strategic partner. An executive commented: "We spent time and money training our salespeople in how to sell solutions. But we never got this message across to service people, who are constantly on customers' premises and often know more about customer needs than the salesperson does."

Second, because of how training is funded, the need to develop skills across marketing units often goes unrecognized and, when recognized, unfunded at the appropriate levels. Product, sales, and service units have their own training budgets, in-house management development personnel, and external sources of training and expertise. "Innovative" programs are those that find effective (or, at least, novel) ways of transmitting needed functional expertise. The broader business management skills needed for concurrent marketing are seen as the focus of programs reserved for top executives or for those attending a university-sponsored course on generic strategy frameworks. But as market changes place more emphasis on customizing and decentralizing important marketing tasks, reserving such training for top executives leaves many firms with an appreciation for, but not the organizational ability to deal with, new marketing requirements. Further, programs offered by universities and most large training firms are commonly off-the-shelf courses that take little if any account of the specific company context in which these managers work.

Third, common sales-training practices are, ironically, often unintended barriers to the development of a company's concurrent marketing abilities. These practices tend to develop the sales force in the image of the previous generation of successful salespeople in the firm, not with a vision of the new marketing environment. The issue here is not money: most marketing training expenses already go to sales training, and the money spent is substantial. By the late 1980s, the average cost of training a salesperson in the United States was estimated at $11,600 in consumer goods firms, $22,200 in industrial companies, and $14,500 in service businesses while in 1993 sales training accounted for 13% ($6.4 billion) of the estimated $48.2 billion that U.S. companies spent on training.[8] But the overwhelming focus of this training is on new salespeople and on developing skills such as time and territory management, presentation skills, and product knowledge.[9] With new field-marketing requirements, however, there is a growing discrepancy in many industries between what is needed and what sales training programs actually deliver. A study of 235 companies found that customer service and relationships with other areas of the firm were seen by sales managers as essential for effective selling. But only 1% of sales-training time in these firms focused on these areas. Generic selling skills constituted more than 50% of the training content in these firms while product and industry knowledge accounted for the remainder.[10]

Some leading-edge companies I examined have altered the form and content of their training programs. They used redesigned programs as a way to build recognition of the need for better linkages, develop a shared understanding of each area's contribution to customer satisfaction, and broaden the individual relationships needed to institutionalize better coordination at marketing interfaces. These initiatives shared certain characteristics: they were typically company-specific in design, cross-functional in terms of participation, and real-world/project-oriented in terms of content.

First, these programs were defined and designed as company-specific initiatives intended to promote a change in attitude and orientation as well as in the skills of managers. The line between cultural transformation and management education blurred, and customization of program content became essential.[11] In line with this approach, many traditional programs—separated among product, sales, and service units—were redesigned as joint activities. In the early 1990s, Motorola realigned the mission and management of its in-house Motorola University program in this manner. The intent was, in part, to create and sustain a companywide language for quality initiatives, and to develop quality consciousness and capabilities across its multiple customer-contact units. What one exective described to me as, previously, "one of the best nonaccredited MBA programs in the world—a nice distinction but not really our business," has become an agent of company-specific cultural change. Koch Industries, a privately held energy and financial services firm, has made significant investments in its Koch Management Center to develop "management technology"—a common vocabulary and shared understanding across functional units, including marketing interfaces.

Second, while top management attended, these programs were not limited to top executives. They typically included managers from different levels and functions. Indeed, a major benefit was often the education *of* top managers *by* front-line managers about changing field marketing requirements. An example is a program I attended at a consumer goods firm. There, most senior marketing executives' last sustained exposure to trade selling had been 15 years or more earlier when, as new brand assistants, they spent a few weeks calling on supermarkets. During the program, workshops with lower-level sales and merchandising personnel alerted these managers to the many changes in trade buying and service requirements since their own firsthand experience.

A third characteristic of these programs (and another reason they tended to be company-specific) was complementing classroom instruction with actual projects about ongoing issues at the firm's sales interfaces. Often billed as exercises in "action learning," these programs were influenced by TQM initiatives in other areas of the firm and what Deming called the "Plan, Do, Check, Act" cycle required for systematic problem solving. The assumption is that, especially in raising awareness of interdependencies among busy marketing managers, an effective learning program must develop skills and shared awareness in the context of meaningful business issues. Either alone is inadequate.

A development initiative illustrating these characteristics is the Work-Out programs begun at General Electric in 1989. Company-specific in focus, cross-functional in terms of participants, and project-driven in agenda, these sessions deal with various issues within GE's many businesses. Many involve the need for better integration of product, sales, and service units in the context of global competition, lower-priced alternatives, a consequent emphasis on value-added product service packages, and flat or shrinking headcount in many GE businesses. Chairman John Welch has been explicit about the organizational challenge facing his firm: "Even in a horizontal structure you'll still have product managers, still need accountability. But the lines [between product and other functional units] will blur."[12] Hence, many Work-Out programs concern the development of concurrent marketing skills in a corporation with a heritage of autonomous, functionally oriented product, sales, and service units.

Work-Out programs first involve in-depth interviews with managers at all levels of a business unit, often by outside facilitators. Company-specific case studies and other materials may be developed as part of this process. Then, at programs lasting from two to five days, managers from different functions and levels consider research about the issues in question and address actual business problems. The format is analogous to a town meeting and the customer is a visible participant. Most Work-Outs utilize specific data from customer service surveys or other sources. Customers make presentations at the outset of the sessions, in person or on video, to give participants in nonfield functions a firsthand feel for what customers are saying about doing business with GE. Managers in various GE marketing and other functional groups then work on, and "work out," the issues identified by the customer. In recent years the emphasis has increasingly shifted to using Work-Out as a mechanism for real-time, collaborative problem solving *with* customers.[13] The output is a preliminary plan for reorganizing responsibilities and activities (often codified in a written "contract" between individuals or functional groups), and a schedule for reviewing implementation results.

Other companies opt for less structured approaches. At some firms, joint assignments at trade shows are opportunities for product, sales, and service personnel to establish relationships and learn more about another area's impact on their activities. An executive at a medical products firm noted that these "are ideal settings to qualify prospects, conduct research with customers, and learn about potential new competitors. By sharing these activities at shows and conferences, sales and marketing can compare notes and individuals in each area often develop an important esprit de corps."

Changes in marketing information systems can also be training and development opportunities. At a consumer goods company, a shift to scanner data was implemented by having brand personnel visit sales offices to explain the nature of the data and the numbers that brand managers expected to monitor closely. "In turn," a market researcher explained, "brand groups were educated by salespeople about how the trade uses this data, caveats concerning brand's intended analyses, and activity that could help improve marketing effectiveness in certain regions and accounts." At a telecom firm, a task force of product, sales, and service managers was charged with developing a customer database. Initially intended for use by sales and service in forecasting territory potential and planning service calls, the task force discovered uses for product marketing in areas ranging from promotion design to pricing and direct mail campaigns. Product managers also learned about selling requirements, and therefore stressed different kinds of applications in product development plans.

BENEFITS AND VULNERABILITIES

These career path and development initiatives can reap significant benefits. But, in most firms, they also generate conflicts that can limit or negate their usefulness in building concurrent marketing capabilities.

Consider the comment of a manager who, after five years in brand management, moved to a sales position in her company:

> In product marketing, I had represented our brand at three national sales meetings and, each time, thought my 30 minutes in front of the sales force had an impact. But last month I attended my first meeting on the sales side. By noon, a half-dozen brand groups have told you why their program is fantastic, but little relates to Monday morning in the branch office. I felt sorry for the people scheduled to present after lunch.

Meanwhile, BDD's Bob Short noted that "When I was in sales, I had no appreciation for what product marketing does. In sales, there are visible wins and losses, but 80% of product management is invisible to sales, yet essential to effective selling." As these comments suggest, one benefit of having worked both sides is increased awareness of another unit's operating conditions, constraints, and contributions.

More generally, these assignments and cross-functional training help build what one observer called the "thick informal networks one finds wherever multiple leadership initiatives work in harmony. . . . Too often these networks are either very thin or fragmented: a tight network exists inside [each] group but not across departments."[14] As many studies have demonstrated, managers get much of their work done through dozens of informal networks. This is especially true in time-constrained activities like sales, service, and product management. Even though market changes often require the reformation of existing social networks among these units, standard HRM policies do not encourage the formation of networks across marketing interfaces. A brand manager (one of the few, in her firm, with years of previous sales experience) indicated the value of such networks:

> When I got to Brand, people here would debate the pros and cons of different promotion and merchandising schemes. But I could call district managers in territories where I knew these issues were important, or where competitors had been using a similar program. Those managers could quickly tell me whether something was or wasn't working. Also, because I had worked with these people, they were more willing to help out with a problem or new idea.

In a similar vein, studies of how successful multinational companies manage simultaneous demands for global standardization and national customization have documented the role of management transfers and training in building a common vision. The goal, as one study phrased it, is to create "a verbal information network . . . which results in [coordination] that is personal yet decentralized."[15] This is the sort of coordination by feedback that, as Exhibit 6-1 emphasizes, is more important when markets change rapidly and marketing tasks are increasingly customized. The relationships developed by these career path and training initiatives allow local discretion and flexibility within a context of continuing functional expertise and mutually coherent product, sales, and service policies.

However, these initiatives also require many companies to rethink other HRM policies. Joint development programs usually entail *additional* training beyond the still-required functional training in product management, selling, and service. Therefore, more people in the firm are spending more time in training. Some cost-conscious companies view this expense as unnecessary or infeasible. Unless supported by top management and other processes, the lasting impact of these programs is questionable. At GE, the chairman is the champion of Work-Out programs, and top management of business units attends the sessions. In my experience, however, the more common situation is that top management is only intermittently involved in cross-functional development initiatives. It delegates the design and development of programs to training staff who are often far removed from current field realities. Too often, the result is that described by one executive: "After each program, many people leave enthused. But, back on the job, the enthusiasts still encounter functional stovepipes and management indifference."

Similarly, the career paths discussed here demand sustained commitment, and multiple-year time horizons, from companies and individuals. Also needed is the willingness to assume the risks of a situation where most careers in the firm, including those of current senior management, developed according to a paradigm that stressed within-function expertise. One consumer goods company in my research had instituted many innovative trade marketing programs and reorganized sales around multifunctional account teams. But career systems were untouched by its "close to the customer" campaign. A young brand manager candidly explained that "I recently had an offer to move into a marketing position on one of our account teams. But my boss discouraged me. He said it would set me behind my peers, who would be assuming more responsibility at headquarters while I spent time in the field. I think he was honest with me. I might learn a lot, but I'm not sure it would actually help my career here."

At most companies I examined, cross-functional training and career pathing was usually limited to a small minority of managers. This, in itself, can raise issues. A sales executive at a medical products firm noted that "Product personnel who come into sales are usually younger people slated for more responsibility at headquarters. They're expected to be adequate during their sales stint. But salespeople perceive a double standard, where average-performing product people are favored over outstanding salespeople for promotion. This creates morale problems that many district managers resent." Conversely, cross-functional movement is simply not welcomed by many potential candidates, especially when dual-career households make the geographical mobility that often accompanies a transfer more difficult.

Finally, these initiatives tend to build skill bases that are more company-specific than functionally oriented careers. Historically in many Japanese firms, cross-functional rotation and training occurred in the context of lifetime employment patterns, promotions driven by seniority, and substantial social pressures and other barriers facing managers who sought to switch employers. Hence, Japanese firms had more assurance that returns on long-term investments in individual learning would not be reaped by a competitor while individuals had less incentive to develop careers through functional expertise and more incentive to develop cross-functional skills at a single company.[16] For better or worse, these wider corporate and social conditions do not exist at most Western companies.

KEY DIAGNOSTIC QUESTIONS

Career path and training initiatives in marketing can be more effective if companies first think through certain questions.

- Does management recognize the interrelationship of its career path and training policies with other linkage devices intended to improve concurrent marketing effectiveness?

Part II of this book has discussed three major types of coordination mechanisms: structural devices, such as the formal liaison units discussed in Chapter 4; market research and information systems, discussed in Chapter 5; and the changes in career paths and training programs discussed in this chapter. These mechanisms are interdependent and without the appropriate people and processes, they will have limited impact.

Probably the most common problem I observed was failure to address all three dimensions. Of the three, the human resource dimension was the most neglected. Changes in structure come naturally to top managers seeking to make a statement about the need to change. Investments in information systems have been sanctioned in recent years under the banner of reengineering the corporation. But changes in HRM practices are not glamorous, take time to make their impact felt, and, in many companies, too often stop at the level of vague statements about teamwork and culture. The necessary nitty-gritty of individual learning and skill building is neglected.

This is especially true in sales. Often spending the formative years of their careers in individual contributor assignments, many sales managers do not see connections between HRM policies and "what it takes to sell." Rather, time and money spent on career planning or cross-functional training are often viewed as distractions from achieving quota. Many sales managers are therefore reluctant to go beyond what they think is strictly necessary and, hence, the overwhelming emphasis in most current sales training programs is on basic skills. Indeed, some may view broader development initiatives (especially cross-functional career paths) as ways in which they lose their best salespeople to other functions while having to carry unproven revenue generators on their budgets.

For these reasons, top management involvement is essential. As competition places more emphasis on concurrent marketing capabilities, these HRM issues are vital aspects of strategy design.

- Does the company have mechanisms in place to coordinate
  its training and career pathing initiatives at marketing
  interfaces?

An important factor behind the realignment of BDD's marketing organization was the fact that the corporation had recently included career pathing and training in strategy development. In this annual process, management of each business unit analyzes strategy not only in terms of industry structure and competitive positioning, but also in terms of the organizational tasks to be performed and the particular types of organizational coordination and competencies required. A profile of HRM implications is drawn up and then reviewed with top management, including the CEO.[17] Hence, Gary Cohen could initiate management transfers and joint development programs for marketing and sales personnel in his division knowing that such initiatives were part of business strategy, not just experiments on a few pioneers.

Most companies, however, lack mechanisms for integrating these initiatives with marketing and career planning. Two unfortunate consequences can result. One is that joint training programs for product, sales, and service often have little to do with the participants' promotion aspirations and prospects. The other consequence is that managers may pay lip-service to the need for better coordination but, recognizing organizational realities, resist assignments that broaden individual and organizational learning at marketing interfaces. A senior executive in one firm spoke for many when he noted that "We do all this strategy development work and we do a lot of financial planning, but so often the unknown factor is the people and the process that are needed to implement strategy. Just as we reduce our planning to specifics in marketing, manufacturing, and technology, we also need to reduce it to specifics in what we're going to do with people development and staffing. Otherwise, those plans are not going to get implemented."

- In getting to specifics, has the company analyzed the kinds
  of joint activities where management transfers and training
  are likely to add value?

The message of this chapter is *not* that firms should simply scuttle functional departments and adopt cross-functional career paths and training for all product, sales, and service personnel. As Part I emphasized, specific expertise remains important, and the key issue in building concurrent marketing capabilities is how to link effectively knowledge and actions that necessarily reside in different units in most firms.

Companies must make conscious choices about the kinds of crossfunctional learning their marketing strategies require. Precisely because these career path and development initiatives take significant time and resources, companies must be able to specify where and how to forge leverageable linkages along the continuum of activities in value creation and value delivery.

At some companies I studied, getting to specifics involved an audit of marketing activities as a way of surfacing strategic interdependencies while underlining what one executive called the "clarity of purpose required for effective implementation—organizational clarity about what each unit uniquely contributes to overall business performance."

Exhibit 6-4 provides an example of the output of such an analysis at a consumer goods company. In this example, four increasingly interdependent organizational units are distinguished along certain criteria:

- The major joint activities in which coordination is necessary between two or more of these units;
- Each unit's key contribution to customer satisfaction in the performance of these activities;
- The primary external focus and responsibility of each unit (in this case, trade customer or end-consumer); and
- Specific elements of the marketing mix over which each unit has final decision-making authority.

In this company, product management and sales must coordinate pricing, promotion, and merchandising activities. But each group retains decision-making authority over different aspects of these activities with trade customers or end-consumers. Product management is responsible for consumer advertising, promotion, packaging, and pricing decisions; sales is responsible for distribution, merchandising, shelving, and promotion at trade customers. Similarly, sales and prod-

Exhibit 6-4
Joint Activities and Functional Responsibilities at a Consumer Goods Firm

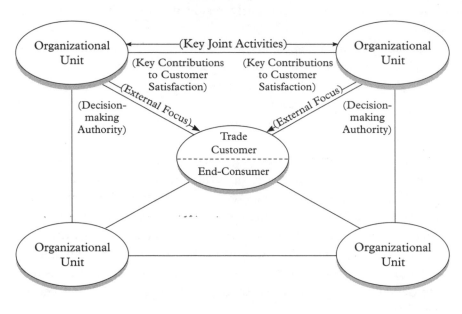

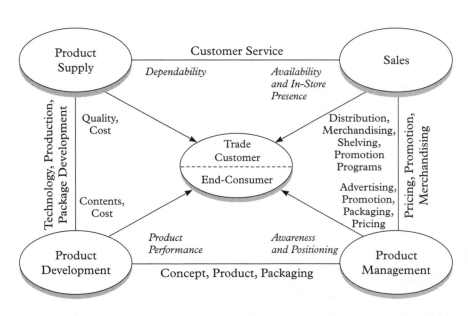

uct supply (logistics and service units) must coordinate service efforts in different classes of trade. Sales makes decisions about distribution and merchandising activities within the quality and cost parameters established by product supply managers

An executive at this firm explained: "These units have more cross-functional requirements but less time to execute. A chart like this doesn't 'solve' conflicts. But it has helped to expedite decision making and resource allocations while underlining where accountability for joint activities resides." In turn, this framework has helped both line managers and HRM staff to specify what kinds of transfers and cross-functional development programs build long-term learning while speaking to the day-to-day realities of particular units. "Before we performed this analysis and got down to specifics," an HRM executive noted, "we were randomly encouraging all kinds of career moves that had the net effect of diluting functional expertise in each area. And we were running training programs where talk about 'excellence' or 'empowerment' tried to substitute for an actionable understanding of the business and changing field realities. Now, we can pick our shots and leverage the investments in time and people that these moves entail."

CONCLUSION

Career pathing and management development programs have important roles to play in addressing new marketing requirements. Their impact on individual learning is crucial in forming, and reforming, the organizational capabilities required for concurrent marketing. But, like the other internal linkage devices discussed in Part II, these initiatives are meant to add value in external customer encounters. Part III, therefore, focuses on the role of account management systems, sales compensation policies, and service procedures in the daily execution of field sales and service tasks.

III
MANAGING FIELD
MARKETING
REQUIREMENTS

■

7

Account Management
Systems

■

P ART I concerned new marketing requirements generated by
market developments. Part II discussed what firms are doing organizationally to build concurrent marketing abilities. Part III focuses on
getting the marketing job done through field sales and service
people—in most firms, the front line of customer contact.

This chapter considers account management systems and other
issues involved in building relationships in situations where concurrent marketing capabilities are most needed. Chapter 8 discusses a
vital part of a company's field marketing system: sales compensation policies. Chapter 9 then focuses on ways to achieve better coordination of service tasks with sales and product management
activities.

I begin with the topic of account management because the developments outlined in Part I lead to significant changes in day-to-day selling tasks. Traditionally, selling involved the management of individual
efforts. Now, selling is more often the province of a team which
must work across product lines (the products often made by different divisions and sold from different locations) and with customers
that demand an integrated product-service package. This chapter
focuses on the role of the account manager, clarification of account
selection criteria, and the coordination challenges posed by key
accounts.

KEY ACCOUNTS

For most companies, all customers are *not* equal; some account for disproportionate shares of a firm's sales or margins. Many managers refer to this as the 80/20 rule, meaning that about 20% of customers may generate as much as 80% of sales. Numerous studies support this intuition. An extensive survey of companies in business-to-business markets found that the top 20% of customers contributed a median 75% of sales volume for these firms, that 50% of a typical company's sales volume came from 10% of its customers, and that 90% of sales came from 50% of the accounts.[1] Hence, the 80/20 rule is true enough so that managing key accounts is a core marketing issue at many companies.

Several factors make such customers increasingly important. Mergers, acquisitions, and strategic alliances require vendors to put more emphasis on large customers with complex purchasing processes. Conventional supermarkets, for example, accounted for 75% of U.S. food retail sales in 1980. By 1990, their share of purchases from manufacturers was 25%; superstores, combination stores, and warehouse stores accounted for the majority. Their buying power and internal information systems allow these large chains to insist on specialized services and a coordinated approach from their suppliers, many of whom sell them multiple products through different sales forces. In health care markets, the rise of managed care institutions and integrated delivery networks—where a continuum of care from hospital through alternative site service to insurance reimbursement comes under a single management structure—also affects suppliers.

Global markets too place new account-management demands on sales organizations. In many industrial businesses, suppliers must provide coordinated sales and services at customer locations dispersed throughout the world. At a computer firm I studied, selling to an automobile manufacturer was involved: the formal purchase decision was made by customer personnel in Sweden; applications development was handled by the seller's Italian subsidiary; an independent U.K. software firm was a key subcontractor; and installation and postsale services took place in customer locations in 25 countries.

Finally, the supply chain developments discussed in Chapter 1 also affect account management. Many companies have realigned purchasing to include working with suppliers in product design, development, manufacture, and distribution. These policies place more importance on the selling firm's ability to maintain preferred-vendor status at accounts looking to work more intensively with a smaller but higher value-added supplier base.

Because of these factors, key accounts have the following characteristics:

- They purchase in significant volume from the vendor, both in absolute dollars and as a percentage of the vendor's sales in that product category;
- Purchasing involves multiple buyers and influencers, often from several functional areas;
- Purchasing may also involve a number of geographically dispersed organizations at the account, e.g., multiple stores, branches, or manufacturing plants; and
- The account expects specialized attention and services in areas such as logistical support, inventory management, customized applications, and/or ongoing information about product usage.

These characteristics mean that a long-term relationship between buyer and seller must often be a goal, and organizing principle, in field marketing. The up-front investments in doing business with such customers often cannot be recouped if the buyer-seller exchange assumes a short-term, transaction orientation (see below). The top-line revenue increases and bottom-line cost efficiencies at such accounts are only realized over time, as the buyer-seller exchange broadens and deepens.

By "account management systems," I refer not only to selling in the traditional sense of that term (turning prospects into customers), but also to the process of initiating and developing these relationships with selected customers. At the core of an account management system is the role of the account manager who still performs the sales boundary role described in Chapter 2. But the key-account boundary adds complexity to field-selling tasks because it involves managing a set of internal as well as external relationships.

Exhibit 7-1
Role of the Account Manager

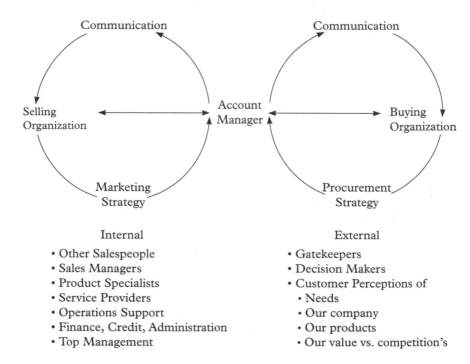

Internal	External
• Other Salespeople	• Gatekeepers
• Sales Managers	• Decision Makers
• Product Specialists	• Customer Perceptions of
• Service Providers	• Needs
• Operations Support	• Our company
• Finance, Credit, Administration	• Our products
• Top Management	• Our value vs. competition's

Externally, as Exhibit 7-1 suggests, the account manager must deal with the gatekeepers and influencers across the customer's organization. Here, the task is to understand and perhaps modify the customer's definition of needs, the selling company's product and service offerings relative to competition, and the customer's perception of the benefits of working with the vendor on a long-term basis. To accomplish these tasks, the account manager must motivate and help align the internal personnel who also deal with the account (perhaps in remote locations or different countries), product managers who often have responsibility for customized terms requested by the account, support and operations personnel in such areas as product engineering (for special applications) or logistics (for just-in-time delivery), and the selling firm's top management when the potential of the contract (or the magnitude of the account's demands) reaches a certain point.

In these circumstances, selling largely *is* the vendor's ability to marshal resources effectively across a range of buying locations, buying influences, and its own product, sales, and service units. The methods used to accomplish this task affect a firm's expense-to-revenue ratio, profitability, and ability to retain or grow business at these accounts. Developing an effective and cost-efficient account management system requires a company to: (1) clarify account selection criteria, (2) understand and influence the dynamics of buyer-seller relations, and (3) manage the formidable coordination challenges involved.

ACCOUNT SELECTION

Key accounts require a resource commitment from suppliers. Delivery systems, applications, and the product line itself may be changed, or developed from scratch, in these situations. Moreover, the selling cycle can take years (and many costly sales calls) before a contract is signed and revenue generated. As one manager emphasized, "No one is really interested in waiting three or four years for a sale. But few customers have budgeting procedures that allow a single person to buy a million-dollar system tomorrow."

These efforts entail resources, time, and attention not allocated elsewhere. Hence, such efforts also mean a sizeable opportunity cost for a vendor as well as direct costs for marketing managers still held accountable for quarterly or annual revenue targets. Clearly, not every current or potential customer can be treated as a key account so account selection is a crucial decision for the seller.

To begin the required analysis, consider what happens when a sale is made to such a customer. Exhibit 7-2 depicts the chain-reaction impact of account selection decisions on a business.

A sale ultimately represents a stream of orders for a supplier, and each order stream comes embedded with transaction costs—the costs of order-acquisition and order-fulfillment associated with that customer. Some orders involve significant presales support while other orders may be for standard items, where incremental transaction costs are low or zero. Often (but not always), these differences align by customer industry. At a telecommunications firm I studied, commercial customers in one industry want service that requires special network

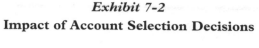

Exhibit 7-2
Impact of Account Selection Decisions

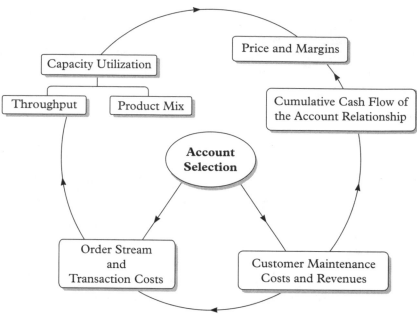

switches and customized software development while customers in another industry are big buyers of the firm's standardized services. Yet, because the firm's accounting system did not capture these order stream expenses as part of customer acquisition costs, account selection policies did not distinguish between the customer groups. Indeed, customers in the first industry group (because of their high usage of telecommunications services and because salespeople were compensated on volume) were considered a prime target for account development efforts while customers in the latter group (despite the lower selling and product modification expenses involved in their stream of orders) received less attention.

In turn, the order stream affects a supplier's business and must be considered in account selection decisions. An account's order patterns influence capacity utilization, both in terms of throughput and product mix. These are very important determinants of the cost of goods sold in most businesses. At the companies I examined, for instance, the top 50 accounts were major drivers of the firms' capacity expansion and product development decisions. Over time, the requirements of serving these accounts affected production economies and core competencies throughout the business. Good account selection builds capabilities by keeping the supplier in touch with market trends. Poor account selection, however, can incrementally lead the supplier to build increasingly obsolete capabilities. Witness the fate of the billions invested in the 1980s by IBM and others in mainframe R&D and manufacturing capacity in order to serve their installed base of key accounts. The problem was *not* that IBM and other leading mainframe firms were insufficiently "close to the customer." Rather, the problem was that they were getting closer and closer to the *wrong* customers: these vendors increasingly tailored their businesses to build and utilize capacity of decreasing relevance to emerging order streams in the industry.

As well as presale transaction costs, customers (especially in industrial markets) generate after-sale costs and revenues for the supplier. In the market for stationary air compressors, for example, accessories, parts, and service generate more revenues and higher margins than sales of the initial equipment. Capturing this value means an investment in a multichannel distribution network and, depending on the account, substantial inventory carrying costs. For leading suppliers such as Ingersoll-Rand, these postsale costs and revenues are major criteria in market segmentation, account selection, and distribution decisions.[2] Across industrial companies, according to a study of 2,400 firms by McKinsey, after-sale business accounts for 10–20% of revenues and a larger portion (ranging from 20% to as high as 67% in some capital-equipment businesses) of total contribution margin.[3] Equally important, during a given product's life cycle, after-sale revenues and costs often are a multiple of original purchase revenue and costs. Hence, account selection decisions that focus only on the order and ignore customer maintenance considerations can lead to serious mistakes.

Finally, these capacity utilization and customer maintenance factors, as well as the account's bargaining power, help determine the supplier's net margins and the cumulative cash flow history of the relationship. In other words, account profitability is the outcome of a series of resource allocations, cash outflows, and cash inflows over time, and not simply the gross margin built into the purchase contract or the vendor's standard costing system for its products.

When customers are viewed this way, many companies are surprised by what they find. After taking into account both pre- and postsale transaction costs, one industrial firm found that 225% of its net income was coming from less than 20% of its customer base, 70% of its customers were breakeven accounts, and 10% were significant money losers.[4] Similarly, a study of five major U.K. corporations, in businesses ranging from equipment leasing to specialty chemicals manufacturing, found that between 15% and 30% of customers were unprofitable when their customer maintenance costs were properly allocated.[5] The cumulative findings of newer activity-based costing systems, moreover, suggest that these are not isolated instances. In fact, the deviation between profitable and unprofitable customers may be widening as bigger, more powerful accounts invest in information systems that allow them to monitor suppliers' costs and services on a global basis.

In practice, there is no easy alignment of the factors depicted in Exhibit 7-2. But key-account selection sets off this chain reaction of vendor commitments that affect transaction costs, profitability, and wider organizational skills and capabilities. How do companies manage this crucial decision? My experience and research suggest that, unfortunately, most companies *don't* manage account selection well. Most firms leave this decision to the field sales force, whose aggregate call patterns essentially determine who becomes a key customer and who doesn't. And, when one examines sales compensation policies in many firms (see Chapter 8), the implicit message to salespeople concerning account selection is a variation on the Biblical injunction to "Go forth and multiply"—sell to anyone. Salespeople therefore bring back a variety of customers, each with very different order patterns, transaction cost, capacity utilization, and maintenance needs. This account base then pulls the company in several directions at once. Strategically, the firm gets "stuck in the middle":[6] attempting to build varied customer relationships without a clear competitive advantage and with conflicting account requirements vying for limited investment funds.

AN ACCOUNT SELECTION PROCESS

What is needed is a process that makes explicit the near-term potential *and* the longer-term resources required to maintain vendor value and reap profits from an account relationship. Without such a process, key accounts can become increasingly unprofitable to serve over time, as their buyer power allows them to demand higher levels of support at lower prices. In recent years, for example, many firms have focused on customer retention in their marketing efforts. The typical assumption, however, is that a satisfied customer is (in financial terms) an annuity—a stream of steady-state payments. But buying behavior is not passive. Over time, most customers tend to make more demands on their suppliers. Account selection, therefore, must be explicit about which demands the seller can meet *and* leverage in dealings with other customers. Otherwise, the seller risks overserving unprofitable accounts and wasting resources that might be allocated to other customer groups.

Exhibit 7-3 describes a three-phase account segmentation process.[7] The phases are a screening process for key-account selection. That is, only accounts that qualify through phase-one criteria move on to phase two, and so on. Phase one focuses on profit potential, measured in terms of incremental sales potential and how much a customer values the vendor's support services. Most companies segment their customer base by sales volume. But there must also be *incremental* volume to justify investing in a key-account opportunity. Put differently, the 80/20 rule merits attention in allocating marketing resources but, by itself, says little about where and how to allocate resources. Indeed, if their customer base already conforms to the 80/20 rule, managers hardly need the expenses of key-account programs to indicate that big customers are big. Beyond the current volume a customer represents, the seller needs to assess sales potential across its product line.

It must also assess the extent to which potential accounts value the support services that it can provide. Some accounts cost a great deal to serve but are willing to pay for support, either because the seller's product is critical in their finished product or because the vendor provides important services more effectively and so minimizes the costs of product failure. Other accounts do not value ancillary ser-

Exhibit 7-3

Three-Phase Account Segmentation Process

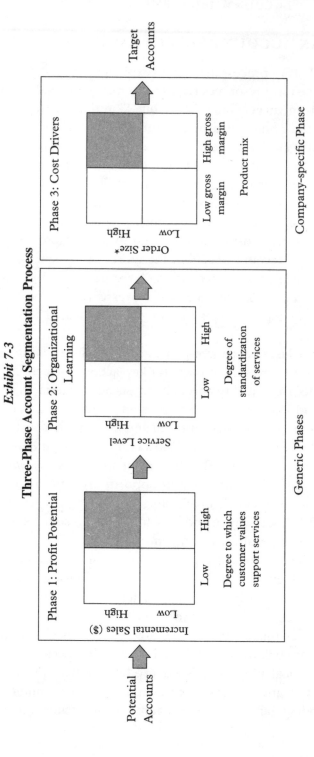

* Cost drivers listed are those important for a specific vendor.

vices and are usually price-sensitive, especially in rebuy or trade-up purchases.

Air compressors, for example, provide power for equipment ranging from drills and screwdrivers to jet engines and other pneumatic machinery. Pharmaceutical and food manufacturing, high-technology plant systems such as microchip assembly, and textile weaving also require compressed air in their production processes. The cost of downtime in some applications can be a hundred times or more the price of spare parts and service for the compressors. These accounts are very willing to pay for support contracts that minimize downtime, boost customer satisfaction, and build repurchase loyalty for vendors. At the opposite extreme are accounts whose buying volume and usage patterns give them the bargaining power and incentive to unbundle the product service offering. Many compressor customers use the equipment on an intermittent basis for noncritical applications. These accounts also buy many compressors, but they tend to buy lower-quality spares and cut-rate service from "pirate parts" vendors that sell at a discount. Strategically, these two customer groups have very different lifetime values to an air-compressor manufacturer even though both may purchase similar amounts of equipment.

Phase two focuses on identifying those accounts that, because of their support requirements, provide profitable organizational learning opportunities for the seller. High service levels can generate lucrative after-sale opportunities, but only if the vendor makes the investments in facilities and expertise required to provide excellent support. For key accounts, support often includes modification of existing information systems, field and technical service, multisite distribution logistics, product development and design, and billing. After determining which customers value such support services, in phase two firms screen accounts according to common support priorities. The goal is to identify similar needs so that the vendor can (1) invest aggressively in those support capabilities valued by multiple key accounts, and (2) in so doing, accelerate learning and support excellence in selected areas so that the selling company can cost-effectively standardize the provision of customized support services to its key accounts.

In effect, phase two requires a vendor to select carefully which types of demands it will respond to, using a coherent support strategy.

Without this explicitness in the account selection process, support capabilities tend to develop in response to average customer needs (many of which are not shared by key accounts) or to proliferate expensively in response to each big account's demands. By making demand explicit, the vendor is in a better position to institutionalize organizational learning at customer interfaces around certain support needs, and to know which support areas it can delegate to resellers or other partners without jeopardizing the account relationship.

Phase three is the final screen in account selection. Phases one and two focused on issues relating to customer value criteria, and the extent to which that value corresponds to the seller's current or potential capabilities. Phase three focuses on the transactions that compose the buyer-seller exchange, and whether they complement the seller's economics. In most businesses, the cost of sales transactions is driven by a few factors that, after analysis, can be isolated. These might include order size, order frequency, the product mix, or another characteristic of customer buying patterns. These cost drivers vary among vendors, and so phase three is a company-specific stage of account selection.

Moore's Business Forms Division, for example, sells a range of products to a wide variety of customers. Through its key-account program, Moore sells to a select number of "enterprise" accounts that buy at least $25 million annually and receive special attention. In choosing these customers, Moore looks beyond volume to the nature of the orders placed by that account. It performed a detailed cost analysis, which found that the leading transaction cost drivers for Moore are product mix and order size. Some of its products are forms and equipment for specialized applications where Moore is often the only supplier; others are for standard uses, where low-price bids are the major purchasing criterion. Not surprisingly, the former are higher-margin products for Moore than the latter. In terms of order size, Moore's manufacturing facilities can accommodate both short- and long-run orders, but long-run orders are more efficient to produce. Hence, accounts that buy a significant number of the higher gross-margin products, in long-run orders, are important accounts for Moore.

For many companies, large orders are also proportionally less expensive to fulfill than smaller orders because of scale economies in production and delivery. For other firms, however, order size may not be a crucial cost driver. In many high-fixed-cost service businesses, the variable costs of fulfilling large versus small orders are low and a number of products may share the same production and delivery system. But in these businesses, customer benefits and price elasticity often vary greatly across service offerings while the vendor's transaction costs are driven more by *when* the capacity is utilized by an account, rather than by capacity allocation. Similarly, with flexible manufacturing systems, production costs in many businesses are driven more by economies of scope than by traditional batch-size considerations.[8] Customers who order special options, or across the product line, are often more profitable than those who order a single item in big quantities.

Having identified the drivers of its customer transaction costs, a company can then influence the nature of transactions with key accounts. Moore has pricing and distribution policies that encourage larger orders as well as support services that demonstrate the value of sourcing specialized equipment from the company. These policies help Moore build account relationships while leveraging fundamental cost drivers in transactions with key accounts. At other companies, where inventory and physical distribution are major cost drivers, investments in on-line automated replenishment systems can profitably shape transactions with key accounts.

This is one approach to key-account selection. What is important is that an account management system have a process that incorporates both customer value and vendor-specific costs. In many situations, cash flows for the vendor may be negative until reorders and support revenues begin to materialize. When there are clear criteria for determining the profit potential, learning benefits, and cost drivers associated with customers, the firm knows when (and when not) to incur the substantial commitments required for effective key-account relationships. When these factors are not explicit, however, account managers will be driven by competing proposals at important customers. They can chase volume but hurt profits, they have more difficulty in coordinating resources across functional groups, and the firm may become prey to competitors that *do* manage account selection effectively.

Exhibit 7-4

A Spectrum of Accounts

Transaction Buyers	Relationship Buyers
Short time horizon	Longer time horizon
Contract terms specify all obligations	Development of tacit norms and obligations
Small investments in specialized procedures or assets	Large investments in specialized procedures or assets
Low switching costs and systems benefits	High switching costs and systems benefits
Buying a specific product's price/performance features	Buying a partner and its organization
Consistency and coordination are minor marketing requirements	Consistency and coordination are major marketing requirements

DEVELOPING ACCOUNT RELATIONSHIPS

Selection decisions are only the starting point in managing key accounts. The goal is developing a cooperative relationship rather than a series of transactions. This distinction is more than semantic. Account relationships include specific transactions, but the characteristics of each type of buyer-seller exchange can be distinguished along several dimensions (Exhibit 7-4).[9]

Relationships develop over time, and purchase decisions are made with an eye toward the vendor's past performance and future capabilities. On the other end of the spectrum are transaction sales, which have a distinct beginning, short duration, and a sharp ending. Because of the duration and continuity of exchange in relationships, there are tacit norms and obligations that often go beyond the formal contract terms. No contract can foresee the many circumstances that may arise during a multiyear account relationship. Relational norms between buyer and seller provide the flexibility needed in a changing environment. By contrast, standard sales transactions tend to focus on the price and other formal terms and conditions relevant to the specific transaction, with little or no attention paid to performance above and beyond contract terms.

In long-term relationships, dependencies develop as each party invests in specialized procedures and assets. These investments increase switching costs *and* systems benefits. On one hand, duplicating the exchange conditions with another party will be costly and/or require much time, and so the investments are unlikely to be treated as sunk costs. On the other hand, returns on these investments depend on the optimization of multiple aspects of the exchange, ranging from product design to delivery and after-sale service. In turn, these dependencies lead to deeper communication and cooperative planning aimed at anticipating problems in areas like source of supply, inventory costs, or the purchasing levels required for efficient production and distribution by the vendor.[10] Hence, social and interpersonal factors—the chemistry of the relationship—are important aspects of the process. By contrast, transactions predominate when performance is easily measured and product specific, where few specialized investments are required, and where personal relationships may be cordial but not an important part of the bargaining, problem solving, or setting of specifications.

Finally, because of the time horizons and switching costs involved, the relationship buyer is "buying" a vendor and its organizational capabilities. Conversely, the relationship marketer finds that consistency and coordination are important account-management requirements. The transaction buyer is less concerned with its vendor's long-term capabilities and more concerned with current price/performance features of individual products. In turn, the transaction marketer finds that longer-term consistency and coordination of its marketing programs are not important account-management requirements. What *is* important in these exchanges is price and availability.

In general, the more critical the impact of the supplier's products on the buyer's business, the more customized the specifications need to be. The more customization requires investments not easily transferable to another vendor or customer, the more there is potential and need for relationships rather than transactions.

In the early 1980s, for example, disk drives were a critical component for computer OEMs yet product standards were still evolving.
For an OEM, choosing a drive vendor was a major decision since its
own product line was dependent on the product plans and capabilities
of its suppliers. Conversely, a big OEM customer could easily account
for 50% or more of a drive supplier's business, making the supplier
dependent on that OEM's product plans and marketplace performance. So buyers and sellers sought to develop longer-term relationships, dependent on what one executive called "head-of-state selling":

> As well as a set of technical specifications, the OEM is buying a trusted
> supplier. Because the product is technically complex and so important
> to the ultimate performance of the OEM's system, delivery, reliability,
> quality control procedures, and many other aspects of the supplier's
> business are crucial.
>
> As a result, a number of sales are concluded with the top manager
> from the OEM looking across the table at the top manager of the drive
> vendor and saying, "I understand the technical specs and the pricing
> arrangement, but can you *promise* me this product will in fact be deliv-
> ered on time and without any bugs?"

In this market, intensive communication was required between
both firms' design engineers, product managers, production personnel, sales and service units, and top management. Further, OEMs'
systems established performance expectations in the end-user market
and proactive knowledge of an OEM's product strategy allowed a
drive vendor to channel its R&D investments effectively. Conversely,
the OEM's costs of qualifying a new drive vendor were extensive,
ranging from a battery of product tests to numerous plant visits
and discussions about product design, specifications, and compatibility with other parts of the OEM's system. Once an OEM had
become familiar and confident with a drive vendor's engineering
team, production personnel, and top executives, that vendor's
chances of winning contracts for next-generation products were
greatly improved.

At the other extreme is the situation in some financial and commodities markets. The products are well known and available in essen-

Exhibit 7-5
Success and Failure in Account Management Systems

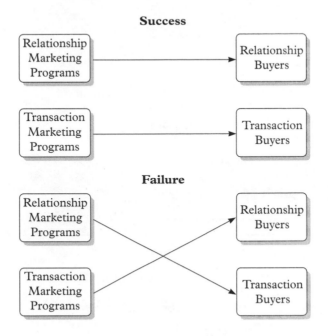

tially the same form from multiple sources of supply; moving from one source to another is facilitated by an active trading infrastructure; and product performance (e.g., the interest rate on a bond offering or the price and availability of a quantity of pork bellies) is easily measured. Here, as the saying goes on Wall Street, "Loyalty is a basis point" (.01 percent).

It would therefore be a mistake to conclude that the goal of all marketing programs should be a relationship rather than a transaction. I referred to a spectrum of accounts because most companies have both types of buyers in their customer base. As Exhibit 7-5 emphasizes, sellers can be profitable with both types, provided they understand the differences and do not commit either of two common errors in account management systems: wasting time-consuming and price-inflating relationship programs on transaction buyers or approaching relationship buyers with transaction-oriented strategies. These differences affect account management, ranging from pricing (e.g., pen-

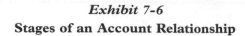

Exhibit 7-6
Stages of an Account Relationship

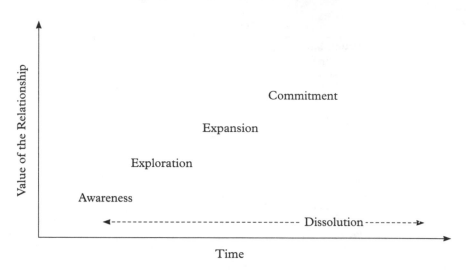

etration pricing to develop a relationship versus skim or supply/ demand pricing to maximize transaction revenues), to product policy (e.g., the relative willingness of the seller to devote time and resources to product customization and the willingness of the buyer to share confidential information) and distribution (e.g., investments in on-line systems and warehousing facilities).

Stages of an Account Relationship

For those customers selected as key accounts, these differences underscore the importance of understanding the circumstances and tactics that transform transaction selling into exchange relationships or vice versa. Exhibit 7-6 outlines five stages in the evolution of an account relationship.[11] Analyzing the dynamics of buyer-seller relations at each stage can help avoid the two types of errors mentioned above.

Awareness refers to one party's recognition of the other as a potential partner. The vendor's account-selection process is part of this stage, as are the roles performed by purchasing and engineering personnel in many industrial firms. In this stage, there may already be substantial transaction volume between buyer and seller. But these have been discrete sales that required few or no investments beyond selling and purchasing time for each party. Alternatively, there may not have been direct sales closed between buyer and seller, but new product technology at the supplier, new sourcing requirements at the customer, or a reseller's or competitor's activities may make each aware of the potential benefits of closer exchange.

Many disk drive firms, for example, initially sold through independent manufacturers' rep channels. These resellers sold items besides drives and, because they worked on commission, allowed drive vendors to devote more resources to R&D rather than selling expenses. Also, as a vice president for one drive vendor explained, "When we started, we didn't know which doors to knock on at a big OEM customer like IBM, DEC, or Hewlett-Packard. But our manufacturers' reps did." As sales to an account increased, however, drive vendors replaced rep channels with a direct sales force. Once an OEM had purchased significant numbers of a disk drive, that buyer often represented a large portion of a volume for that vendor. Meanwhile, any manufacturing problems or product allocation decisions at the drive supplier could disrupt or even halt production at that buyer. Both desired more information, and influence, on the other's plans.[12]

Exploration is a search and trial stage, where each party investigates the feasibility of a long-term relationship. Depending on the products and companies involved, this may be a brief or a prolonged testing and evaluation. If no sales have been made, this stage might involve the buyer opening a second source of supply to the vendor on a trial basis. The vendor may approach the buyer with special terms or promotions. The buyer may give the vendor information about capacity expansion or product development plans.

In corporate telecommunications, MCI has developed many account relationships through this route. Until the mid-1980s, MCI's primary market was residential long-distance buyers. But, for many reasons, big corporate buyers became more important for MCI. At the time, AT&T controlled an estimated 95% of the long-distance traffic in *Fortune* 500 companies. The exploration stage for MCI meant acting as the second source of supply for initially low-risk applications and/or providing special billing features that AT&T could not provide. Good performance in these areas eventually allowed MCI to escalate its presence in many accounts and trade up to more sophisticated applications and larger portions of the customer's traffic.

The exploration stage provides mutual learning for buyer and seller. But relationships in this stage are fragile. There are minimal interdependencies, and so termination (or the playing off of one vendor versus another) is not costly. For MCI, it was relatively easy to open doors at corporate accounts and gather a portion of their traffic. For telcom managers, giving MCI a piece of the business was often a signal to AT&T. But transactions revolved around price and, as an MCI executive explained, "When you're handling only a small percentage of a large company's telecom traffic, you're about as important as the envelope supplier. Also, for us, large accounts demand about the same overhead expenses whether you're handling 10% or 80% of the traffic." Hence, the firm had an incentive to expand the scope of the relationship.

Expansion is a stage of continually increasing investments, interdependencies, and benefits obtained by buyer and seller. The knowledge and trust accrued in the exploration stage lead to more risk taking, financial exposure, and allocation of resources to the specialized procedures and assets required by the exchange. Motivation to maintain the relationship increases because the goods and information being exchanged have important outcomes for each party and because these interactions have reduced the feasible alternatives for buyer and seller. In this stage, standards of conduct develop, which may go beyond the terms of a formal supply contract.

One aspect of expansion is often a change in the decision-making unit at the customer—a change that may be initiated by the customer or the vendor. For disk drives, OEMs' purchasing managers were key decision makers during earlier stages. But as a drive vendor became important in an OEM's product planning, design and engineering managers wielded more influence. For MCI, account expansion often meant dealing with a corporation's IS department or chief financial officer instead of the telcom managers. Telcom managers were, in the words of one account manager, "high-inertia customers, reluctant to go beyond a certain level of business with a new vendor. Meanwhile, our network allowed us to provide voice/data combinations that could lower telcom overhead while impacting use of other corporate information systems. For a telcom manager, this might mean fewer staff and a lower budget. It became necessary to make an end run around the telcom department and deal directly with other functions." Knowing when and how to initiate this end run is often a crucial phase of an account relationship. In many instances, the original decision makers may not be in a position to expand the seller's presence in other areas, but they can exercise veto power over the account manager's attempts to do so.

Commitment refers to an explicit or implicit pledge of continuity in the relationship. This may take the form of a multiyear contract. Or it may involve a noncontractual recognition by both parties that their investments make this a particularly effective and hard-to-alter exchange. The key point is that the criteria for evaluating the exchange depend more on determining whether the relationship as a whole is desirable than on the monitoring of individual transactions. In this stage, both parties are purposefully devoting resources to maintain the relationship. A customer might provide a supplier with capital for development and testing; the supplier might build a plant close to the customer's manufacturing locations; participation in one another's heretofore proprietary plans becomes part of joint problem solving.

The buyer may still deal with multiple sources of supply in the product category. But for the seller, the value of committed account relationships is threefold: the account provides the access needed to understand and shape opportunities; the account pays attention to the vendor's proposed solutions; and there may be less price competition because, in return for the resources devoted by the seller, the account will limit the search among alternative suppliers. For the buyer, the benefits of the partnership are: lower transaction costs and higher value-added from a smaller but more committed supplier base; customized services along the supply chain; and tapping external sources of innovation.

In many industries today, movement to this stage is motivated by developments in technology and global competition. Before the 1980s, for example, U.S. automakers' dealings with outside suppliers were characterized by short-term contracts (usually one year), arm's-length bargaining with six to eight suppliers per part, and a large portion of sourcing requirements allocated to internal components divisions. In the past decade, automakers have moved through the stages discussed here to a different system. Only a few suppliers provide each type of part and information is exchanged extensively. Contracts with outside suppliers are increasing in length (three- to five-year contracts are now common in the industry), and automakers have reduced sourcing from internal components divisions, in some cases divesting them completely. At Chrysler under the Integrated System Supplier program, a supplier for instrument panels was chosen before a single drawing was made. That supplier is responsible for product design and negotiations with subcontractors for the plastic moldings and gauges. Ford has put TRW in charge of safety systems for its cars. Safety devices are a complex technology and affect other parts of the car (e.g., warning lights and air bags must be integrated with the car's electrical system). Hence, Ford and TRW must be in close communication over the years involved in designing and manufacturing a generation of automobiles. Substantial joint investments are also involved.

As Susan Helper has documented, these changes are not motivated by a desire for relationships per se. Rather, before the import challenge of the 1970s, GM, Ford, and Chrysler "were free to choose a supplier relations strategy that favored buyer bargaining power over technical change. With the entry of Japanese and European automakers, however, U.S. automakers no longer were able to make profits by minimizing supplier bargaining power at the expense of quality and innovation."[13] Also, advanced electronics (a technology outside auto companies' core expertise) became important in engines, safety devices, and other aspects of automobile design. As one Ford executive put it, "The thing which is driving us to new relations with our suppliers is the desire for more coordination, which will lead to more innovation. . . . We must find ways to use the capabilities of our suppliers, which we have ignored in the past because of NIH [not-invented-here]."[14]

Dissolution, as Exhibit 7-6 indicates, is possible at any stage of exchange. Awareness and exploration may lead one or both parties to conclude that transactions are preferable to more complicated relations. Expansion may generate self-limiting investments that require no longer-term commitments. Or an established relationship may be strained by decreased obstacles in altering sources of supply or changed competitive goals at the seller. With key accounts, the process of dissolution is more important than in most selling situations. How and why such relationships are terminated often affect the vendor's ability to establish partnerships at other accounts or pursue another relationship (based on another product or new technology) at the same account.

Two factors are especially salient in short-circuiting relationships. One is inability to manage the coordination issues discussed below. The other is indifference to the impact of standardization and customer experience on buyer behavior. As customers gain knowledge (in part through their relationships with key suppliers) about the technology and their usage patterns in a product category, they often unbundle aspects of the exchange not directly related to their primary needs. Over time, moreover, product design standards get established, the quality threshold rises, and competitors enter with plug-compatible products that they will sell to big accounts at lower prices. The disk drive market of the 1980s was the focus of many new entrants as well as the gradual development of standards and base quality levels, which made close dealings with a few suppliers less important for computer OEMs. By the end of the decade, many partnerships dissolved as OEMs moved to a price-oriented supplier strategy. A similar process is occurring in some hardware and software markets in the 1990s. The databases required for making airline reservations, hotel bookings, or withdrawals from ATMs have been held on mainframe computers with software tailored for each application. But client-server systems, and new programming tools that allow software programs to interact, are eroding partnerships between mainframe vendors, companies that license proprietary database software, and many airline, bank, and hotel customers.

This dimension of buying behavior has important implications for account management systems. The purpose of an account relationship is to allow buyer and seller to maximize joint value. Once a good customer relationship is established, however, many vendors often tend to cherish the staus quo. But talk about "the relationship" is not a substitute for continued innovation to enhance it.

ACCOUNT COORDINATION

A crucial aspect of an account relationship is the seller's ability to coordinate its personnel who deal with the customer. Surveys of key-account programs rank this among the most important factors affecting success of these programs. Conversely, a lack of systems for coordinating the vendor's efforts is among the most common complaints by customers and account managers.[15]

With large multilocation customers, two types of coordination are important. One is coordinating the salespeople who may be involved with the customer's different locations and buyers. The other is coordination between sales and other parts of the vendor's organization. For the latter, many companies now employ multifunctional account teams.

Sales Coordination

It's important to distinguish among three common situations:

1. *Geographical.* In this situation, salespeople selling the same product line call on different account locations. In industrial markets, this approach is often used to sell to companies with multiple plants or to big distributors. In consumer markets increasingly characterized by local marketing programs, this situation occurs when a large retail chain is sold by regional sales forces at the manufacturer. In both markets, geographical coordination is essential in selling to global customers through multiple country sales forces.

2. *Across product lines.* Here, salespeople (perhaps different sales forces), selling different product lines, call on the same account. This is often the case when a vendor sells both capital equipment and compatible supplies. Many large-volume customers want to coordinate their equipment and supply purchases because of the impact both have jointly on production processes. But the vendor sells through different sales organizations because each product line has unique selling dynamics, requiring different types of expertise. Equipment sales are higher-priced transactions than supplies, occur less often, and involve contact with more functions in the customer's organization, thus requiring more sales calls, a longer selling cycle, and different postsale support. Here, the issue is coordinating these different types of sales efforts at the same account.

3. *Organizational.* In this situation, a salesperson is responsible for aligning a vendor's efforts at an account that is also sold and serviced by the vendor's field sales offices. For example, a headquarters key-account manager (KAM) or account executive (AE) must work with local sales reps. The KAM or AE is usually dedicated to one or two customers, but these accounts are among dozens or hundreds that the local reps call on.

In each situation, different factors become more or less important. When coordination means spanning geographical boundaries, efficient communication among dispersed sales personnel should be a priority. At companies I studied, only 11% of the salespeople involved with key accounts were located in the same building; 43% were in different sales districts and 7% in different countries. This dispersion erects time, expense, and scheduling barriers to coordination. Effective communication relies on electronic networks and new groupware that enable salespeople to collaborate on documents, send electronic mail, and organize information in databases that can be updated by many users. When sales coordination involves different product lines, cross-product training can develop a shared understanding of account needs. Finally, in the third situation, the ability of the KAM or AE to manage a host of dotted-line reporting relationships is crucial. Here, careful selection of account managers is particularly important.

In all team-selling situations, however, four areas of account management are vital: sales compensation policies (discussed in Chapter 8), account planning processes, performance measurements, and account staffing.[16]

Account planning is important because the makeup of the buying and selling units is changing constantly. Developing a key account can take years. During this time, purchasing people and criteria change while many field reps who call on different parts of that account also change assignments during crucial stages of the relationship. Many people must be updated about the account's business, new decision makers and their concerns as well as the vendor's history with the customer. But account planning at many companies is a perfunctory ritual, where salespeople, in isolation from other functions, produce diaries of what was sold last year rather than prospective analyses of the accounts' needs and the role of the vendor's programs at the customer. As a result, coordination suffers.

By contrast, Teradyne, a maker of automatic testing equipment, holds semiannual meetings where salespeople and senior executives discuss joint sales work at specific accounts. Teradyne's equipment is often bought as part of a total quality-control system at multiple customer locations. Hence, customization and integration with customers' information and production systems are important sales tasks. Top management considers its meetings with salespeople an input to strategic planning in a business where product development costs and a multinational customer base make incremental sales to key customers a core aspect of strategy. For their part, account managers use these sessions as a major tool for coordinating work at customers.

At a medical equipment supplier, fast delivery is important to hospitals trying to reduce product-handling costs. So, account planning meetings now include the truck drivers who regularly deliver to customers. "Knowing the warehouse," they can make the difference in expediting orders with key accounts.

Performance measures aid account coordination. Some firms respond to the more protracted and complicated nature of key-account sales by relaxing or ignoring performance measures in the name of relationship development. But when this happens, salespeople in the divisions or regions often feel that "We do the work while the account managers play golf and get the glory." It is *because* key-account sales demand sustained attention that measures are important. Without them, the gravitational pull in most sales organizations is toward shorter-term, individually assigned accounts.

Sales volume is only one potential measure of performance. Given the impact of key accounts, cross-selling, new product introductions, and/or support revenues are often more appropriate measures, depending on the vendor's strategy. In addition, qualitative as well as quantitative measures are useful. At many investment banks, a source of data for evaluating an individual's performance at bonus time is input from colleagues. Such evaluations keep busy people sensitive to the team nature of their interactions with customers and aware of potential problems. The process also helps bridge their different marketing dialects, as discussed in Chapter 3.

Account staffing affects sales coordination in a number of ways. One concerns the transition of salespeople, from lone ranger seller to account manager as the relationship develops. Some are incapable of this transition, and this has staffing implications. Teamwork in sales, as in sports and many other endeavors, is the sum of individual efforts working toward a common goal. And just as most ballplayers play better under some conditions than others, so do different salespeople perform better in certain circumstances. Salespeople accustomed to transaction marketing are unlikely to thrive in relationship development. Moreover, the salesperson who is successful in moving an account to the exploration stage is not necessarily the person to manage the cross-functional linkages of the later stages of account relationships. Transfer to an account at an earlier stage of business development can be a better and welcome use of this kind of person's skills.

Another staffing issue is whether to hire internally or externally. External hires can bring expertise about the customer's industry or even long acquaintance with the customer through their experience at another firm. But most companies I found to be successful in account management preferred to promote from within. As Exhibit 7-1 emphasizes, key-account managers must work with many other people who affect customer satisfaction. Further, their line authority is often ephemeral since the field sales, service, and other personnel also dealing with that account may report to another manager. Effective performance calls for account managers who know internal systems as well as they know the customers' buying processes. In these situations, things get done through persuasion, a detailed knowledge of how the organization sets budgets and allocates resources, and a network of acquaintances cultivated over time. Outsiders, however knowledgeable and competent, are at a disadvantage in these areas.

Multifunctional Account Teams

A development at many companies is the establishment of multifunctional account teams composed of individuals from product marketing, sales, service, and often manufacturing, finance, IS, and logistics. This approach may build on a firm's existing sales program. But it tends to differ from traditional account management programs in two ways.

Exhibit 7-7
**Multifunctional Account Team: Consumer Goods
Manufacturer**

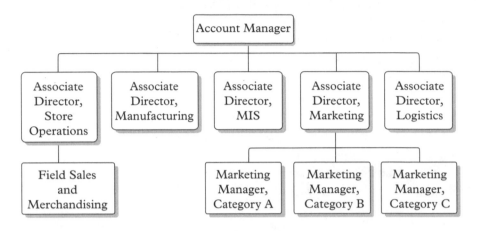

First, the buyer-seller exchange stresses effective supply chain management and the spectrum of cost-in-use components outlined in Chapter 1. A dedicated unit may be established to optimize acquisition, possession, and usage costs for key customers. Procter & Gamble has combined purchasing, engineering, and distribution functions into product supply units, which focus on logistics requirements at major retail accounts. For large managed-care customers, Becton Dickinson has a corporate supply chain management group, which combines many divisionalized sales, product marketing, customer service, materials management, and IS activities.

Second, because of this emphasis, account management requires the alignment of multiple areas of expertise at buyer and seller. Exhibit 7-7 is a partial organizational chart for one such team at a consumer goods manufacturer. Customer personnel who work with the team include the corporate controller, three regional directors of store operations, three merchandising directors, the vice president of merchandise support systems, a director of transportation, the accounts payable manager, and buyers in multiple product categories. Account managers here are not necessarily from sales because core tasks involve integration of product programs, logistics, and pre- and postsale services at buyer and seller. In this case, for instance, the team manager is a finance executive (with no previous "sales" experience) because new MIS and distribution links between these companies make payment terms a source of increased penetration at this account; in turn, these terms affect the vendor's marketing, manufacturing, and merchandising programs.

One benefit of these arrangements is that they focus information flows on the ultimate source of profits: the customer. The multifunctional team is a way of dealing with the data transmission problems discussed in Chapter 5.

Another benefit is the impact on business planning. Key-account salespeople are often first to recognize emerging market trends and opportunities, but lack the means to respond with more than tactical (usually, price-sensitive) programs. One reason is that, in many account-management systems, sales efforts are fragmented, hampering the vendor's ability to track the costs and benefits of multiple product and service programs at key accounts. In 1992, for example, P&G consolidated 14 sales forces into four and established multifunctional teams for key accounts such as Wal-Mart. A sales executive explained that "We had many different ordering, shipping, and billing procedures at the same customer. So, account managers really spent most of their time rectifying variances, not developing programs that optimize our shelf space and store support. Because of this fragmentation, the golden rule in account management was, 'Stack it high and price it low.' We sold, and if that created problems for other functions like manufacturing or logistics, so be it." By contrast, the multifunctional account-management structure encouraged broader and deeper information sharing with accounts, the development of automated replenishment systems that improved carrying costs for the customer and production scheduling for the supplier, lower landed costs for P&G, and profit for both parties.

Important issues in managing multifunctional teams concern decision making, staffing requirements, and account selection criteria.

In these arrangements, functional reporting procedures usually remain intact. Hence, when resources must be allocated, the lines of authority are often unclear and this can inhibit a timely response. At one firm I examined, a dozen executive signatures were required to approve team initiatives. At another firm, team funding was allocated by product group, and this raised concerns in each group about "who works for whom" when account management goals and product group goals did not coincide. An account manager provided an example:

> When we established a multifunctional partnership with [account A], people here were thrilled. But that account recently decided to source in one of our product categories from a competitor. That product group is outraged. "Partnering" often connotes across-the-board agreement to many managers, and that's unrealistic. We have many common goals and conflicts with this account. And the trade-offs differ for individual product units in our firm.

Multifunctional teams also raise human resource challenges. Rotation of team members from different areas must be managed even as the team seeks to build continuity and relationships with customers. After experience with this approach, one firm outlined staffing criteria for its account teams. A report noted that the relevant criteria "expand beyond those traditionally used [because of] the structural and cultural changes we are undertaking with major customers," and included the following:

> Technically competent in their disciplines; has the trust and confidence of senior management, peers, and subordinates in their discipline; able to communicate effectively up, down, and laterally in both the customer and our internal organizations; knows how to "work the system" to create the capacity required to execute; has the appropriate management style: works effectively in a team, has good project management skills, able to coach and counsel, and manages against "principles" versus "rules."

This combination of necessary skills is not easy to find and, as Chapter 6 indicated, takes time (and organizational change) to develop.

Finally, the multifunctional approach accelerates the customer-specific investments of key-account management. At firms I examined, major IS and distribution investments, in particular, were required to provide supply chain services to these accounts. But, as one manager explained,

> Which customers *don't* become multifunctional partners? That's a tough issue. Inevitably, other accounts want the customized services that account X is getting. And if we don't give that service, a competitor will. Also, many of the product-sales-service linkages required to implement the concept are specific to an account, and the benefit for individual product and sales units in our firm differ widely by key customer. The customer doesn't incur the same switching costs we do.

These factors reemphasize the importance of rigorous account selection. "Partnering" is a frequently used term but less frequently successful. Many longer-lasting and well-publicized multifunctional team relationships (e.g., P&G and Wal-Mart, IBM and Boeing) share certain characteristics: (1) initiation of the approach at top levels of both buyer and seller; (2) a buyer who buys, and a seller who sells, across the product groups involved (e.g., Wal-Mart bought in 39 product categories sold by P&G in 1992); and (3) customers considered to be leading-edge in a market or application (e.g., computer-integrated manufacturing at Boeing), so that—as emphasized in the discussion of account selection—the necessary account-management investments yield transferable learning benefits for the seller.

CONCLUSION

Most top managers now recognize the importance of strategy and devote considerable time to strategic planning. But relatively few strategic plans actually focus on the systems required to build and maintain profitable relationships with those accounts that have a profound impact on resource allocations and strategy implementation. Attention to account management systems should be a central concern in these decisions and in managing marketing linkages. Otherwise, strategizing remains a set of interesting ideas, not a pattern of action that affects customers.

Clarifying the role of the account manager, key-account selection criteria, and coordination issues in these relationships is crucial in managing field marketing effectively. The next step is influencing the behavior of the salespeople who deal with current and prospective customers. Compensation policies—the focus of the next chapter— are among the most powerful, and misunderstood, tools for managing field sales behavior.

8

Sales Compensation

∎

O F all sales issues, compensation is probably the most discussed. It is now the focus of a vast and varied literature with enough folk wisdom and quantitative studies to satisfy most managerial temperaments. One stream of essentially theoretical research concerns the design of "optimal" sales force compensation systems.[1] These models focus on the amount of variable incentive pay versus fixed salary. Another stream concerns administrative aspects of compensation and techniques for setting quotas, establishing commission rates, and designing sales contests.[2]

But the great bulk of this literature emphasizes what might be called "compensation hydraulics": push this pay lever and get this kind of field behavior. Lost in this approach is the recognition that sales compensation is an area in which data analysis, strategy, values, and human motivation are inextricably linked. Managers, focused on the hydraulics, often forget that addressing the question "How should we pay the people responsible for dealing with customers?" inevitably involves a wide range of business issues. The emphasis of the sales compensation plan will affect the quantity and kinds of orders received by manufacturing, the cash flows managed by finance, the recruitment and training needs of HRM, and daily organizational interactions among product, sales, and service managers.

This chapter concerns matters that should be addressed *before* worrying about the specific numbers or debating the precise weighting between incentive-based and fixed-salary plans. It discusses: (1) important links among compensation, evaluation, and motivation; (2) an analytical process for developing a sales compensation plan; (3) key choices in setting goals and rewarding results in sales; and (4) the relevance and limits of compensation policies within a healthy and effective sales management system.

COMPENSATION, EVALUATION, AND MOTIVATION

"We pay for product, not process," is a sentiment often voiced. This aphorism nicely emphasizes the importance of results, not just good intentions, in business. But it should not obscure the fact that compensation is primarily a motivational tool and, in most companies, an evaluation mechanism as well. One can still design a sales compensation plan on the basis of outputs rather than inputs—a separate issue which is discussed later in this chapter. But, when effective, *compensation is a tool for achieving sales performance consistent with marketing strategy,* a key means of guiding effort toward desired results.

This view has two important implications. One is that compensation, evaluation, and other motivational procedures should be linked coherently in a sales management system. The other is that, despite the salience of individual abilities in sales, the salesperson is not an "individual contributor" in the organization. He or she should be viewed as the agent of the firm's marketing strategy, and the compensation plan designed accordingly.

Connections among compensation, evaluation, and motivation do not of course have strict cause and effect relationships. They affect one another in ways that might more accurately be described as a web of interactions. Also, a common assumption in compensation design—that all salespeople will react similarly to a pay plan—may not be warranted. However, it is useful to risk oversimplification and, as Exhibit 8-1 outlines, consider motivation, evaluation, and compensation as links in a chain in order to illustrate certain connections that might otherwise be ignored.

Motivation is a core function of management. At the heart of most

Exhibit 8-1
Links among Motivation, Evaluation, and Compensation

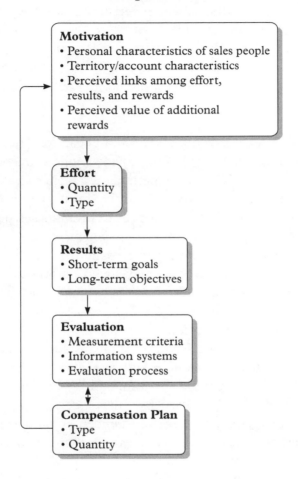

managerial responsibilities is the question, "How do I get other people to do as much as possible of the right kind of work?" In recent years, an "attributional" theory of motivation has received much support in selling research, and this view underlies the discussion here.[3] This approach sees people as motivated to maximize rewards, but also "to attain a cognitive mastery of their environment"—that is, people want to know why an event occurred, why they succeeded or failed at a task, and to what to attribute success or failure. Answers to these questions—based on objective data or subjective conjectures—affect future behavior.

In sales, motivation has many factors. One is recruitment policies, which influence the personal characteristics of the salespeople (e.g., knowledge, skills, and attitude) that sales managers must manage. Some people work harder than others, and some are smarter than others. Training can increase skill levels and mitigate some of these differences. But in most sales forces, the normal distribution curve pertains: there is a range of personal abilities that must be developed and managed.

A second factor is territory and account characteristics, which define the opportunities available and provide implicit direction for sales efforts. Some territories and accounts have a higher yield rate, independent of the salesperson assigned to that territory or account. The relationship between territory characteristics and sales performance lends itself well to quantitative modeling, which, in turn, can be a useful input to quota setting and compensation design. A number of territory-design models have been developed, and the declining costs of information technology make them increasingly available and practical.[4]

The salesperson's perception of the connections among effort, results, and rewards is a third factor. In some instances, working harder or smarter may not translate into better sales results because of the firm's product policy, pricing, or competitive situation. In other instances, more effort by the salesperson may indeed lead to better sales results, but the firm's measurement, compensation, and recognition systems may not acknowledge or reward incremental results. Either way, motivation is not enhanced.

Finally, a fourth factor affecting motivation is the perceived value of additional rewards. Effort, results, and rewards may be linked, but salespeople may perceive the required effort as disproportionately high relative to the rewards received. Many incentive systems, for example, pay salespeople for incremental volume increases over the previous year's results. The intention is to motivate experienced salespeople to develop new business. But in many situations, the effort required to develop this business is seen as "not worth it" by sales reps who have a base of mature but steady accounts in their territories.

They are essentially managing the installed base of customers as an annuity. The issue is whether to design a compensation plan that increases the value of additional rewards *or* redeploy the sales force so that new business has its own focus.

An outcome of motivation is effort, which, in sales, has two dimensions: quantity and type. Quantity refers to the sheer amount of effort expended by salespeople as measured by call frequency, orders booked, or other relevant activities. Traditionally in the pharmaceuticals industry, for instance, call frequency on busy doctors was highly correlated with sales results, and maximizing this "face time" has been an important component of sales incentive plans in the industry. As managed care organizations dramatically decrease the number of relevant call points, call frequency becomes a less important measure of productivity. Type refers to such factors as the focus of the sales force's account development versus account maintenance, the relative emphasis on new versus established products, or, in some situations, an emphasis on selling products that generate revenue and manufacturing volume versus products that have higher margins but lower unit sales. Compensation plans influence both types of effort.

Effort leads to results. The key issue in sales compensation is deciding what goals should be established in order to guide efforts toward desired results. Some important choices in setting goals and rewarding results are discussed later in this chapter.

Once goals are established, results must be measured, raising issues of the appropriate (or feasible) measurement criteria, the information systems available, and the process by which performance evaluations are made. There are many possible criteria for evaluating sales performance. Often, however, the company's information systems do not gather the relevant data, or sales force call reports (a key source of information about selling activities in most firms) are notoriously noisy and unreliable. Equally important, but often overlooked, is the process for administering the evaluations. At many companies, salespeople receive big bonuses as a result of their efforts. But the process of providing this additional compensation is at odds with the company's formal performance-evaluation criteria. That is, the basis of the bonus (e.g., orders booked or cases sold by an individual rep) often contradicts what the company and its sales managers *say* they want in performance evaluation sessions (e.g., referrals, joint presentations, or other cross-selling efforts). The result is demotivation or, worse, motivation toward the wrong type of sales effort.[5] Managers may "pay for product, not process," but if they ignore process in a sales environment, they often don't get what they pay for.

Finally, managers must indeed consider the mechanics—both the type and quantity—of the compensation plan. Here, type refers to such issues as the relative emphasis on base salary or incentive pay. While compensation models tend to posit a choice between salary or variable incentive pay, surveys indicate that 80–90% of sales forces in North America and Europe are paid by a combination of salary and commission or bonus. The practical issue for most firms is adjusting this mix in the face of changing marketing conditions and sales tasks. Quantity refers to the total amount of compensation provided relative to industry norms and, within a sales organization, the amount of money provided for performing a given sales-related task. Both topics are discussed in the next section.

The key point here is that sales compensation should not be approached in isolation. There are always links (intended or unintended) among compensation, evaluation, and motivation. The framework outlined in Exhibit 8-1 contains the following advice: start with the engine (the types of efforts and behavior desired of salespeople) and *then* design the transmission (the specific compensation plan aimed at encouraging these efforts).

DEVELOPING A SALES COMPENSATION PLAN

Developing and implementing an effective sales compensation plan requires answering five questions.

What Are the Sales Tasks of the Firm?

The starting point for analyzing field-marketing requirements, including compensation, should be identifying the nature of the sales task. This means considering the competitive environment, the firm's marketing strategy in that environment (overall and by major segment), and the essential functions of the salespeople. Selling, directly or indirectly, is almost always a key function. But compensation design requires disaggregating this factor into its constituent parts. In sales forces that deal with retail trade customers, for example, there is a range of tasks that can often be divided into three categories:

1. Volume-Influencing Activities:
   Selling new items
   Getting more shelf space for established items
   Selling/managing point-of-sale materials
   Selling/managing in-store displays
   Selling/managing co-op advertising features
   Selling/managing trade promotions

2. In-Store Service Activities:
   Shelf audits
   Handling of damaged merchandise
   Ensuring product freshness
   Pricing adjustments or corrections
   Handling queries or complaints from store managers

3. Supply-Chain Management Activities:
   Ordering/sales reporting systems
   Coordination with product groups
   Analysis of account/store patronage patterns
   Sales forecasting
   Ad hoc management of deliveries

The sales compensation plan, informed by an understanding of the company's marketing strategy, should set priorities among these tasks. As discussed in Chapter 1, the relative importance of these tasks now differs among classes of trade, and sales incentives should recognize these differences.

In industrial businesses, managers must monitor what portion of selling in a market segment is attention to delivery, price negotiations, building distributor network relationships, technical expertise, personal relationships with customers, postsale service, cold calling, and sheer persistence? In industrial markets, these aspects of selling change over the course of a product life cycle or as competition in an industry evolves. Early in a product's life cycle, customer education and applications development are often key sales tasks, especially for technically complex products. But as the market develops and standards emerge, salespeople spend more time selling against functionally equivalent brands or developing working relationships with intermediaries as well as end-users. All too often companies' compensation systems fail to keep pace with these changes.

This was the case at many computer manufacturers during the 1980s. As hardware margins declined, computer firms franchised distributors, value-added resellers (VARs), and other intermediaries, often establishing a certain order-volume size below which sales were to be made through resellers. Then, as common product standards began to emerge, manufacturers found it difficult to differentiate themselves on the basis of hardware performance characteristics. Software applications and the bundling of products into networked packages became crucial in many segments. VARs, focused on specific industry or occupational groups, often had the expertise and customer contacts for these sales functions. But many manufacturers provided little incentive for their direct salespeople to work with influential resellers through cross-referrals, training, joint sales calls, or help with specific applications. Indeed, at some companies, the compensation plan encouraged salespeople to sell *against* the manufacturer's authorized reseller. Frequently, both parties lost the sale with consequent acrimony between the manufacturer's product and sales groups as well as between direct and indirect channels of distribution.

One reason for this misfit in a changing marketplace is that, in many firms, the people making important sales-compensation decisions base their decisions on an obsolete vision of field-marketing tasks. The lesson here is that there is no substitute for ongoing field interaction, including actual sales calls, by those responsible for sales compensation policy. This qualitative input is a necessary complement to aggregate data about the company's customers and markets, and a key part of maintaining a coherent, relevant picture of important sales tasks.

What Must the Salesperson Do to Succeed?

After analyzing the tasks that are important in a segment, consider the activities necessary to perform them. If wining and dining or attending industry trade shows and conferences are important aspects of selling, the plan's treatment of expenses should not discourage salespeople from developing the contacts and relationships accrued through such activities.

The selling cycle, as Chapter 7 indicated, often varies by key account or major segment. So a plan that focuses only on short-term incentives will almost certainly discourage attention to the longer-term (and often higher-margin) accounts and segments.

Salespeople cannot control many elements that affect sales results (e.g., macroeconomic developments, a customer's financial problems, competitive products and pricing). In many instances, the compensation plan can and should encourage attention to these factors by rewarding accurate forecasting or market intelligence. But it should focus on the factors that salespeople *can* control. If not, important links among motivation, effort, results, and compensation are broken.

In analyzing sales tasks, management must be clear and up-to-date about how, fundamentally, the salesperson can make a difference with the company's current and prospective customers. That difference is what the compensation plan should reinforce and support.

What Is the Labor-Pool Frame of Reference?

A firm with uncompetitive pay levels will eventually lose its best sales personnel, and perhaps inadvertently fuel what one sales manager called "the finishing school syndrome": "At my previous company, we hired relatively new people, trained them, gave them experience selling in this industry, and then, like me, they moved on to better paying jobs at competitors."

Many companies spend considerable time and personnel department overhead in determining comparative pay levels. Yet, this information is often available through trade publications or industry surveys. In the United States, for example, *Sales and Marketing Management* magazine publishes an annual survey of pay levels, by industry groupings, for different types of sales personnel by region, educational level, and other variables. Other sources include the biennial surveys published by Dartnell and TPF&C's annual "Sales Compensation Survey," a data bank that covers different types of sales positions and looks at companies' policies concerning benefits, expense reimbursement, and incentives. These sources usually provide different numbers in a category because each defines and aggregates its categories differently. But this differentiation can be useful, spurring thinking about the activities that are and are not relevant for a given sales position.

Another issue in determining pay levels concerns the salesperson's potential influence on the buying decision and the abilities required to exert that influence. In many industries, selling requires technical skills, which means companies must recruit highly trained personnel who have opportunities in different industries and in functions besides sales. This affects pay levels independent of competitors' wage rates. More generally, what economists call "transaction-specific assets" are also relevant to sales compensation.[6] These assets are expertise and working relationships built up over time by the people selling a product, and specialized to the task of selling that product. When salespeople possess such assets, the costs of replacing them can be significant, and the compensation plan should reflect this.

An example is the private banking business, which provides specialized services to high-net-worth individuals. In the past decade, many commercial banks aggressively pursued the sizable fee income and stable deposit base that a productive private banking group can generate. These banks often established private banking as a profit center and altered their compensation programs in the process. The key to this business is the private banker, who must possess an array of company- and client-specific skills. Private banking requires knowledge of multiple banking products and areas, including credit, marketing, and operations. Referrals, leads, and support from other parts of the bank are crucial. Hence, the private banker must be adept at maintaining goodwill and communications with people in these other areas. At the same time, personalized service is the heart of the business, especially since any one bank's products are easily imitated and not highly differentiated from competitors' offerings. Thus, trust, compatibility, and the other elements of good chemistry are the essence of the client relationship. Indeed, over time, many clients see themselves as doing business with an individual private banker rather than the bank.

This combination of skills is rare, narrowing the pool of qualified candidates, and highly dependent on accumulated transaction-specific expertise with the company and the client. As a result, compensation plans for private bankers are different from the traditional pay policies of commercial banks. By the 1980s, private bankers' compensation had increased at annual rates two to three times that of other bank personnel.[7]

What Should the Salary-Incentive Mix Be?

Management must also determine the relative emphasis on fixed salary and incentive compensation. Some sales forces receive straight salary and some straight commission. But most receive a combination of salary and incentive pay.

Several factors make a higher salary component attractive: the relative difficulty involved in measuring an individual salesperson's performance in a reasonable period of time; the need for salespeople to coordinate efforts (see below); the complexity and length of the selling tasks; the amount of missionary selling involved;[8] the importance of such nonselling activities as pre- and postsale service; and the volatility of demand in a market.[9] These factors tend to make fixed salary a higher component of total sales remuneration than incentives. But a company can have a highly leveraged (i.e., high-commission or variable bonus component) compensation plan and still sell technically sophisticated, complex products in a market environment where nonselling activities and long-term relationships are important—*if* other aspects of the sales management system support the required sales tasks. A number of manufacturers' rep firms selling high-technology products operate very successfully with such plans.

Many sales managers I know stress the fact that the sheer amount of incentive compensation is often a less important influence on sales behavior than issues such as: the time frame for compensation payouts and performance evaluations (are they congruent or do they conflict?); whether and how sales credit is divided among a dispersed account team or different sales groups (see below); the unit(s) of measurement used to calculate incentive pay (e.g., volume sold or gross margin); and the role of any compensation plan in the context of the organization's more general reward and recognition systems. For example, while they often represent substantial earnings opportunities for their members, many commissioned direct-selling organizations such as Avon or Mary Kay also carefully orchestrate sales meetings to reward and motivate their sales forces.

Nonetheless, salary plans are easier to administer. For this reason, they often become the default option for companies that lack the information systems or managerial skills required to administer more complex plans.

How Should the Incentive Component Be Designed?

Bonuses, a form of incentive compensation, are lump sums paid for the attainment of specific objectives. They can be based on a quantitative formula or on qualitative objectives or they can be administered at the discretion of a particular manager. Commissions, another form of incentive compensation, are typically based on a percentage of sales volume or margins. Some companies apply a standard commission rate to all sales while others vary the rate by product or category of customer in order to reflect profitability or competitive objectives. Sometimes commissions are only paid for sales above quota, or different rates apply above and below quota.

Management must pay close attention to these details. Salespeople study their plan closely. Many look for what managers often call loopholes and what a salesperson might well call "the best use of my time to maximize income." Apparently incidental matters, such as paying commissions when orders are booked instead of when shipped, can make major differences in the company's cash flow, production schedules, and focus of selling efforts. Hence, the specific company context is crucial. However, there are still some general observations to be made about sales incentives.

First, sales incentives have three allied purposes:

1. To communicate management's goals and direct sales force efforts toward the most profitable opportunities;

2. In so doing, to increase return on investment in the firm's sales capacity; and

3. To provide competitive pay levels to salespeople.

As well as a vehicle for payment, sales compensation plans are always important company communications. Many managers worry about whether a complex incentive plan will be understood by the sales force. But, in my experience, salespeople are usually very adept at understanding the implications of incentive plans. As one sales executive noted, "I've yet to meet the comp plan that my salespeople won't understand in detail within days of its announcement." The issue is, what behavior is encouraged, or discouraged, by the plan? A related issue concerns how sales incentives encourage incremental efforts. In effect, the purpose of incentives is to maximize the firm's return on its investment in sales resources by directing effort toward areas where both the firm and the individual salesperson can prosper. Hence, an important principle in designing effective incentives is to establish win-win goals for both parties. In addition, the incentive system should be structured so that, given a good performance, total compensation is at competitive pay levels. And, given varying performance levels in the sales force, the spread in incentive pay should be meaningful.

Second, the time frame for incentives must be considered. In general, it should be short enough to make an impact but long enough to make each payment significant. The principle here is that the incentive structure should make the cause-and-effect relationships among effort, results, and rewards visible to the sales force. Generally, this means trying to establish incentive plans that conform to the firm's typical selling cycle.

Also, the incentive plan should not unwittingly discourage sales effort in a given year. Many companies base incentives on achieving "all or nothing" minimum thresholds of sales performance on certain products. That is, unless sales of product X reach a certain level, the salesperson is not eligible for incentive payouts tied to sales of other products. The firm's intention is to focus efforts on particularly profitable or strategic products. But, unless the "all or nothing" goals are set carefully and with achievable targets, this approach can backfire.

Exhibit 8-2
Four Variables That Affect the Salary-Incentive Mix:
An Example

% of Target Pay at Risk	Sales Force Perception	Degree of Management Control	Degree of Fixed-Cost Reduction
<10%	Barely noticeable	High	Low
10–25%	Gets my attention	Good	Some
25–50%	Drives behavior	Only key things	Significant
>50%	Make quota or quit	Minimal to none	High

Note: The particulars here are used by a senior sales manager at an office
products company. The arrangement should change to reflect individual
companies' selling environments.

At one consumer goods firm I examined, it became clear to many
salespeople that the sales target for a particular product would not be
achieved by the end of the year. During the fourth quarter of 1993,
many salespeople therefore saved orders on this and other products
for the first quarter of the next year, when these orders *would* help
them achieve incentive targets. The result was a terrible 1993 (with
much idle capacity at the firm's manufacturing plants), a dramatic
upsurge in first-quarter 1994 sales (with expensive manufacturing
overtime), and loading of trade channels that negatively affected sales
later in 1994—results all arguably tied to the timing and structure of
the sales incentive plan.

Third, establishing the mix between incentive pay and salary involves judging the interplay of four key variables: the percentage of
total compensation at risk with incentives; sales force perceptions
about this proportion of incentive pay; the degree of desired management control; and the degree of fixed-cost reduction attainable
through variable incentive compensation. As an example, a senior
sales manager in an office products business (where the average total
compensation per salesperson was about $70,000 in 1992) uses the
rules of thumb outlined in Exhibit 8-2 as a way of judging these interactions. He noted that "We vary the mix between incentive pay and

salary every other year or so, in response to competitive conditions, new business initiatives, and cost pressures from corporate."

Fourth, the performance measures on which incentives are based should reflect important managerial objectives. While sales volume is the most common measure used for incentive systems, there are other performance measures. For example:

- Product Mix. This is especially important when the company sells different items often used as a system.
- Pricing. This is important when negotiations are a key part of the sales task and the salesperson has discretion over price-exception requests.
- Bad Debt or Returned Goods. In many firms (service merchandisers or cable TV companies), these are major components of selling expenses and of firm profitability.
- Type of Sale. The type of sale (outright sale versus rental) often has a big impact on cash flow, the nature of the company's installed base, and after-market revenues.
- Training. In some industries (computers and corporate software), user training is both an important aspect of the sales task and a significant source of revenues and profits for the manufacturer.

Clearly, no one form of sales compensation is optimal for all companies, or even for different business units within the same company. The nature of the sales tasks, and the nature of the salesperson's influence on the buying decision (a factor affected by the role of personal selling in the company's marketing strategy and the alignment of sales with product management and service activities) help indicate the most suitable form of compensation.

SETTING GOALS AND REWARDING RESULTS

A key choice in any compensation system is the process adopted for setting goals and rewarding results. This issue is a complex one, involving the mechanics of the particular plan, the information available to the company, and questions about the basic social contract a firm

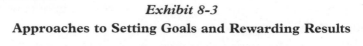

Exhibit 8-3

Approaches to Setting Goals and Rewarding Results

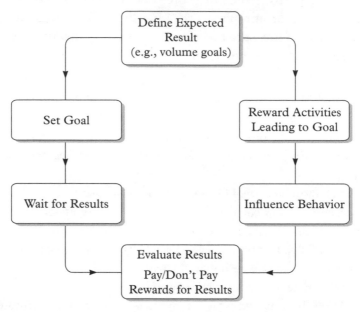

tries to establish with its sales personnel. But there are two basic approaches.[10]

An emphasis on product over process generally leads to the approach on the left side of Exhibit 8-3. Management sets goals, sends the sales force out into the field, and waits for results. It rewards on the basis of whether or not the goals are met. The reasoning here is that (1) the salesperson can best decide how to meet those goals ("Isn't that what we pay them for, anyway?"); (2) over time, natural selection will retain the "best" salespeople while others leave for lack of rewards; and (3) salespeople are entrepreneurs who resist attempts to control their activities.

In the approach outlined on the right side of Exhibit 8-3, management rewards specific activities aimed at achieving the desired results and attempts to influence the performance of those activities. This approach assumes, first, that in the absence of clearly defined and prioritized sales activities, the salesperson may *not* be the best person to design a strategy for reaching goals. As Chapter 2 discussed, salespeople most often work from limited, account-specific bases of market information. Sales managers should understand the nature of the sales tasks and improve the performance of those tasks ("Isn't that what managers get paid for, anyway?"). Second, over time, the former approach can waste effort, especially when the most productive sales activities are likely to change over a product's life cycle or as a market matures. Third, salespeople may well be entrepreneurs, but successful entrepreneurs endorse processes that increase their earnings. The issue is not whether salespeople like to be told what to do, but whether the company influences its salespeople to move in the right directions. Management should optimize the allocation of resources, including sales resources, to indicate that direction.

These philosophical differences have actionable implications. The choice of approach affects all major dimensions of sales management: recruitment criteria, training initiatives, first-level sales supervisory tasks, performance evaluation criteria, and compensation. It also has a significant impact on the culture of the sales organization since the former approach rewards results independent of means while the latter focuses on means. At its best, the former approach allows for necessary degrees of freedom with a diverse customer base; at its worst, salespeople are encouraged to scant service activities in favor of short-term sales. At its best, the latter approach keeps people focused on key revenue- and relationship-enhancing activities; at its worst, salespeople become excessively process-oriented—more concerned with the quality of call reports than the quality of the call.

The interdependencies created by international markets and the need to sell product service packages put pressure on the essentially laissez-faire approach outlined on the left hand of Exhibit 8-3. However, many companies adopt this approach without considering the alternative method, either through force of habit or because they lack the information and sales reporting systems needed to implement the activity-based approach. Especially in fast-changing markets, the lack of required information systems is often the major reason for adopting the "wait for results" approach to goal setting. At medical products firms I studied, for example, information systems were established on an individual division basis. Meanwhile, their customers are increasingly demanding sales efforts across previously independent divisions.

The situation is similar at consumer goods firms, where information systems have long been driven by individual brand demarcations. More and more, however, trade buyers are making purchasing, stocking, and merchandising decisions on a cross-brand category basis. An important top-management choice facing these firms is whether to invest in new sales information systems or to continue the current alignment of sales force deployment and incentives. Unfortunately, high-level executives in some of these firms are too far removed from actual field events to grasp the choices involved. Indeed, their reliance on current sales information systems often prevents them from monitoring market changes and the potential benefits of a new approach to goal setting.

COMPENSATION AND TEAM SELLING

For many firms, the account management requirements discussed in Chapter 7 raise special compensation issues. Differences in tasks and selling cycles between key accounts and others mean that a single compensation plan for all salespeople is often impractical and counterproductive. Where coordinated sales efforts to large, geographically dispersed accounts are needed, important compensation considerations include the basis of incentive bonuses, the time frame used, and whether and how sales credits are shared.

If there are multiple salespeople calling on key accounts and teamwork is necessary, a bonus based on total account sales or profitability often makes more sense than individually oriented incentive arrangements. Interep is a large radio rep firm in the United States. Its salespeople call on ad agencies and advertisers to sell time on the more than 3,000 radio stations it represents. To maintain an entrepreneurial spirit in the field, Interep uses six sales forces. At the same time, mergers among big ad agencies and advertisers have made customers increasingly responsive to a rep firm that can act as a coordinated supplier across radio markets for different product categories. In response, Interep uses a team approach to selling that cuts across each sales force. A prime element of this approach is the compensation system. Unlike most rep firms, where incentives focus on the individual commission-oriented sales representative, Interep has salespeople with shared-account responsibilities participate in a bonus pool based on the account's total sales volume. The approach has been effective: Interep's sales have grown faster than the industry's and, according to market surveys, ad agencies view Interep as more responsive than its competitors.

Another important team-selling compensation issue is the time frame. Sales efforts at key accounts can take years. But most sales compensation plans tie incentives to quarterly or annual snapshots of performance. The usual result, as one salesperson noted, is this: "Because our compensation plan is short-term oriented, I put my efforts where there are short-term benefits. Also, many short-term sales goals can be met with minimal teamwork. The longer-term sales require the hassle of working with lots of other people." Coordination between field salespeople in local offices and the account manager is lacking. Bonuses for multiple-year performance, and/or for shorter-term qualitative objectives like building relationships with certain account decision makers, are often required in such situations.

Sharing of sales credit is a third issue that must be resolved. Surveys of key-account sales programs indicate that only a minority use credit splitting to help coordinate field and headquarters selling efforts. One reason is the administrative difficulties involved in assigning portions of credit to a geographically dispersed sales effort. Also, people have a tendency to mark up their own contributions to a joint effort and mark down the contributions of others. As one sales manager put it, "Many of my salespeople feel that when the split is 50/50, they're losing 50% instead of gaining 50% of the incentive pay. A lot of time and energy is wasted arguing over splits." But where sales coordination is required, split credits are often better than mutually exclusive ones.

More important, many companies can give full credit to salespeople involved in a team-selling situation and still not (as many managers fear) "pay twice" for the same sale. The key is having a good understanding of the sales tasks and an information system capable of tracking performance so that shared volume can be taken into account when assigning accounts and setting targets. Consider the following example: two salespeople last year sold about $500,000 each to individual accounts and about $500,000 to shared accounts. Thus, their combined sales amounted to about $1.5 million. Two approaches to goal setting and rewarding results are possible:

1. The selling company sets targets and bonuses so that each person receives, say, $25,000 for $750,000 in sales, with credit from shared account sales split 50/50. If each sells $500,000 individually and $500,000 to shared accounts, each makes the $750,000 target and receives a bonus.
2. The selling company pays a $25,000 bonus for $1 million in sales with all shared-account sales volume double counted and fully credited to both salespeople. Each must then rely on team effort for about 50% of target sales, but each also receives full credit for joint sales efforts.

A participant in the first plan may well reason that an incremental $250,000 in individual sales (perhaps developed at the expense of time devoted to more complicated joint sales efforts) could reach the $750,000 target. Thus, he or she might decide to concentrate on individually assigned accounts, encourage colleagues to continue to work hard on team accounts, and hope to gather those half-credit sales with little or no effort. Coordination and major account penetration are likely to suffer and so is sales force morale as, over time, free riding becomes apparent. Under the second plan, there is at least no compensation barrier to expenditure of effort on the more labor-intensive team sales and there is an implicit incentive for individuals to collaborate on accounts that deliver big sales.

Sales incentives alone won't deliver teamwork if the other account management systems described in Chapter 7 discourage coordinated efforts. But poorly designed incentives will almost certainly kill teamwork even if other systems support it.

PLACING COMPENSATION IN CONTEXT

"You won't get what you don't pay for" is a fact of life in most sales organizations. But appropriate compensation policies are what some have called organizational "hygiene factors"—necessary, but not sufficient, conditions for motivating people to do what you want them to

Exhibit 8-4
How Poor Management Can Affect Sales Results

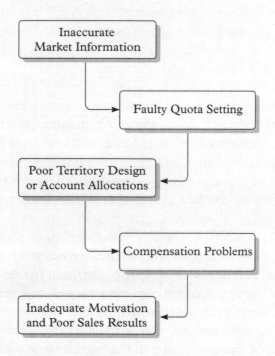

do. A compensation plan is a part of, not a substitute for, a coherent sales management system. This fact merits emphasizing because many managers, appreciating the power of incentives in affecting sales efforts but often underestimating the role of other factors, practice what I call "management by algorithm." That is, they implicitly assume that a well-designed compensation plan virtually ensures desired field behavior. Further, because compensation plans are visible and relatively malleable in the short run, they spend much effort on redesigning incentives when the problem really lies in other areas.

In the final analysis, developing an outstanding sales force is a function of the firm's ability to integrate its organizational systems and capabilities with market conditions. While the compensation plan affects the company's revenue stream and its pattern of resource allocations in many areas besides sales, many factors besides pay affect sales results. For example, in the scenario illustrated in Exhibit 8-4, compensation problems reflect larger deployment, information, and strategy problems. Attempting to fix sales compensation without addressing these other issues is fruitless. Hence, it is important to recognize both the relevance and limits of compensation decisions. In doing this, consider the following four factors as part of a quick audit of sales management policies and practices:

- **Marketing Strategy.** In weak sales systems, the firm's marketing strategy is often implicit, interpreted differently by various parts of the sales force, and so implemented in an ad hoc manner. In strong sales systems, marketing strategy is explicit, widely communicated, and (at any given time) executed with a high degree of consistency by the sales force.

- **Role of Personal Selling in the Strategy.** In weak sales systems, definitions of sales tasks are often frozen for years despite important changes in customer-buying processes and in key functions performed by channel intermediaries. In strong sales systems, managers continually reexamine the role of personal selling in the marketing mix to determine which sales tasks are still important and at what level of the distribution channel they can best be performed.

- **Sales Performance Expectations.** In weak sales systems, there is often an "everything is important" attitude, reflecting a managerial inability or unwillingness to establish priorities. In strong sales systems, there are a few key requirements that are defined, clarified, and emphasized at a point in time.

- **Sales Compensation Plan.** Because the marketing strategy is vague, the role of personal selling taken for granted, and sales expectations ill-defined, weak sales systems manage sales compensation on a "tweak the formula" basis, letting incremental changes in commission rates or the salary/incentive mix substitute for the analytical process outlined in this chapter. In strong sales systems, the compensation plan is the focus of frequent cross-functional reviews. These reviews define the necessary trade-offs, establish current priorities, and use the discussion of sales compensation as a way to clarify the responsibilities of management, not replace them.

CONCLUSION: A SALES MANAGEMENT SYSTEM

Evaluating comparative pay levels and the mix between fixed-salary and commissioned compensation are among the outputs of the process outlined here. But establishing a sales compensation plan always includes consideration of such fundamental issues as motivation, evaluation criteria, strategy, and goal setting and rewarding results. Managers sensitive to the choices and linkages discussed here can avoid unpleasant surprises and direct strategy to maximize sales efforts.

For that reason, Exhibit 8-5 serves two purposes. First, it suggests a framework that places many of the topics discussed in this chapter in context. Second, it includes aspects of a coherent sales management system that were *not* discussed here but that are nonetheless important in analyzing field-marketing requirements and developing concurrent marketing capabilities.

"Sales force control systems" refers to aspects of sales management that are relatively quantifiable, and so susceptible to policy guidelines and management-by-objective initiatives. These include performance measurement, evaluation, compensation, and training programs. "Sales force environment" refers to more qualitative issues concerning human resource practices, the amount and type of communication (communication among sales personnel and between field reps and relevant product and service personnel), interactions of personnel, and management style. Policy and process affect each other. For example, what a company measures and rewards will affect its sales process. Conversely, the human resource and communication patterns in the sales organization affect what a company decides to

Exhibit 8-5

A Sales Management Framework

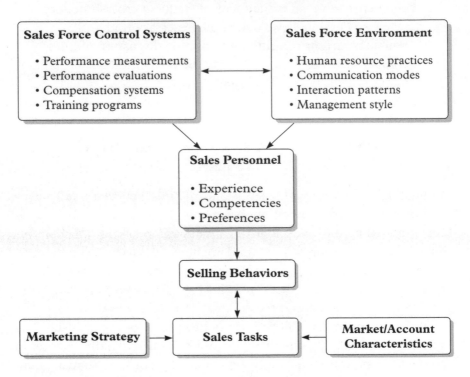

measure, train, and reward. In turn, both the control systems and the environment in field offices will affect the focus of the company's sales personnel, their selling behaviors, their interactions with product and service units, and their performance.

Using this framework, a manager contemplating a change in sales compensation might first want to consider the following diagnostic questions:

- How does the firm's marketing strategy affect personal selling? What specific tasks must field personnel accomplish to implement the strategy?

Although it is field salespeople who are the prime agents of strategy execution in most firms, many so-called strategic plans do not make meaningful reference to the sales force's role in implementing strategy. Indeed, the strategies that result from top management analyses and negotiations are often kept secret from field salespeople because of fear that wide dissemination of these plans would unwittingly include competitors. But in most cases, withholding such information is counterproductive. If salespeople are not selling in accordance with goals, withholding information about strategy will not help; and if salespeople are selling in accordance with strategic goals, competitors will learn about them anyway.

- Who are all the important salespeople at the company? What are their competencies, experience, and selling preferences?

As Chapter 9 will discuss in more detail, many people outside the formally designated sales force are increasingly involved in customer acquisition and retention. And as Part I of this book indicated, customer requirements increasingly include sales and service personnel in marketing. As one branch manager put it, "Not everyone here is called a salesperson, but everyone is directly or indirectly involved in selling." Do compensation and other sales management practices encourage or discourage the necessary coordination among these groups?

- What control systems, besides pay, influence sales force behavior? To what extent are productivity measurements, performance evaluation criteria, and training programs consistent with the analysis of required sales tasks?

It is the rare situation where compensation alone will generate the desired selling behaviors. Other factors must be actively managed. As one executive said, "I can pay my salespeople any way I want. But if market coverage is inadequate [a deployment issue] or they don't know what to do when they're in front of customers [a training and development issue], the world's best pay-for-performance system is of only limited use."

- How well or poorly are these control systems being implemented?

In most sales organizations, the branch manager (or similar first-line sales supervisor) is a key player in a sales management system, but often overlooked. Who gets this job? What steps, if any, does the company take to help these people make the transition from sales representative to sales manager? How do career paths and interaction patterns between sales reps and sales managers affect selling behavior?

- Finally, what gaps exist between the requirements of sales tasks and current selling behaviors? How, if at all, can a change in sales compensation or incentives help eliminate these gaps?

The basic idea behind the framework in Exhibit 8-5 is that an effective sales management system must integrate three internal factors of the sales organization with two external factors. The internal factors are the people involved; the systems established to influence their behavior (sales force control systems); and how those systems are applied or misapplied in the field (sales force environment). The external factors are the vendor's marketing strategy (push versus pull emphasis and the consequent impact on the role of sales personnel); and market/account characteristics in key segments (buying processes and market structure).

The external factors largely determine the nature of sales tasks. The internal factors influence field behavior so that these tasks are performed in a way that is consistent with the firm's strategy. When there is coherent integration among these elements, the company focuses on customer encounters, and selling begins to turn into effective concurrent marketing.

9

Customer Service

∎

BECAUSE marketing is about getting and keeping customers, customer service is a goal (and often the raison d'être) of marketing organizations. Indeed, the word customer itself comes from the Old English "custumer": one who customarily frequents a particular craftsperson. In recent years, the word's roots have been emphasized in numerous articles, books, and workshops that highlight the importance of service and customer retention in achieving competitive advantage.

Yet, while service has become a popular topic, surveys repeatedly find that good service is still the exception. Why? Is it, as many discussions now stress, primarily an issue of attitudes and the lack of a "service obsession" at companies? Or are other factors more relevant? What *is* customer service in a given situation, and how can managers diagnose the activities that help or hinder responsiveness?

The fact is that meetings and workshops about customer service are usually preaching to the converted. Most managers realize service is important, but interactions at key marketing interfaces often impede good service. Honoring individual service heroes may momentarily galvanize the firm, but it will not help much if management preaches service without addressing its components.

This chapter considers core organizational factors that affect the provision of service in most firms. It discusses: (1) a perspective on customer service that stresses its interfunctional requirements; (2) the tasks of a marketing organization in its attempts to manage service levels; (3) the steps involved in building better sales-service coordination; and (4) a framework for analyzing customer retention dynamics and the marketing tools relevant at different stages of customer relationships.

WHAT IS CUSTOMER SERVICE?

Many companies define customer service as product delivery and repair accompanied by friendly behavior on the part of their front-line service providers. As a result, they tend to focus on delivery time, order fill rates, and attitudinal fundamentals in defining "good" or "bad" service.

But many elements determine the value of a purchase and the level of customer satisfaction. The most obvious relate to the product itself: its price/performance characteristics, quality ratings in terms of industry standards or a respected rating agency (e.g., Underwriters Laboratories for electrical equipment or *Consumer Reports* for many consumer durables), and product specifications relative to the purchaser's requirements. Other elements are prepurchase and postpurchase activities that add value to the item. These nonproduct activities include whatever the vendor can do to reduce the customer's information search and ordering costs, in-bound logistical costs, operation and maintenance costs, and, in many product categories, disposal or trade-up costs. Customer service should always refer to these broader elements of value creation and customer satisfaction.

When evaluating service efforts and goals, managers must remember the importance of cost-in-use and the inevitable variability of service criteria across customer groups.

First, as the discussion of cost-in-use in Chapter 1 emphasized, a firm's product offering is the total package of benefits that customers receive when they buy. The package includes the functional utility of the good or service; assistance in applications development provided before the sale; training or repair services provided after the sale; timely delivery; and any brand name or reputation benefits that help the buyer promote its own products or services. Through its Intel Inside campaign, for example, Intel has used this last benefit to leverage accumulated brand equity and add value to the functional products it sells to OEMs. Recognizing the threat to this value component, Intel's management offered free replacement of its Pentium chips in 1994, despite the low probability of actual computational error at most of its end-users. In other situations, as discussed in Chapter 7, benefits might include the account relationship itself. Especially in industrial markets, the relationships that develop among people in buying and selling organizations have intangible but real value.

Conversely, the package of benefits in some situations might involve the *absence* of personal contact because reorders or other transactions are more efficiently conducted through automated systems. Many suppliers have added value to their customers' materials-management functions by placing on customers' premises terminals that provide automated replenishment services. In ordering supplies, for example, a 500-bed hospital spends more than $30 in overhead each time it places an order while suppliers spend $24 to $28 to process an order. Estimates are that electronic data interchange can reduce these costs to about $12 an order for hospitals and to less than $1 for many suppliers.[1] Hence, in an effort to improve service and reduce their own distribution costs, major hospital suppliers are trying to establish a standardized electronic ordering system. In this context, "keeping close to the customer" does not mean courteous human contact and physical proximity. These are important qualities in marketing. But so is efficiency. And in many cases, good service means less interaction but more economic value for buyer and seller.

One advantage of approaching service from this perspective is that it encourages a vendor to develop value-based pricing policies that reflect the costs and benefits of the total product offering. This can enable a firm to differentiate a product or service traditionally viewed as a commodity.[2] L. E. Muran sells office supplies in a market made even more competitive in recent years by the entry of high-volume, low-priced superstores. In response, Muran and selected corporate clients jointly produce a catalog of regularly ordered items and Muran distributes it to each client's purchaser of supplies. They check off what they need, and Muran sales representatives pick up their orders daily. Muran delivers individual orders to each customer location within 48 hours, along with regular usage-by-department reports.

The director of purchasing at one customer noted: "We used to buy stationery, allocate space for a stockroom, and pay four people and a supervisor to run it. Now we order all these supplies from Muran and call it our 'stockless stationery' policy."

The second key idea embedded in this perspective on customer service is that service has different meanings for different customers. Many companies continue to struggle with customer service because they treat it as a constant quality between buyer and seller—a discrete set of characteristics that buyers are looking for—rather than as a variable across exchange settings. As a result, they often spend much time and money developing customer satisfaction indices that are really exercises in pseudo-specificity and mock quantification. With the laudable aim of benchmarking service performance, these indices typically average various characteristics into a single set of factors that satisfy few individual purchase and service criteria, or, in an effort to avoid such averaging, the index becomes a mere checklist of activities that is oblivious to any trade-offs between services offered and cost-to-serve.

Critical elements of service vary by type of customer and, for the same customer, across phases of the order cycle and account relationship. For example, applications engineering or other technical services may be especially valued by companies that have few R&D or in-house service personnel. But they are valued less by large companies with established development and in-house service organizations. These customers put a higher value on ease of ordering and prompt delivery.

A few years ago, General Electric conducted an extensive audit of service factors in its industrial business units.[3] The findings are applicable to many other firms that also sell a variety of products into diverse markets. GE managers distinguished between what they called "flow goods" (standardized products ordered frequently from stock and sold in large part through distributors) and "project business" (semicustomized orders with substantial engineering content, often involving multiple products assembled as a system not only by different GE business units, but also other firms). The results indicated marked differences in the service expectations of customers in each category. Further, these differences meant contrasting service requirements across flow goods and project business order cycles.

Exhibit 9-1

Critical Elements of Customer Service Typically Vary by Phase of the Order Cycle and by Type of Business

	Preorder	Order-to-shipment	Postshipment
Flow Business	• Accurate, timely quotations • Knowledgeable sales force	• On-time, complete, accurate shipments • Accurate, timely order tracking/status reports	• Timely, responsive complaint resolution • Quality, timely in-warranty and out-of-warranty service
Project Business	• Accessibility and responsiveness of personnel • Quality, timely application support • Product availability information	• Flexibility to react to customer changes to the order • Experienced project managers • Ownership/authority for multiproduct department orders	• Competent installation support • Accurate, timely billing • Effective spare parts support

As Exhibit 9-1 indicates, accurate and timely quotations, and salespeople knowledgeable about pricing and delivery terms and conditions, are particularly important in the preorder stage of flow business. These products are sold by distributors as part of a larger package of goods (most not manufactured by GE). Fast and accurate quotations are crucial to both end-users and intermediaries. In the project business, by contrast, the lead times and selling cycles are longer. Important preorder services hinge on making applications specialists and other support personnel accessible and responsive to customers, whose product specifications are often ill-defined at this stage.

In the order-to-shipment phase, punctual and accurate deliveries, as well as shipment tracking reports, are valued services in flow businesses. While the products are often relatively inexpensive and standardized, their availability can be crucial to throughput and efficient run lengths at customers' manufacturing plants. Consequently, efficient, routinized, and predictable distribution procedures are important for these products. However, in project businesses there is more uncertainty in the order-to-shipment phase. Because specifications are customized and must be compatible with other components of the systems package, changes are frequent and often continue right up to the shipment date. Thus, project customers value a supplier's flexibility and ability to react to changes in the order. Here experienced project or account managers are often key to a successful relationship.

Postshipment, quick response to complaints and warranty claims are the most important components of after-sale service for flow goods. In fact, providing out-of-warranty or extended-warranty service as well as premium pricing opportunities for seemingly price-sensitive products, often distinguishes one vendor from another in these product categories. As a result, an extensive distribution network and good working relationships with intermediaries are prerequisites for good service in this type of business. For project business, important postshipment services involve a range of direct supplier-user activities such as installation, training, and the maintenance of spare parts.

These differences in service criteria must be identified and managed. They influence the time period to use in measuring service levels as well as the amount and type of services involved in achieving customer satisfaction in each type of business. The worst response is to approach all customers with a level of service that represents an average across these activities—a response that has been encouraged in recent years by a misapplication of benchmarking studies. The best response is for a vendor to understand product and customer differences well enough to distinguish its service and pricing policies. FileNet, a leader in the image-processing industry, places its service emphasis on applications development, systems configuration, customer training, installation, and postsale maintenance. It offers different levels of responsiveness, based on the customer's relative sensitivity to downtime and the availability of in-house programmers able to assist FileNet support reps in applications development.

Most companies are simultaneously involved in both flow and project exchanges with customers. The differences in the businesses influence the degree and type of coordination required among product, sales, and service groups to provide effective service. Hence, rather than use homogeneous measures of customer satisfaction, these firms must develop a portfolio of service strategies.

Exhibit 9-2
Customer Service Involves Most
Organizational Functions

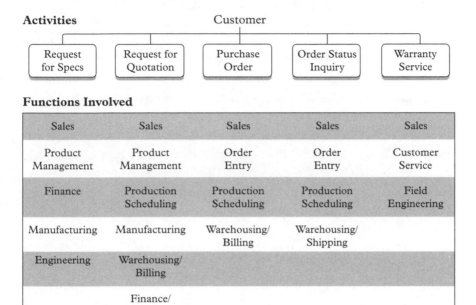

Activities		Customer		
Request for Specs	Request for Quotation	Purchase Order	Order Status Inquiry	Warranty Service

Functions Involved

Sales	Sales	Sales	Sales	Sales
Product Management	Product Management	Order Entry	Order Entry	Customer Service
Finance	Production Scheduling	Production Scheduling	Production Scheduling	Field Engineering
Manufacturing	Manufacturing	Warehousing/ Billing	Warehousing/ Shipping	
Engineering	Warehousing/ Billing			
	Finance/ Billing			

CUSTOMER SERVICE AND INTERNAL MARKETING

In the broader sense outlined here, customer service is a multifunctional activity. This can be illustrated by considering the typical order cycle in many industrial businesses (Exhibit 9-2).

For the selling company, from a customer's request for specifications to the actual purchase order and through after-sale warranty service, the progress of an order involves numerous groups and functions. Two aspects of this order cycle are particularly noteworthy. First, field sales is involved in most activities of the cycle, if only because, in most businesses, it is the salesperson who hears from the customer with a question or complaint about order fulfillment. Therefore, service initiatives that do not recognize the central role played by salespeople (and the impact on service initiatives of the sales training and compensation issues discussed in earlier chapters) are likely to be short-lived.

Second, in spite of their centrality, salespeople have little direct authority over the many activities involved in filling an order. Therefore, those most directly involved in managing customer encounters must often persuade personnel in other areas to help customize the order and services for a particular customer.

For these reasons, service problems persist at many companies, despite speeches and investments in culture building. The marketing dialects discussed in Chapter 3, as well as different incentives and operating procedures between marketing groups and other functions involved in service provision, generate different views and a fragmented approach to the customer. But external responsiveness requires internal coordination across these areas, placing customer service squarely in the crossfire between necessary cooperation and potential conflict.

This situation is further complicated in many firms because product-related elements receive the bulk of managerial time and attention, even though nonproduct elements of customer value are often crucial in service differentiation. Consider the following areas, which are usually fundamental to completing tasks in any complex, time-constrained organization.

Management Responsibility

In many companies, the product elements of customer service are the responsibility of product or brand managers, but the nonproduct elements are not. If good service can be likened to a well-executed performance,[4] consider that in movie making one person is responsible for continuity—making sure the background in one take is congruent with that of the next day's filming of the same scene. However, in most firms no one function or manager is responsible for overseeing all the required activities of order fulfillment.[5] The closest thing to an order overseer in many firms is the formal customer service staff, which often plays a reactive role and has little authority to alter the flow of customer orders. The result, as one service manager described it, is making this group the firm's "Florence Nightingale brigade: The customer service staff tries to patch up and soothe a customer wounded in an internal war that neither of them started."

In the computer industry, for example, nearly every major vendor now stresses some form of systems integration for clients that have increasing needs for networked communications. But many of these vendors sell and service this offering through separate hardware, software, and peripherals organizations formed at a previous stage of competition. The result is often uncoordinated service, with components arriving at customer sites at different times and in different quantities. Another result, as one angry customer of such a vendor complained to me, is a "pass the buck situation, where several product divisions are involved but nobody has control over the complete system."

A promising approach for dealing with this aspect of service is case management, in which, as part of business process redesign, individuals or small teams perform a series of tasks (such as order fulfillment) from beginning to end, with the help of information systems that gather and disseminate relevant data from multifunctional sources.[6] Organizations like Citibank, Dell Computer, Georgia Pacific, IBM Credit Corporation, MCI, Pacific Bell, and Xerox have implemented this approach, often with dramatic improvements in efficiency as well as customer satisfaction.

Plans and Budgets

Management responsibility means developing formal business strategies and plans, complete with budgets and financial tracking of activities. Again, companies have controls in place for product-related elements of service. But the nonproduct elements are managed on a more ad hoc basis, often without any financial controls or method for making trade-offs among different customer groups. Indeed, the emphasis during the past decade on a service culture has motivated many firms to eschew budgets and financial controls for service activities. "We want our service people to be action-oriented zealots for the customer," is the reasoning here, "and not fettered by plans and budgets that put them in a short-term, bean-counting frame of mind."

But the unintended result of these good intentions is that service initiatives are driven by the most pressing needs at the time. The importance of service is usually stressed when a new product is introduced, when new salespeople are hired, or when a major customer complains. But the firm's ongoing procedures and budgeting processes do not reflect the importance of continuity of service, and the upshot is an essentially reactive, intermittent approach characterized by periodic outbursts of programs aimed at service excellence. In many instances, these programs actually damage the firm's service reputation: they raise customer expectations without delivering consistent levels of quality and, as research now demonstrates,[7] the customer tends to focus on lapsed promises.

These programs can also damage management morale and create a self-defeating cycle. At one corporation in my study, the CEO had grown concerned about customer complaints, and appointed a senior vice president to head a task force to fix service problems. The vice president soon found that the quality of customer service was not a new issue. The corporate marketing files quickly coughed up numerous internal and consultant reports on service dating back more than 20 years. "In fact," the vice president noted, "customer service has been the most studied issue in this company, and the recent top-management attention [is] perceived by middle managers as just another fad."

This is in fact the situation currently facing many companies: how to prevent talk about service from becoming a fad—an important issue that engages people's energies for a while but then dissipates, leaving customer and employee cynicism in its wake. Precisely because service components are dispersed throughout a company, budgets and financial controls are important means for service realization. These seemingly bureaucratic mechanisms also make tangible activities easily perceived as intangible (and therefore "unimportant") to busy and resource-constrained functional groups.

Measurements and Evaluation

One reason service programs are difficult to sustain is that few managerial measures actually relate customer support expenses to profit-and-loss criteria. As discussed in Chapter 3, cost accounting systems in most firms are set up to allocate costs by product volumes. This, in turn, drives the firm's salient financial and performance measurements. Manufacturing managers can track variances by product item while marketing information systems can track product sales by region and channel. But customer-level data are still the exception in most companies, leaving managers with little knowledge of account profitability and the support components of account management discussed in Chapter 7. Even when companies do track expenses at the account level, their accounting systems often make it very difficult to allocate SG&A costs or other relevant activities in meaningful terms.

Further, responsibility for overseeing account service is often vested with sales managers, whose compensation (as discussed in Chapter 2) is generally tied to revenue goals. These managers therefore have an incentive to endorse same-day service or no-fault/money-back service guarantees that "increase our share," regardless of the impact on profitability. This situation has been exacerbated in recent years as sales automation efforts, implemented at great cost and with meticulous attention to user-friendly technology, have tended to freeze in place systems that generate little actionable data about customer maintenance costs. The frequent result is what one executive called "the service boomerang: based on our accounting measures, we charge toward providing 'value-added' services to customers. But then we charge right back when the actual ROA is disappointing."

Culture-building activities may be resoundingly successful, and everyone may well realize that service is important. But in the absence of specific measures, and with continual pressure to make quarterly earnings goals, service expenditures tend to become discretionary, allocated when budgets allow and dropped when cost pressures increase. This is analogous to a typical cycle of advertising expenditures in many companies: the level of ad spending is actually the result, rather than a cause, of historical sales volume. That is, ad expenditures are set as a percentage of sales volume, and these firms tend to cut ad spending when sales are flat and cost pressures most intense. But it is often precisely at this juncture that advertising, and service, are most important in brand building and market development.

Perhaps worse, in many companies the absence of specific service measures means that the actual measures used to allocate resources to service activities change from year to year (perhaps from quarter to quarter), depending on the business unit's earnings or other elements of its financial performance. In turn, this can breed a "Do what I say, not what I do" ethic among P&L managers as they perceive that top management is sending mixed signals that undercut the official exhortations about service.

At one of the flow businesses mentioned earlier, for example, field-stocking levels were a crucial aspect of customer service because distributors depended on the quick availability and wide assortment of many different spare parts. But despite a corporate customer-satisfaction program, the general manager of one business unit cut production and field inventories in the fourth quarter, lengthening order fill rates and delivery times. These moves provided immediate cost reductions under the accounting system and, as this manager candidly explained, "As a company, we live on our measurements. It's tough to trade a tangible addition to this year's bottom line for intangible benefits in service that are not reflected in the printouts that corporate executives study at our quarterly review meetings."

Accountability

This is the scarcest resource in organizations, and its dearth is often apparent in customer service. In an effort to manage the multifunctional efforts required to provide good service, companies have increasingly defined service as the responsibility of all employees. Indeed, a scan of annual reports, popular books on team building, and the Baldrige Award citations quickly reveals how prevalent are incentive systems that try to reward employees on the basis of company-wide customer satisfaction measures. The unintended result is to exacerbate the lack of accountability that plagues service efforts at many companies.

At GE, for example, one of the first steps taken by corporate managers charged with improving service was simply to locate people in each business unit responsible for customer service. "We were surprised by what we didn't find," noted one executive. "There was no one person responsible for these matters in the businesses, and so no champion to raise awareness of the issues involved." This situation can be debilitating in terms of actual service provided because, as another manager described it, "Customer service is an optics issue: it must remain visible and a central part of someone's agenda. Otherwise, things don't happen, or they consistently happen after the fact."

In most Western companies, de facto responsibility for service resides with the marketing organization. As noted, dissatisfied customers complain to the field salesperson, and yet it is product marketing managers who often have primary influence over many activities that comprise the order cycle outlined in Exhibit 9-2. Indeed, most definitions of marketing in Western business schools cite customer service as central to marketing efforts. When pressed for a description of their fundamental role in the organization, most marketing practitioners are likely to cite "customer service" or its fraternal twin, "serving customer needs."

By contrast, responsibility for service is a less specialized function in many Japanese firms, where engineering and manufacturing managers pursue more continuous contact with customers after the product has been purchased. When a Japanese company learns that a customer is dissatisfied with the design of its product, it is not uncommon for it to dispatch a design engineer, who determines if the problem is significant enough to warrant redesign. In Western companies, customer complaints are usually handled much farther downstream in the value chain, in sales or service, and then brought upstream through manufacturing and product development.

Many factors account for these differences, including the now well-known historical differences in employment policies, manufacturing policies, and rate of adoption of quality practices.[8] But despite statements to the contrary by some Western observers, service is *not* everybody's business at Honda, Toyota, or other successful Japanese firms. The engineer (or manufacturing manager or product development leader) in these firms is often held personally accountable for customer reactions. When service is an issue, the tasks of these managers is the same as in the West: to expand and maintain their colleagues' understanding of customer needs, priorities, and preferences. It is the worst of both worlds, however, to remove product design and delivery from production and field sales, where current knowledge of customers and products is often highest, and then declare that customer satisfaction is everybody's business. This is, in fact, the gist of many recent

Exhibit 9-3

Typical Management Approach to Product versus Nonproduct Elements of Customer Value

PRODUCT	NONPRODUCT
Focused management responsibility	Fragmented responsibility
Formal business strategies and plans	Ad hoc planning
Budgets and financial tracking mechanisms	No or after-the-fact financial tracking mechanisms
Cost accounting systems provide product-costing data	Cost accounting systems rarely provide nonproduct data
Formal, visible performance measurements of product technology, quality, revenues	Few performance measurements
Cost/benefit trade-offs often made by managers with profit-and-loss responsibility	Few cost/benefit trade-offs tied to P&L impacts and results

reengineering efforts. But the longer-term impact is to destroy accountability and, despite the teamwork rhetoric, generate "pass the buck" behavior rather than customer service.

Exhibit 9-3 summarizes the different types of management attention given to the product versus nonproduct components of customer value. Given these circumstances, it is not surprising that complaints about customer service are still common. But specifying these circumstances indicates where an actionable emphasis on improving service should start: first, with management clarity about both the product and nonproduct components of customer value in the business, and second, attention to the structures, systems, and processes that aid the coordination of these components.

BUILDING THE SALES SERVICE TEAM

Implicit in this perspective on service is the supplier's ability to forge effective links between the two groups that, in most companies, have primary responsibility for customer encounters: sales and service. As Part I emphasized, coordination between sales and service units becomes more important and more complex in an increasingly segmented, fast-response marketplace. To achieve better sales-service coordination, companies are devoting new attention to structural, training, budgeting, and compensation issues that affect how and when these groups interact during the order cycle.

Structurally, some firms are using customer team approaches aimed at melding sales and service efforts more closely. As part of its corporatewide emphasis on customer satisfaction, Xerox reorganized its regions and districts into customer relations groups (CRGs) that are partnerships of sales, service, and business operations.[9] Previously, these units had reported to regional and headquarters levels, and there was not much coordination at the local district level. Now, the CRG at each district consists of two to six people who have direct customer contact. Problems reach the CRG by multiple routes: customer surveys, internal problem referrals from a salesperson or service technician, contract cancellations, and nonconformance costs such as machine replacement, accommodation, and sales refusals or reversals. The objective is to resolve issues better and faster with a cross-functional, closed-loop process that can both analyze and implement service initiatives.

Similarly, some consumer goods firms have restructured marketing, sales, and distribution/merchandising units into business groups that, among other things, are responsible for trade servicing activities. At Pillsbury, teams of this sort have been formed around various product groups. Each involves managers from production and sales as well as marketing. "In the past if anything went wrong," noted one executive, "marketing would blame sales and sales would blame operations." The aim of the new structure is to make all these groups brand champions, with the brand defined in the sense discussed above as including both the product and nonproduct elements of customer satisfaction. One advantage of this approach is that service personnel deal with many of the same internal managers, developing an in-depth knowledge of product marketing and channel requirements. Hence, expertise is not sacrificed in the name of teamwork.

A variation on this structure is the specialist program at apparel manufacturer Liz Claiborne. Started in 1984, the program included more than 100 marketing specialists in the United States by 1993. They do field work in stores, and report to headquarters on "What's hot and what's not." The company assimilates this information and gives it to design and purchasing teams. Then, as the fashion season approaches, the specialists come to headquarters to learn about the new lines. They return to their regions to brief retail sales associates on features of the line and merchandising ideas. Moreover, on announced days in each store they work behind the counter with customers. This service structure is in keeping with Claiborne's store-within-a-store merchandising concept. The specialists train retail salespeople in the clothing's construction, upcoming design changes, ways to mix and match the pieces, and how to handle customer inquiries responsively. The result is remarkable trade and consumer loyalty in a notoriously fickle fashion industry and, as one study noted,[10] a higher percentage of full-price sales for Liz Claiborne clothing compared to the industry average.

Training programs also help build coordinated sales and service. As Chapter 6 indicated, training for marketing, sales, and service managers has traditionally moved along separate lines in most firms. But the importance of the product service package has altered training initiatives in some companies. At Reader's Digest, in addition to 12 weeks of classroom training (broken into two 6-week sessions) during their first year, new customer service reps meet monthly with marketing and sales managers. This training focuses on the service requirements of different items in the product line (in addition to *Reader's Digest* magazine, the company also sells books, records, videos, and other products). Further, for the first two months of employment, new service reps observe other service and sales personnel doing their jobs. Conversely, at an industrial products firm, new and experienced salespeople now receive order placement training. "Previously," noted a regional sales manager with 20 years' experience at the firm, "this wasn't viewed as important. But while our product development and manufacturing cycles shrunk, our product line grew and order-processing time lengthened. The net result was that, from the customer's perspective, our time-to-installation had not improved."

An emphasis in some training programs is the "service as a product" concept. As software becomes embedded in the product and/or its delivery system, service features can be customized. In turn, customer value is increased—*if* the customer understands the impact on its business operations. In telecommunications, new network software allows some carriers to offer customized billing and usage reports, which have become a source of product differentiation. At MCI, sales and service personnel are trained together in the options available so that these services can be sold as products. At other firms, EDI investments in the distribution channel allow on-line links with customers. For some firms, this capability greatly improves order entry, invoicing, rebate procedures, forecasting, delivery, and other cash flow dimensions of buyer-seller relationships. Some suppliers have altered sales training to emphasize how such services affect customer operations. The goal is to translate seemingly neutral features of the transaction (order entry and invoicing) into benefits that customers can measure and appreciate (continuous inventory replenishment that lowers carrying costs). The impact, as one marketing manager explained, can be especially big for firms that rely on distributors to get their products to market: "Resellers live or die on working capital and inventory turn improvements. Making these services visible has increased our share of shelf and sales support at resellers, and helped us and our distributors in price negotiations with key accounts. But both sales and service personnel must first understand how service can be a product, and that takes training."

SYNCHRONIZING SALES AND SERVICE INCENTIVES

As Chapter 8 indicated, making any structural or training initiatives work requires attention to metrics that influence field behavior and resource allocations. This, in turn, often requires a company to gather and maintain more activity-based costing data than that available in most standard cost-accounting systems.

For years at a computer firm in my study, customer service (composed of field engineering and software development units) was measured as a profit center. Service managers faced ongoing choices between dedicating resources to field engineering "fixes" (which typi-cally required engineers at customer locations for some time to fulfill warranty contracts on sales whose revenues were already credited to the account's sales team) or to development of software applications (the sale of which *did* generate revenues credited to the service organi-zation). In practice, junior service resources were allocated for fixes while more experienced senior resources were reserved for software development. The result, from the perspective of a sales manager, was that "repeat sales, trade-up buying, and other aspects of customer re-lations were jeopardized by service's reluctance to provide timely on-site response to customer problems." The result, from the perspective of a service manager, was that "salespeople had little incentive to worry about the service implications of what they sold, and continu-ally argued for more generous warranty contracts whose costs were incurred by another part of the company. Meanwhile, service had much incentive to focus on development and saw mainly expenses, not rewards, in making fixes."

A reallocation of credits and expenses is a first step in breaking this logjam. Dow Chemical U.S.A. has more than 200 service reps based in a center at company headquarters. Dow allocates much of their time to field work and carries much of their expense budget as selling costs. This treatment of service resources results in frequent joint cus-tomer calls by sales and service personnel not only to resolve current problems, but also to diagnose emerging account needs and act as a proactive sales-service team.

A next step is attention to congruent compensation and evaluation procedures. Renex Corporation markets computer interconnectivity products, a business where technical service to a dispersed customer base is crucial. For its sales force, commissions represent up to 60% of total compensation. Technical service reps also receive a bonus (up to 25% of total compensation, paid quarterly) based on an evaluation procedure which combines a measure of the service rep's success in solving or preventing any customer problems with feedback from cus-tomers, service management, and the salespeople with whom the tech rep works. Based on mail and telephone surveys, the customer and management ratings represent a certain percentage of the evaluation each quarter. Sales reps, whose rankings compose the remaining portion of the evaluation, complete questionnaires that rate tech reps on attitude, professionalism, responsiveness, and contribution to customer satisfaction. Sales reps also participate in the performance evaluations and are required to explain their ratings along these subjective but crucial dimensions of service.

Similarly, Western Stone & Metal, an importer of precious gems, pays a bonus to all employees at each of its stores. A percentage of the store's profits over a preestablished threshold goes into a store bonus pool which is distributed quarterly, 50% going to sales employees, 35% to support staff and supervisors, and 15% to the store manager. Salespeople's bonuses are calculated on how much they exceed a target base. Bonuses for sales support employees are based on a point system which takes each employee's responsibility into account and factors that against the store's performance. The company also has an annual bonus plan for all full-time corporate employees, from hourly workers to top management. This bonus is tied to net sales and "earning power" (a performance measure used in retailing which is based on operating margins and inventory turns). Under the plan, employees can earn 40–125% of a target award. The aim, according to Western Metal's CEO, is to provide an opportunity for all employees to share in the rewards of increased sales since all are required to support the sale in different ways.

But most companies have been relatively slow to adopt incentive plans for service personnel. One reason is concern over the impact of incentives on core service activities. A well-publicized example of a poorly implemented sales-service incentive was at Sears in 1992. At its auto repair centers, service advisers were accused of padding their commissions by falsely diagnosing brake and alignment problems. At the time, these people both inspected cars for defects and sold motorists on repairs. Legal proceedings cost Sears $15 million in refunds and other settlement costs. The company restructured its service centers to separate the problem diagnosis and selling activities and, in 1993, began paying commissions again to service consultants for sales of tires, batteries, and other components whose failure is obvious to most motorists.

However, a more common reason for the relative lack of congruent sales and service incentives is that, as noted, most firms lack budgeting systems that are informed by customer-level data. Implementing the service concepts discussed in this chapter requires that costs be considered in light of their impact on repeat purchases and customer relationships over time—a perspective not recognized in most established accounting systems. Here, activity-based cost analyses are useful because many service costs vary, not with short-term changes in output (as assumed by the overhead allocation procedures built into most traditional costing systems), but with changes over a period of years in the design, mix, and range of a company's products, customers, and channels of distribution.[11] After conducting activity-based analyses, a number of companies in my sample found that service costs behaved in ways that changed their assumptions about how to manage marketing resources and customer relations.

For one thing, these analyses often revealed the true selling and support costs in these firms. In the computer industry, for instance, the cost of direct labor in producing products is now often less than 10% of the total cost of delivering the product. The cost of sales and support is several times that amount. In addition, for many companies, the cost to serve customers does not vary proportionally with the sales volume a customer represents. Rather, as a percentage of sales, cost-to-serve is often a near constant amount beyond a certain revenue threshold. That is, in many cases an account purchasing $100,000 costs half the percentage effort to service as a $10,000 account while a $1 million account often has an even lower percentage. Conversely, at low revenue levels, the cost-to-serve can exceed 100% for many accounts, leading to unprofitable sales.

Armed with this knowledge, managers can adjust elements of the marketing mix to accommodate the facts. Individual product items can be repriced to reflect their call on key support resources; quantity discount pricing and minimum order-size rules can be instituted; offloading intermittently used support resources to third parties can often lower cost-to-serve without lowering customer service. Without this knowledge sales and service personnel lack the means to argue for appropriate resources while top management often views coordination mechanisms between the groups as expensive luxuries for seemingly low-margin sales.

MANAGING CUSTOMER RETENTION

I have argued that realigning internal activities to provide better product-sales-service integration is justified by long-term market developments and competitive pressures. However, in the short run management must understand the economic value of customer retention and the factors that build and extend buyer-seller relationships. Research has established that, in a variety of businesses, customer retention is linked to increased profitability.[12] Less well-established is *how* different elements of a company's marketing program affect customer retention. Also, retention discussions usually assume a static relationship between buyer and seller, and ignore the impact of customer experience on buying criteria and other aspects of account relationships discussed in Chapter 7.

A useful method of analyzing customer retention in many businesses is to distinguish between two types of customer defections:

- Those related to the product (customers dissatisfied with product quality or elements of the price performance offering discussed in previous chapters); and
- Those related to the nonproduct elements of customer value discussed in this chapter (customers dissatisfied with any transaction or support services that are, or are not, provided by the vendor).

Moreover, in most businesses, there are two time periods during which the seller can influence the behavior of customers: before and after installation or implementation of the product or service.

Exhibit 9-4 arrays these factors in a matrix, along with the marketing tools most relevant to different stages of buyer-seller exchange. The dynamics of customer retention at a familiar business—cable television—can help illustrate the relationship of the various factors outlined in Exhibit 9-4.

A cable company's up-front costs of property, plant, and equipment can only be recouped if customers stay on the system for some time. For example, one cable franchise found that a basic cable cus-

Exhibit 9-4
Marketing Dynamics of Customer Retention

	Preinstallation	Postinstallation
Product	I	II

• Quality	Account Selection
	  • Market Segmentation
	  • Customer Education
		Product Policy
		  • Product Improvements
		  • New Products

• Price Performance	Sales Management
	  • Training and Deployment
	  • Sales Incentives
		Communications Policy
		  • Follow-Up
		  • Complaint Resolution

Nonproduct	III	IV

• Transaction Services	Order Entry Procedures
	
	Inventory Management
		Account Management
		  • Team-Selling Efforts
		  • Sales/Service Coordination
		  • Solutions Orientation

• Customer Support	Delivery Performance
	
	Technical Assistance/
	Applications Development
		• Responsiveness
		  • Customer database
		  • Internal information
		    systems

tomer had to be a subscriber for six months before the franchise recouped its costs of installing that customer. Factoring in the amortized costs of plant construction, the firm had to retain the basic customer for 11 months before it returned a profit. By contrast, given the cost structure of a cable franchise, the variable costs of serving an installed customer are minimal. Ideally, these customers should become virtual annuities, generating monthly fee revenues. To ensure that they do and to avoid what in the cable industry is called "churn" (disconnection of service), these companies have developed marketing programs aimed at minimizing churn's potentially devastating effects on supplier profitability.

What is especially salient for cable firms is increasingly the case in other businesses. In many other high-fixed-cost service businesses, customer acquisition costs can only be justified if the customer "stays with us" beyond the initial transaction. Banks, credit card companies, and airlines were among the first to stress repeat-customer programs.

But, as I argue, this imperative is also true of traditional manufacturing businesses, where production technologies and changing buying criteria mean that suppliers must often sell a system whose costs require customer retention over time to be economically viable.

In quadrant I of Exhibit 9-4, account selection and field-sales management policies are the primary marketing tools for managing retention. The goals are to attract customers whose product preferences are in line with the supplier's product offerings and to establish sales systems that focus on these customers. In the cable business, for example, management can take some relatively simple actions at this juncture: educating potential customers about specific program offerings so that their expectations are fulfilled, and structuring sales incentives that discourage salespeople from selling program packages that customers later cancel. In other businesses, rigorous and continuous market-segmentation decisions (implemented through pricing and promotion policies) are the key means for appropriate account selection.

In quadrant II, a company's preinstallation transaction services and customer support procedures should be the focus of marketing attention. Here, easy and reliable order entry procedures, delivery performance, technical assistance with installation, and the administrative procedures associated with order processing are key factors in customer satisfaction. In the cable business, joint work between the cable vendor and apartment complex managers (or other important intermediaries between the supplier and end-user) has meant better performance along these dimensions of customer value. In other businesses, cooperation between the supplier and distributors, strategic alliances, and development of information systems to expedite these transactions are critical at this juncture of buyer-seller relationships.

In quadrant III, the supplier's evolving product policy becomes the primary marketing lever for customer retention. Many cable franchises have found that programming alterations that reflect changing demographics in a franchise area are key to preserving the subscriber base. Similarly, postinstallation follow-up by sales or service personnel can lower churn in the first months after installation, which, in cable and many other businesses, is an especially critical period for customer retention. Direct mail, 800 numbers, and other vehicles aimed at promoting and explaining new products and follow-on services in greater detail are also important at this stage.

Finally, in quadrant IV, the vendor's long-term value as a supplier is the key determinant of customer retention. In marketing, this means paying attention to policies and programs that continually improve the supplier's ability in two areas: (1) gathering and exchanging information useful in developing solutions to the customer's evolving requirements, and (2) maintaining the internal systems that are a prerequisite for external responsiveness. In the cable business, this means developing and maintaining a customer database that helps the supplier track usage patterns and develop appropriate programming packages and promotions. In many other businesses the task is more complex, requiring the kinds of changes in both the supplier's sales programs and internal alignments among product, sales, and service units discussed in Part II.

The framework in Exhibit 9-4 is a general look at customer retention dynamics and requires adaptation to specific company circumstances. But this framework can help operationalize what "keeping close to the customer" really entails. By breaking down this worthy but often ephemeral advice into manageable segments of the buyer-seller relationship, marketing, sales, and service managers can focus their limited time, attention, and resources on those areas and actions likely to provide the best returns on customer investments.

CONCLUSION

How do firms improve customer service? In large part, they improve it by effectively managing the market orientation paradox: external responsiveness (the ultimate test of marketing efforts in any firm) requires internal coordination and attention to the product, sales, and service linkages discussed in this book. These are structures, systems, and processes that customers rarely see or explicitly care about. But how companies manage these organizational functions are the ultimate causes of customer praise or complaints.

10

Building Concurrent
Marketing Capabilities

■

CONCURRENT marketing is both a challenge and opportunity for companies competing in the twenty-first century: a challenge because market developments in many industries require new types of flexible integration in customer contact activities, and an opportunity because few firms have yet perfected the structures, systems, and processes needed for concurrent marketing capabilities. Developing these capabilities requires more than slogans ("keep close to the customer"), simple solutions ("pay everyone the same way"), or packaged programs ("more communication and lots of cross-functional teams"). It requires an understanding and implementation of themes that have been developed throughout this book:

- The forces that make the coordination costs of concurrent marketing competitively necessary for many—but *not* all—firms;
- The continuing importance of specialization and expertise in the effective execution of more cross-functional tasks;
- The analysis of key interdependencies among the product, sales, and service units that develop and deliver customer value;
- The creation of appropriate linkages in order to manage these interdependencies efficiently and effectively; and
- The vital importance of "going the final mile": focusing and rallying the diverse field-marketing resources needed for effective account management.

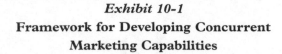

Exhibit 10-1
**Framework for Developing Concurrent
Marketing Capabilities**

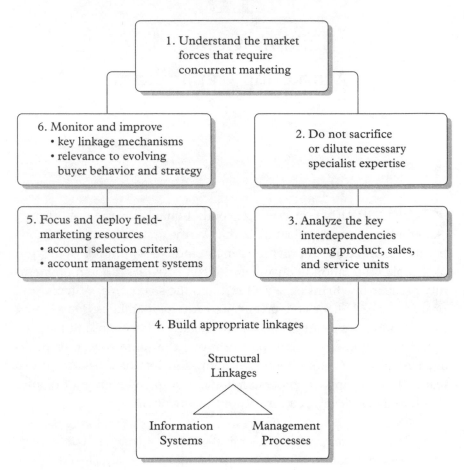

Along with the perennial relevance of continually monitoring and improving efforts, these themes serve as a framework for action and a direction for change (Exhibit 10-1). In any given company, the framework will have to be modified to reflect particular competitive circumstances and culture. As argued in Chapter 3, "one size fits all" approaches to organizational redesign are rarely successful, and, along with the nonparticipation of front-line marketing personnel, are a major reason for the failure of many reengineering efforts.[1] But, together, these themes raise issues that will help companies get started in building concurrent marketing capabilities.

UNDERSTAND THE FORCES THAT REQUIRE CONCURRENT MARKETING

Chapter 1 discussed four factors that make concurrent marketing capabilities a competitive necessity in many businesses: changes in what is being sold (the nature of the product offering), to whom it is sold (market fragmentation), how it is sold (supply chain management demands), and under what competitive conditions it is sold (accelerating product life cycles). In different ways, each of these developments increases integration requirements among product management, field sales, and customer service groups.

In more industries, the global diffusion of technology and quality improvements have given the core product only a temporary competitive edge at best. Customers more often choose suppliers that, in addition to technical excellence and quality in the core product, provide ancillary services and support, both before and after the sale. In addition, new opportunities for sellers in many industries require the combination of systems rather than innovation around a stand-alone product. These developments mean that profits and margins now come from an offering that puts a premium on the seller's ability to coordinate its own product, sales, and service units.

Exhibit 10-2 summarizes some of the key implications for managing marketing. This kind of competition requires the seller to be able to develop longer-term relationships with selected customers. The upfront costs of this approach, as well as the ongoing coordination costs among functional areas, are usually too steep to make transaction-oriented exchanges worthwhile for the seller. If these costs do not result in a future stream of orders, competing in this manner is unprofitable.

To develop these relationships the seller's field-marketing units need to know more about their customers' business processes in order to analyze and optimize the cost-in-use components of the exchange. Further, since the buyer is not only purchasing a product but also

Exhibit 10-2

Market Developments: Some Key Implications

- Transactions vs. Relationships
- Product and Process Knowledge
- Realignment of Value-Added Components

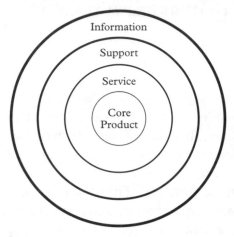

organizational prowess, field sales and service personnel require more familiarity with their own company's business processes across a variety of functional areas.

Finally, this type of competition means a fundamental realignment of value-added components in many industries—a realignment suggested in the series of concentric circles in Exhibit 10-2. Increasingly, customer value is a function of what sellers can provide in the outer rings of the circle. And, because pricing is that aspect of marketing in which a seller extracts some of the value it provides to customers, pricing is more often a function of what is, or isn't, provided along these dimensions. This emphasis does *not* mean that the core product or service is unimportant or that expenditures for continuous technical and quality innovations in the core offering should be viewed as unnecessary or discretionary. Quite the contrary: without that solid core, the concentric circles will become a dark star and the outer rings will collapse. But, as I have stressed in this book, quality and innovation are table stakes in many industries, a necessary prerequisite for effective competition.

Not all product strategies require concurrent marketing efforts. Indeed, no-frills, low-price/low-service strategies will always be viable in many businesses, especially for those firms that can develop or utilize low-cost distribution channels for their core offerings. The decision about how to compete remains a fundamental strategic choice. But once a firm decides to meet market developments with a value-added rather than no-frills strategy, management must recognize the implications for the alignment of product, sales, and service processes in the firm.

MAINTAIN NECESSARY SPECIALIST EXPERTISE

Chapter 2 discussed the roles and responsibilities of product, sales, and service units, and how their joint activities form a marketing gearbox. Chapter 3 discussed how these responsibilities can generate separate marketing dialects that often impede necessary coordination. Both chapters also explained how and why specialist expertise in each area is crucial in the new marketing environment.

As a firm's offering becomes a product-service-information mix that must be customized for diverse segments, organizational interdependencies increase and marketing groups in particular are involved in more cross-functional tasks. But specialty expertise is still vital in this environment. Indeed, contrary to currently fashionable pronouncements about future organizations as boundaryless collections of ad hoc project teams, a division of labor that develops and maintains appropriate product, sales, and service expertise is even *more* important as more work becomes knowledge work. This is especially true in marketing, where the supply chain and information factors outlined in Part I are ratcheting up significantly the analytical components of product, pricing, promotion, and distribution tasks. To dismantle or diffuse this necessary expertise in the name of undifferentiated notions of teamwork is to short-circuit the continuing organizational learning required in the new market environment and to unwittingly encourage lowest-common-denominator approaches to the marketplace.

Such expertise, it must be stressed, is also a prerequisite for the higher-level capabilities required, including cross-functional coordination and concurrent marketing. As strategy theorists have begun to point out, company competencies typically exist in layers, the performance of a higher layer being dependent upon competent execution of lower layers of skills.[2] Company coordination skills (layer 2) and new marketing capabilities (layer 3) can only be developed when layer 1 skills (effective product development, sales, and service operations) are in place. For these reasons, concurrent marketing organizations are built around a combination of world-class functional specialists, customer-driven information flows, and appropriate integrating structures and processes. All three dimensions are required.

The reality for most companies is that their business environment truly *is* more complex, simultaneously demanding both more functional expertise and more cross-functional coordination. And, in a world characterized by shorter product life cycles, there is also less time available to form and reform necessary linkages. Addressing this complexity with simple (often, simplistic) nostrums is, in the long term, self-defeating. Building concurrent marketing capabilities requires top management to seriously consider F. Scott Fitzgerald's remark that "A first-rate intelligence [can] hold two opposed ideas in mind at the same time and still retain its ability to function," and then do the detailed work required to embed this ability in the firm.

ANALYZE KEY INTERDEPENDENCIES

Because integrating the activities of product, sales, and service units takes time and resources, the next step involves choices about where and how to attempt links along the continuum of customer contact tasks discussed in Part I. Getting to specifics often requires an audit of marketing activities as a way of surfacing key interdependencies while underlining the types of functional expertise that remain necessary. Without this analysis, and the consequent choices about where integration is most important, coordination remains the perennial off-site meeting topic rather than the actual stuff of marketing practice. Moreover, on the job time-constrained marketing personnel (especially field salespeople) are likely to fall into the competency traps discussed in Chapter 3: getting better at their own specialized procedures rather than developing mutually reinforcing coherence at the customer interface.

The example cited in Chapter 6 is a useful model of the kinds of analysis required. In that example (cf. Exhibit 6-4), a consumer goods company analyzed the tasks of its increasingly interdependent brand, sales, and product supply units in order to clarify the following:

- The major joint activities in which coordination is necessary between two or more of these units;
- Each unit's key contribution to customer satisfaction in the performance of these joint activities;
- The primary external focus and responsibility of each unit: in this case, whether a unit's focus and responsibility was the end-consumer or trade customer for the company's products; and
- Specific elements of the marketing mix over which each unit has the final decision-making authority and accountability for implementation and results.

In this company, product management and sales must integrate their pricing and promotion activities with increasingly segmented consumer groups and increasingly powerful retail customers. But, while each organizational unit has input into another's activities, each retains final decision-making authority over different aspects of these activities with trade customers or end-consumers. Product management is responsible for consumer advertising, promotion, packaging, and pricing decisions; sales is responsible for distribution, merchandising, shelving, and promotion programs for trade customers. The groups engage in joint planning and implementation. Similarly, sales and product supply (i.e., logistics units) must coordinate service efforts across different classes of trade. The analysis of key interdependencies gives sales final decision-making authority over stocking and merchandising activities within the quality and cost parameters established by product supply managers.

A computer manufacturer distinguishes between "resource owners" (responsible for functional excellence in product development, manufacturing, and field service) and "market owners" (responsible for identifying account requirements and then contracting with resource owners to define and deliver a customer solution). With this framework, joint activities are identified and, for key activities, each unit is assigned decision-making authority, recommendation responsibilities, or concurrence rights (i.e., a unit's agreement or disagreement is a matter of record and thus part of the organizational database for continuous improvement of this marketing activity). An executive commented: "We always had ad hoc agreements among our product, sales, and service units. But that doesn't develop a repeatable process, which is important when time-to-market is a bigger aspect of competition. Surfacing the key interdependencies clarified responsibilities and got resources moving, while sharpening accountability for the timely performance of joint activities."

As these examples indicate, the analysis of key interdependencies will differ among companies. But the point is to make visible where, along a given firm's continuum of relevant customer-contact activities (cf. Exhibit 2-1), integration and accountability are necessary, not discretionary. Concurrent marketing capabilities develop out of this attention to detail, and not just out of a generalized concern for coordination for its own sake. In addition, this analysis is important for the next step: building appropriate linkages where integration is required.

BUILD APPROPRIATE LINKAGES

Part II discussed what firms are doing organizationally to enhance their concurrent marketing abilities. These initiatives include: an emphasis on structural devices such as formal liaison units; changes in research and information systems utilized by product, sales, and service units; and alterations in management processes, especially new career paths and training programs. Each can be a platform on which firms can build complementary mechanisms for integrating sales, service, and product management. But these initiatives form a linked triad of options. New structures without supporting information systems, or new information systems without the appropriate people and processes, have limited impact.

The chapters in Part II focused on individual companies as a way of evaluating the benefits, vulnerabilities, and marketing environments associated with each set of linkage devices. From those companies' experiences emerged certain implications for building appropriate linkages. Three seem particularly critical.

The Importance of Boundary Roles

Formal liaison units are often viewed skeptically by line managers and have typically been among the first units to go when downsizing programs are initiated. These units are viewed skeptically because they rarely have direct line authority, yet do have influence over the resources sought by functional managers who *are* responsible for P&L results. They are often cut in downsizing because their value cannot be linked directly to current revenue-generation routines. But, without such units, the coordination required for concurrent marketing capabilities is often nonexistent, treated as a secondary priority by each unit, or simply takes too long to accomplish in a marketplace where product life cycles are accelerating and a given window of opportunity is shortening.

This is one of the lessons of the IBM experience discussed in Chapter 4. There, the symptoms were product-sales conflict, slow time-to-market, and uncoordinated product introductions. But the underlying problem was an organization unable to deal with a shift from a general-purpose to a solutions market that required deeper and faster coordination among multiple product, sales, and service units. IBM's initial response was a common one: create ad hoc project teams. But this response had minimal impact on product development processes and involved more people spending even more time in meetings aimed at promoting cross-functional teamwork.

The next response was the establishment of a formal liaison unit. The Assistant General Manager of Marketing position involved additional overhead costs and staffing issues. But this unit legitimized product-sales-service collaboration in a company where each was traditionally managed in isolation. Equally important, this boundary position provided a single point of contact and visible means for specifying required information and resource flows among multiple product labs and field-marketing units; it also provided a specific decision-making mechanism in an environment where important trade-offs reside at the interface between these groups, rather than primarily within each area.

Relevant Information Systems

The diverse marketing dialects discussed in Chapter 3 have their roots in the distinct tasks facing product, sales, and service units. But market research and broader marketing information systems in most firms are geared to the information needs of product management, not field sales and service. This is a major problem in an environment where customization needs are growing and where local field knowledge must inform product strategy. Without a relevant and accessible information infrastructure, "more communication" through more teams or task force meetings will not result in concurrent marketing capabilities.

This lesson is implicit in the experience of Packaged Products Company, discussed in Chapter 5. There, the symptoms were a gradual erosion in the market shares of key products as well as a loss of shelf space and in-store merchandising support at retail accounts. The underlying problems were an organization unable to manage new information sources that altered the flow of timely consumer data throughout the distribution channel, the buying process at trade customers, field selling and services, and brand-sales coordination requirements. PPCo's initial response was a reengineering of its product development process. This indeed generated more new products, but not commensurate gains in profitability or market share. Direct and indirect sales groups, now dealing with buyers who evaluated category movement and not just individual product margins, found themselves responsible for an even broader set of line extensions from various brand groups. The result was more trade promotion spending but continued share declines.

Productively grappling with new marketing requirements required a redefinition of the role and organization of marketing information systems. At PPCo, this involved dismantling the traditional market research unit and creating a new Research & Analysis group, which was integrated with corporate MIS capabilities. This, in turn, led to the development of more field-responsive information flows, account reviews as a product-sales-service integrating mechanism, sales training initiatives, and new marketing strategies for product lines. As the PPCo example indicates, a common information base provides a shared vision of customers and is both a means and motivation for joint activities.

Individual Understanding and Commitment Are Crucial

This is an aspect of all genuine solutions to complex organizational challenges, and no amount of restructuring, investment in information technology, business process redesign, or pay-for-performance programs will make it less so. Concurrent marketing requires many individuals along the firm's value chain to work together on different nonroutinized tasks, which involves many decentralized changes to generic plans and strategies. Structures that allow for the repeatable processes required for organizational learning, and information systems that disseminate pertinent data across the firms' marketing dialects, are enabling means for such work. But, by themselves, they are not the solution. In a complex external marketplace, it is unrealistic to expect that reengineered work processes alone will make individuals become market-driven and customer-focused.[3] Conversely, line managers in marketing units must have the skills and perspective required to make decisions in terms of an interdependent business system.

The value of HRM initiatives that build these skills and commitment is exemplified by the experience of Becton Dickinson Division (BDD), discussed in Chapter 6. In an attempt to deal with a changing health care environment, BDD repeatedly reorganized its marketing activities—by product, then by market segment, then by products and programs. But none of these organizational restructurings addressed the underlying issue: how to get sales managers (whose field tasks involved more customized product-service packages at key accounts) and product managers (whose headquarters tasks involved more work across functional lines and whose P&L metrics were under pressure) to understand their complementary roles and to solve potential customer conflicts cooperatively. Those abilities, which are ultimately driven by individual skills and relationships, were embedded in the division through new recruitment criteria, joint management development initiatives, new career paths and performance evaluation procedures for product and sales personnel, and attention to cultivating the informal social networks that pervade all time-constrained organizations.

Companies learn and change through the behavior of their individual members. Concurrent marketing needs individuals who have the skills to implement customer solutions that are as integratively complex as the demands of their marketplace. No linkage mechanisms can substitute for the absence of those skills.

FOCUS AND DEPLOY FIELD-MARKETING RESOURCES

Marketing's raison d'être is to add value in customer encounters, value that redounds to the seller's benefit in terms of customer satisfaction, pricing, and profitability. Internal organizational capabilities are the necessary conditions for external responsiveness. But this value is delivered in most companies by field sales and service personnel. Part III focused on account management issues, sales compensation policies, and customer service procedures in the development and daily execution of concurrent marketing capabilities. For salespeople in particular, this manner of going to market involves a significant change in their selling activities. Two aspects of this change are especially noteworthy: the importance of clear account-selection criteria, and the role of account management systems in mobilizing and delivering value to selected accounts.

An old, street-smart aphorism describes traditional sales processes in many firms: "Know your customer; know your product; see a lot of people; ask all to buy." With its haiku-like finality, this adage nicely encapsulates the kinds of activities that are fundamental to selling: customer knowledge, product knowledge, market coverage, and closing skills. However, in a concurrent marketing organization account selection becomes an additional important part of the selling process.

As Chapter 7 indicated, the seller can still "ask all to buy." But the seller's marketing programs must recognize and operationalize the differences between relationship and transaction exchanges. The former require concurrent marketing capabilities; the latter do not. Most companies have both types of accounts in their customer base, and they can be profitable with both types, provided they understand the differences and avoid the two common errors: wasting time-

Exhibit 10-3
Three Dimensions of Account Management

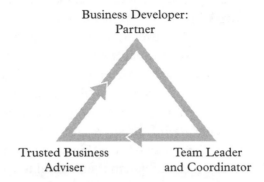

Business Developer:
Partner

Trusted Business   Team Leader
Adviser   and Coordinator

consuming and price-inflating relationship programs on transaction buyers, or approaching relationship buyers with transaction-oriented strategies. For this reason, clear, well-understood, and constantly up-dated account-selection criteria are fundamental in building concurrent marketing capabilities.

Top management can begin the process of clarifying those criteria with a simple exercise. Look over the list of those customers designated as key accounts or national accounts. Speak to sales and service managers about the buying and order fulfillment processes that characterize exchanges with these high-priority customers. Then, using both the explicit and implicit account-selection criteria surfaced by those conversations, ask: which customers *wouldn't* be key accounts, given this criteria. In my experience, most companies' account selection criteria do not provide sufficient guidance to field personnel in making the required crucial distinctions.

For those customers that do merit these efforts, the seller must then deploy the appropriate account management systems. Exhibit 10-3 can help put this issue in perspective and underscore its importance for concurrent marketing initiatives. The discussion of buyer-seller relationships in Part III reveals three dimensions of effective account management: the partnership between buyer and seller that leads to incremental business opportunities for both parties; the information exchange that builds the trust and business advice which, in turn, helps build the partnership; and the vendor's ability to coordinate its resources and account team in developing and implementing those business solutions. From the customer's perspective, there is no hierarchy or priority among these three dimensions: key accounts expect a seamless interface with their suppliers, and their buying power allows them to enforce this requirement. However, as a seller, a vendor must first be an effective coordinator of its resources before it can perform the business adviser's role which, in turn, is a prerequisite for transforming transactions into a profitable long-term relationship. Many customers want the ability to outsource part of their infrastructure to suppliers by sharing information and tighter linkages across the vendor's product, sales, and service units. A key task in account management is to make the selling firm transparent to these customers by effective deployment of the supplier's efforts across the portfolio of opportunities available at such accounts.

The staffing, compensation, training, and sales-service coordination tasks required to do this were discussed in Part III. They are the "going the final mile" part of concurrent marketing and the part that most directly affects customers. It cannot be omitted. The pressing need in many firms to integrate their internal processes should not be an excuse for neglecting the nitty-gritty of field account management systems.

MONITOR AND IMPROVE

Having built linkages and focused field resources, a firm must monitor the progress of concurrent marketing efforts. First, as discussed in Part II, many linkage mechanisms, appropriate at the time of their establishment, can become progressively inappropriate over time. Liaison units must remain conduits for cross-functional efforts rather than checkpoints; information systems must be kept current with evolving segmentation schemes and data sources; training and career-pathing programs must be relevant to customer contact tasks.

Second, as Part III discussed, customers are not static entities and buying behavior is not passive. Over time, the market segments and specific accounts that once required concurrent marketing capabilities may no longer do so. Standardization of once customized services, or a change in the buyer's business strategy, can alter the market forces that do, and do not, require concurrent marketing. When these changes occur, the seller's marketing approach should also change. Hence, the framework in Exhibit 10-1 describes an iterative process.

When concurrent marketing capabilities are viewed this way, companies can take concrete actions that aid integrated monitoring, improvement, and ongoing allocation of these efforts. Firms can proactively gather the information necessary in making the account selection decisions so crucial to profitable concurrent marketing. GE, for example, places microprocessor chips on many of its power distribution and control products (e.g., motors, electrical switches) to gather data about its customers' manufacturing processes, usage patterns, and service requirements. This information improves the efficiency of GE's account management systems as well as the integration of its own product, sales, and service activities in these business units. Technology is making accessible many other low-cost, real-time approaches to gathering such information.

In other situations, as discussed in Chapter 9, service personnel are ideally positioned to gather information to monitor and improve concurrent marketing efforts. They are often the seller's personnel most infrequent contact with the buyer. For that reason, Xerox and other companies have realigned sales service interactions to create a closed loop that combines their local pre- and postsales knowledge with account selection and account management decisions.

More generally, concurrent marketing requires firms to view customers as assets and then actively manage the dynamics of customer retention (cf. Exhibit 9-4). In turn, this may require a change in internal accounting systems. Magazines, for example, often capitalize subscriber acquisition costs rather than expense them as incurred. This approach is in keeping with definitions of an asset as something that offers a future economic benefit, and financial accounting boards are making it possible for more companies. In 1994, for example, the American Institute of Certified Public Accountants issued a new rule that permits the capitalization of customer acquisition and communication costs for certain types of organizations. Under this rule, demand-generation costs incurred today can be amortized over time as the returns from those marketing efforts start to pay back. America OnLine (AOL), one of the firms providing access to on-line databases and other services, uses this approach. According to reports, it costs AOL about $40 to obtain a customer and, given its average monthly subscriber charges in 1994, takes about three months to obtain payback on its customer acquisition efforts.[4] Equally important, such data allow AOL to monitor its marketing efforts, improve its product line to reflect selected customers' usage patterns, and integrate its product, sales, and service activities in order to spur customer retention.

For AOL, customer acquisition costs are primarily direct mail and premium offers to new software purchasers. For other firms, these costs are more varied and involve multiple areas of the business. But the same principle holds: data about response rates to marketing efforts and long-term customer value are increasingly feasible and, once gathered, can be used to build, monitor, and improve concurrent marketing efforts.

MEETING THE CHALLENGE

Probably the most quoted, yet least engaged, insight about management is Peter Drucker's statement more than 40 years ago that: "There is only one valid definition of business purpose: to create a customer. . . . Marketing is the distinguishing, the unique function of the business."[5] Because of its central role in customer acquisition and retention, changes in marketing requirements always have wider organizational implications. Today, those changes are at the heart of many challenges facing enterprises around the world: how to harness new information technologies that alter buyer power? how to respond to multiplying segments made visible and accessible through these technologies? how to deal with shorter product life cycles yet more complex field tasks? how to encourage cross-functional efforts without destroying necessary expertise and accountability?

Concurrent marketing requires managers to develop the organizational capabilities for meeting these global challenges by focusing more attention on those units most directly responsible for customer contact: product, sales, and service. Their interactions remain the basic building blocks of organizational excellence, and, in the current environment, the cutting edge of competitive strategy.

Notes

■

INTRODUCTION

1. Jay S. Kim, "Beyond the Factory Walls: Overcoming Competitive Gridlock" (Boston: Manufacturing Roundtable, September 1994), which reports on research conducted by Boston University in the United States, Waseda University in Japan, and INSEAD in EC countries.

2. Tom Peters, *Thriving on Chaos: Handbook for a Management Revolution* (New York: Harper & Row, 1988), 426.

3. Regis McKenna, "Marketing Is Everything," *Harvard Business Review* 69 (January–February 1991): 65.

4. Theodore Levitt, "Marketing Myopia," *Harvard Business Review* 38 (July–August 1960): 25.

5. For a more technical definition and discussion of the roles of general knowledge versus specific knowledge in markets and organizations, see Friedrich von Hayek, "The Use of Knowledge in Society," *American Economic Review* 35 (September 1945): 310–325; and Michael C. Jensen and William H. Meckling, "Specific and General Knowledge and Organizational Structure," in *Contract Economics,* Lars Werm and Hans Wijkander, eds. (Oxford: Blackwell, 1992), 32–46.

CHAPTER 1

1. See the essays included in John E. G. Bateson, *Managing Services Marketing* (Hinsdale, Ill.: The Dryden Press, 1989).

2. Benson P. Shapiro, "Can Marketing and Manufacturing Coexist?" *Harvard Business Review* 55 (September–October 1977): 121–132; C. H. St. John and E. H. Hall, Jr., "The Interdependency Between Marketing and Manufacturing," *Industrial Marketing Management* 20 (August 1991): 223–229; and for a review of the pertinent

economics literature on this subject, Kelvin Lancaster, "The Economics of Product Variety: A Survey," *Marketing Science* 9 (Summer 1990): 189–211.

3. A study based on a sample of more than 1,400 business units found that firms with broader product lines enjoyed significant market share and profitability benefits without commensurate increases in production costs. See Sunder Keere and Kannan Srinivasan, "Broader Product Line: A Necessity to Achieve Success?" *Management Science* 36 (October 1990): 1216–1231. Another study, of more than 60 auto-assembly plants around the world between 1985 and 1990, found that increased product variety did not significantly hurt productivity or quality in plants with flexible manufacturing technologies *and* commensurate investments in worker training; see Anne G. Perkins, "Product Variety," *Harvard Business Review* 72 (November–December 1994): 13–14.

Similarly, at firms I studied, the number of items assigned to product managers had increased by 50% or more over the past decade—findings in keeping with studies of product variety in other industries. See Steven Wheelwright and Kim Clark, *Revolutionizing Product Development* (New York: The Free Press, 1992), Chapter 1.

For a more general discussion, see Joel Goldhar, Marianne Jelinek, and Theodore Schlie, "Flexibility and Competitive Advantage: Manufacturing Becomes a Service Business," in *International Journal of Technology Management: Special Issue on Manufacturing Strategy* 6 (Fall 1991): 37–51.

4. Stephan H. Haeckel, "Managing the Information-Intensive Firm of 2001," in *The Marketing Information Revolution,* Robert C. Blattberg, Rashi Glazer, and John D. C. Little, eds. (Boston: Harvard Business School Press, 1994), 352.

5. E. Raymond Corey, *Procurement Management: Strategy, Organization, and Decision-Making* (Boston: CBI Publishing, 1978), 22.

6. See John Emshwiller, "Suppliers Struggle to Improve Quality as Big Firms Slash Their Vendor Rolls," *The Wall Street Journal* (August 16, 1991), B1.

7. For more on this topic, see Chapter 9.

8. Frank V. Cespedes, "Channel Management Is General Management," *California Management Review* 31 (Fall 1988): 98–120, provides examples and a discussion of organizational and measurement issues relevant to this topic.

9. For data concerning product life cycles in various categories, see Robert D. Buzzell and Bradley T. Gale, *The PIMS Principles* (New York: The Free Press, 1987), 199–207; C. F. von Braun, "The Acceleration Trap," *Sloan Management Review* 32 (Fall 1990): 49–58; and C. J. Easingwood, "Product Lifecycle Patterns for New Industrial Products," *R&D Management* 18 (Winter 1988): 22–32, which also provides a fine review of factors that alter the prototypical S-shaped product life cycle.

10. Gorman Publishing, *Prepared Foods: New Products Annual* (1990), 159. In this study, a new product was defined as including variations in flavors, colors, or varieties but excluding new sizes, packages, or "simple improvements." Thus, the number cited here is substantially less than the number of new stock-keeping units added during this period, each of which is often treated by trade buyers as a "new product"

because each requires a separate order number, scanning code, and, in many cases, price.

11. Edward W. McClaughlin and Vithala R. Rao, *Decision Criteria for New Product Acceptance: The Role of Trade Buyers* (Westport, Conn.: Quorom Books, 1991), 59–61.

12. This competitive dynamic is discussed, with specific reference to new manufacturing technologies, in Michael J. Piore and Charles F. Sabel, *The Second Industrial Divide: Possibilities for Prosperity* (New York: Basic Books, 1984); and, with reference to new product technologies, in Richard N. Foster, *Innovation: The Attacker's Advantage* (New York: Summit Books, 1986).

13. I am indebted to Joel Goldhar for suggestions on how to visualize the impact of shorter product life cycles on marketing requirements.

CHAPTER 2

1. Raymond L. Manganelli and Mark M. Klein, "A Framework for Reengineering," *Management Review* 83 (June 1994): 10. For a discussion of the pitfalls of excluding the sales force from reengineering efforts, see Mark Blessington and William A. O'Connell, *Beyond Sales and Marketing: Reengineering from the Outside In* (New York: McGraw-Hill, 1995).

2. See Donald S. Tull, Bruce E. Cooley, Mark R. Phillips, Jr., and Harry S. Watkins, "The Organization of Marketing Activities of American Manufacturers," Report No. 91-126, Cambridge, Mass.: Marketing Science Institute, October 1991.

3. For historical perspectives on product management roles, consult Victor P. Buell, "The Changing Role of the Product Manager in Consumer Goods Companies," *Journal of Marketing* 39 (1975): 3–11; and R. D. Fulmer, "Product Management: Panacea or Pandora's Box," *California Management Review* 7 (1975): 63–74.

4. Important studies of product management job tasks include David J. Luck, "Interfaces of a Product Manager," *Journal of Marketing* 33 (1969): 32–36; Gary R. Gemmill and David L. Wilemon, "The Product Manager as an Influence Agent," *Journal of Marketing* 36 (1972): 26–30; A. Venkatesh and David L. Wilemon, "American and European Product Managers: A Comparison," *Columbia Journal of World Business* 15 (1980): 67–74; and Steven Lysonski, "A Boundary Theory Investigation of the Product Manager's Role," *Journal of Marketing* 49 (1985): 26–40.

5. Pertinent studies of industrial versus consumer product managers are W. T. Cummings, D. W. Jackson, and L. Ostrom, "Differences Between Industrial and Consumer Product Managers," *Industrial Marketing Management* 13 (1984): 171–180; and P. L. Dawes and P. G. Patterson, "The Performance of Industrial and Consumer Product Managers," *Industrial Marketing Management* 17 (1988): 73–84.

6. See the results of a survey of more than 500 consumer-goods product managers by John A. Quelch, Paul W. Farris, and James Oliver, "The Product Management Audit: Design and Survey Findings," *Journal of Product & Brand Management* 1 (1992): 45–58.

7. Fritz M. Heichelheim, *An Ancient Economic History,* Vol. I, trans. Joyce Stevens (Leyden: A. W. Sijthoff, 1957); and Thomas L. Powers, Warren S. Martin, Hugh Rushing, and Scott Daniels, "Selling Before 1900: An Historical Perspective," *Journal of Personal Selling & Sales Management* 7 (November 1987): 1–7.

8. Alfred D. Chandler, Jr., *The Visible Hand: The Managerial Revolution in American Business* (Cambridge, Mass.: Harvard University Press, 1977), 287–314.

9. For a more detailed discussion of the salesperson's boundary role, see Frank V. Cespedes, "Aspects of Sales Management: Key Themes," in *Strategic Marketing Management,* Robert J. Dolan, ed. (Boston: Harvard Business School Press, 1991), 403–416.

10. See J. S. Adams, "The Structure and Dynamics of Behavior in Organizational Boundary Roles," in *Handbook of Industrial and Organizational Psychology,* M. Dunnette, ed. (Chicago: Rand McNally, 1976), 317–351; and, for a good review (and application) of this literature in the personal selling context, Jagdip Singh, "Boundary Role Ambiguity: Facets, Determinants, and Impacts," *Journal of Marketing* 57 (1993): 11–31.

11. William C. Moncrief, "Selling Activities and Sales Position Taxonomies for Industrial Sales Forces," *Journal of Marketing Research* 23 (1986): 261–270, and "Ten Key Activities of Industrial Salespeople," *Industrial Marketing Management* 15 (1986): 309–317.

12. Frederick E. Webster, Jr., *Field Sales Management* (New York: John Wiley, 1983), 63.

13. Melvyn A. J. Menezes and Jon D. Serbin, "Regency Facsimile, Inc.," Case No. 9-591-037 (Boston: Harvard Business School, 1991).

14. See the survey data from Forum Corporation and Shycon Consultants cited in A. Bennett and C. Hymowitz, "For Customers, More Than Lip Service?" *The Wall Street Journal* (October 6, 1989), B1.

15. Quoted in Benson P. Shapiro, "The Case of the Tech Service Triangle," *Harvard Business Review* 67 (July–August 1989): 24.

CHAPTER 3

1. E. Raymond Corey and Steven H. Star, *Organization Strategy: A Marketing Approach* (Boston: Harvard Business School Division of Research, 1971), 16.

2. What I call "hierarchies of attention" is analogous to what some have labeled organizational "routines" or "thought worlds": the patterns of activity that characterize different subgroups in a firm, that shape the assumptions and marketplace interpretations of each group, and that over time shape a firm's repertoire of capabilities.

See Richard R. Nelson and Sidney G. Winter, *An Evolutionary Theory of Economic Change* (Cambridge, Mass.: Harvard University Press, 1982), Chapter 5, for an influential discussion of organizational routines; and Michael D. Cohen, "Individual Learning and Organizational Routine: Emerging Connections," *Organization Science* 2 (February 1991): 135–139, for a useful literature review. For a discussion of the various "thought worlds" that characterize groups typically involved in product development, see Deborah Dougherty, "Interpretive Barriers to Successful Product Innovation in Large Firms," *Organization Science* 3 (May 1992): 179–202.

3. Nielsen Marketing Research, *Third Annual Survey of Manufacturer Trade Promotion Practices* (Northbrook, Ill., 1992). Based on returns from 103 companies, this survey tracks expenditures from year to year for various types of trade promotion activities.

4. See M. T. Cunningham and C. J. Clarke, "The Product Management Function in Marketing," *European Journal of Marketing* 9 (Summer 1975): 129–149; and Nigel Piercy, "The Marketing Budgeting Process," *Journal of Marketing* 51 (October 1987): 45–59.

5. Joseph L. Bower, *Managing the Resource Allocation Process* (Boston: Harvard Business School Press, 1970, 1986), 305.

6. For data concerning the design of sales compensation plans, see David J. Good and Robert W. Stone, "How Sales Quotas Are Developed," *Industrial Marketing Management* 20 (February 1991): 51–55.

7. "Theory-in-use" refers to the implicit, inductive, often unarticulated assumptions used by managers to make sense of complex, ambiguous situations. See Chris Argyris, *Reasoning, Learning, and Action: Individual and Organizational* (San Francisco: Jossey-Bass, 1982); and Donald Schon, *The Reflective Practitioner: How Professionals Think in Action* (New York: Basic Books, 1982).

8. Walter J. Salmon and Linda J. Powers, "Organizational Barriers to Department Store Success," Case No. 581-027 (Harvard Business School, 1981), 13–14.

9. Discussions of the connections (and contradictions) between many common features of organizational incentive systems and traditional economic theory are available in J. E. Stiglitz, "The Design of Labor Contracts: The Economics of Incentives and Risk Sharing," in *Incentives, Cooperation, and Risk Sharing*, H. R. Nalbantian, ed. (Totowa, N.J.: Rowman & Littlefield, 1987), 47–68; and George P. Baker, Michael C. Jensen, and Kevin J. Murphy, "Compensation and Incentives: Practice versus Theory," *Journal of Finance* 43 (Fall 1988): 593–616.

10. Bela Gold, "Computerization in Domestic and International Manufacturing," *California Management Review* 31 (Winter 1989): 135.

11. For an analysis of standard costing systems, see H. Thomas Johnson and Robert S. Kaplan, *Relevance Lost: The Rise and Fall of Management Accounting* (Boston: Harvard Business School Press, 1987). Their conclusion about traditional cost accounting practice—"What is missing is an understanding of the costs of reaching and servicing particular types of buyers and the cost of using different distribution channels" (245)—was true at the companies I studied and keenly felt by sales and service managers in those firms.

For an excellent discussion of the means used by managers in various functional areas to bridge gaps between accounting data and the types of information they seek, see Sharon M. McKinnon and William J. Bruns, Jr., *The Information Mosaic* (Boston: Harvard Business School Press, 1992).

12. Michael T. Hannan and John Freeman, *Organizational Ecology* (Cambridge, Mass.: Harvard University Press, 1989) develop this perspective in great detail.

13. Paul R. Lawrence and Jay W. Lorsch, *Organization and Environment* (Boston: Harvard Business School Press, 1986), 8.

14. In a typically illuminating discussion, Peter Drucker has recently stressed the necessary specialization of "knowledge work." See his "The Age of Social Transformation," *Atlantic Monthly* 274 (November 1994), 53–80.

15. Barbara Levitt and James G. March, "Organizational Learning," *Annual Review of Sociology* 14 (1988): 319–340.

CHAPTER 4

1. Thomas J. Peters and Robert H. Waterman, Jr., *In Search of Excellence* (New York: Harper & Row, 1982), 426.

2. Alfred D. Chandler, Jr., *Scale and Scope: The Dynamics of Industrial Capitalism* (Cambridge, Mass.: Harvard University Press, 1990), passim.

3. Frank V. Cespedes, "Agendas, Incubators, and Marketing Organization," *California Management Review* 33 (Fall 1990): 27–53, discusses this point in more detail.

4. Theodore Levitt, "Marketing Myopia," *Harvard Business Review* 38 (July–August 1960): 24–47. The contemporary view of strategy as core competencies, articulated most fully by Gary Hamel and C. K. Prahalad, largely builds on Levitt's enduring insight about marketing and innovation; see their book, *Competing for the Future* (Boston: Harvard Business School Press, 1994).

5. Karl E. Weick, "Organizational Culture as a Source of High Reliability," *California Management Review* 29 (Winter 1987): 112–113.

6. Unless otherwise noted, all information about IBM in this chapter comes from interviews conducted for a Harvard Business School case series; see Frank V. Cespedes and Laura Goode, "IBM: Assistant General Manager of Marketing (A) and (B)," Case Nos. 9-592-066 and 9-592-067 (Boston: Harvard Business School, 1992).

7. T. A. Wise, "The Rocky Road to the Marketplace," *Fortune* (October 1966): 122–135.

8. Mike Ricciuti, "IBM Entry Spans Midrange Gap," *Datamation* (November 1, 1990): 101–102.

9. See Kim B. Clark and Takahiro Fujimoto, *Product Development Performance* (Boston: Harvard Business School Press, 1991), Chapter 9.

CHAPTER 5

1. J. Walker Smith, "The Promise of Single Source: When, Where, and How," *Marketing Research* 3 (December 1990): 3–4.

2. John A. Quelch, *Sales Promotion Management* (Englewood Cliffs, N.J.: Prentice Hall, 1989), 33.

3. For claims concerning the productivity potential of sales force automation and

discussions of the adoption issues, see Louis A. Wallis, *Computers and the Sales Effort* (New York: The Conference Board, 1986), and Rowland T. Moriarty and Gordon S. Swartz, "Automation to Boost Sales and Marketing," *Harvard Business Review* 67 (January–February, 1989): 100–109.

4. From a different perspective, a useful discussion of the differences in marketing versus market research is available in Vincent P. Barabba and Gerald Zaltman, *Hearing the Voice of the Market: Competitive Advantage through Creative Use of Market Information* (Boston: Harvard Business School Press, 1991), Chapter 3.

5. See K. Sridhar Moorthy, "Measuring Overall Judgments and Attribute Evaluations," Report No. 91-116 (Cambridge, Mass.: Marketing Science Institute, 1991); and Raymond R. Burke, et al., "Comparing Dynamic Consumer Decision Processes in Real and Computer-Simulated Environments," Report No. 91-120 (Cambridge, Mass.: Marketing Science Institute, 1991).

6. This is a fictitious title for a well-known firm. The names of managers at Packaged Products Company, as well as some market data, have also been disguised.

7. A plan-o-gram is a schematic diagram of a rack, shelf, aisle, or department in a retail store, indicating the shelf position and facings (i.e., number of packages of an item across the front row) for each product in that section of the store.

8. Slotting allowances are fees charged by many grocery chains for stocking an item. By 1990, these fees ranged from $5,000–$8,000 per item in many of PPCo's product categories. On a five-item line sold through hundreds of chains, this fee quickly becomes a significant cost of doing business.

9. Kate Bertrand, "Navigating Through a Sea of Change," *Business Marketing* (June 1991): 17–19.

10. For useful guidelines concerning these procedures and how such research is conducted at Hewlett-Packard, see Edward F. McQuarrie, "The Customer Visit: Qualitative Research for Business-to-Business Marketers," *Marketing Research* 4 (March 1991): 15–28.

11. For examples of such practices, and suggestions concerning appropriate use of customer information, see Frank V. Cespedes and H. Jeff Smith, "Database Marketing: New Rules for Policy and Practice," *Sloan Management Review* 34 (Summer 1993): 7–22. For discussions of the evolving legal framework of database marketing, see L. R. Fischer, *The Law of Financial Privacy: A Compliance Guide* (Boston: Warren, Gorham, & Lamont, 1991); and Paul N. Bloom, George R. Milne, and Robert Adler, "Avoiding Misuse of New Information Technologies," *Journal of Marketing* 58 (January 1994): 98–110.

12. More than three decades of studies support this generalization. See, for example, Gerald Albaum, "Horizontal Information Flow: An Exploratory Study," *Journal of the Academy of Management* 7 (1964): 21–33; Daniel Robertson, "Communications and Sales Force Feedback," *Journal of Business Communication* 11 (1974): 3–9; and Douglas Lambert, Howard Marmorstein, and Athul Sharma, "Industrial Salespeople as a Source of Market Information," *Industrial Marketing Management* 19 (1990): 141–148.

13. Peter Strub and Steven Herman, "Can the Sales Force Speak for the Customer?" *Marketing Research* 5 (Fall 1993): 32–35.

14. Thomas H. Davenport, Robert G. Eccles, and Laurence Prusak, "Information Politics," *Sloan Management Review* 34 (Fall 1992): 65.

CHAPTER 6

1. Important discussions of this topic, which have influenced my view of the role and components of learning in marketing activities, include: C. Argyris and D. Schon, *Organizational Learning: A Theory-in-Action Perspective* (Reading, Mass.: Addison-Wesley, 1978); B. Hedberg, "How Organizations Learn and Unlearn," in *Handbook of Organizational Design*, P. C. Nystrom and W. H. Starbuck, eds. (London: Oxford University Press, 1981), 3–27; D. A. Kolb, *Experiential Learning: Experience as the Source of Learning and Development* (Englewood Cliffs, N.J.: Prentice-Hall, 1984); and P. Senge, *The Fifth Discipline: The Art and Practice of the Learning Organization* (New York: Doubleday, 1990).

2. Daniel H. Kim, "The Link between Individual and Organizational Learning," *Sloan Management Review* 35 (Fall 1993): 37.

3. For a discussion of the role of marketing in strategy implementation and wider organizational change, see Nigel F. Piercy and Frank V. Cespedes, "Implementing Strategy," in the *International Encyclopedia of Business and Management*, Malcolm Warner, ed. (London: Routledge, 1996).

4. This framework is adapted from Frank V. Cespedes, *Organizing and Implementing the Marketing Effort* (Reading, Mass.: Addison-Wesley, 1991).

5. Charles Perrow, "A Framework for the Comparative Analysis of Organizations," *American Sociological Review* 32 (Fall 1967): 199. The basic distinction was drawn some years earlier by James G. March and Herbert A. Simon in *Organizations* (New York: Wiley, 1958).

6. Information about BDD comes from interviews conducted by Frank V. Cespedes and Laura Goode, "Becton Dickinson Division: Marketing Organization," Case No. 9-593-070 (Boston: Harvard Business School, 1993).

7. See Masahi Kuga, "Kao's Marketing Strategy and Marketing Intelligence System," *Journal of Advertising Research* 16 (April–May 1990): 22.

8. These estimates are, respectively, those in "1989 Survey of Selling Costs," *Sales and Marketing Management* (February 20, 1989): 23, and "Industry Report," *Training* (October 1993): 39.

9. This assertion is supported by numerous surveys. See, for example, Alan J. Dubinsky and Thomas E. Barry, "A Survey of Sales Management Practices," *Industrial Marketing Management* 11 (1982): 136–147; Anthony Allesandra and Philip Wexler, "The Professionalization of Selling," *Sales and Marketing Training* (February 1988): 37–43; and Rene Y. Darmon, *Effective Human Resource Management in the Sales Force* (Westport, Conn.: Quorum Books, 1992), 135–144.

10. Meg Kerr and Bill Burzynski, "Missing the Target: Sales Training in America," *Training and Development Journal* (July 1988): 68–70.

11. The use of company-specific development programs as a socialization device and change agent has been usefully discussed in Noel M. Tichy and Mary Anne Devanna, *The Transformational Leader* (New York: John Wiley, 1990).

12. Thomas A. Stewart, "GE Keeps Those Ideas Coming," *Fortune* (August 12, 1991), 62.

13. For an excellent discussion and analysis of a Work-Out effort between GE's appliance unit and Sears, see Todd D. Jick, "Customer-Supplier Partnerships: Human Resources as Bridge Builders," *Human Resource Management* 29 (Winter 1990): 435–454.

14. John P. Kotter, *A Force for Change* (New York: The Free Press, 1990), 92.

15. Anders Edstrom and Jay R. Galbraith, "Transfer of Managers as a Coordination and Control Strategy in Multinational Organizations," *Administrative Science Quarterly* 22 (1977): 251. The role of career path management and training programs is also discussed in Christopher A. Bartlett and Sumantra Ghoshal, *Managing Across Borders* (Boston: Harvard Business School Press, 1989), Chapter 10.

16. See Masahiko Aoki, *Information, Incentives, and Bargaining in the Japanese Economy* (London: Cambridge University Press, 1988), Chapter 3; and Kazuo Koike, "Skill Formation Systems: Japan and U.S.," *The Economic Analysis of the Japanese Firm*, M. Aoki, ed. (Amsterdam: North Holland Press, 1984), 63–73.

17. A more detailed description of this process is available in "Becton Dickinson (D): Strategic Human Resource Profiling," Case No. 9-491-155 (Boston: Harvard Business School, 1991).

CHAPTER 7

1. William A. O'Connell and William Keenan, Jr., "The Shape of Things to Come," *Sales and Marketing Management* (January 1990): 37–45. Important caveats about how to interpret 80/20 figures are discussed in David C. Schmittlein, Lee G. Cooper, and Donald G. Morrison, "Truth in Concentration in the Land of 80/20 Laws," Report No. 92–117 (Cambridge, Mass.: Marketing Science Institute, 1992). They point out that most reported concentration statistics are based on *observed* purchases (i.e., excluding customers with no purchases during the observation period). Changing the observation period or the definition of nonusers can significantly affect customer concentration indices in many product categories.

2. For a more detailed discussion of how postsale factors affect marketing decisions in this industry, see E. Raymond Corey, Frank V. Cespedes, and V. Kasturi Rangan, *Going to Market: Distribution Systems for Industrial Products* (Boston: Harvard Business School Press, 1989), 336–354.

3. Thomas Knect, Ralf Leszinski, and Felix A. Weber, "Making Profits after the Sale," *The McKinsey Quarterly*, No. 4, 79–86, 1993.

4. See Robert S. Kaplan, "Kanthal (A)," Case No. 9-190-002 (Boston: Harvard Business School, 1990).

5. Abberton Associates, *Customer Base Control* (London, 1994).

6. I use the term "stuck in the middle" differently than Michael Porter in *Competitive Strategy* (New York: The Free Press, 1980), 41–44, where he refers to top management's inability or unwillingness to choose one of three generic strategies. My research indicates that these strategic consequences are often the *result* of firms' tactical account management policies rather than simply a failure among executives to understand the importance of having a consistent strategy.

7. I am indebted to Susan Pieper, a former student in my Marketing Implementation course at the Harvard Business School, for suggesting the ideas on which this approach to account selection is based.

8. See Joel D. Goldhar and Mariann Jelinek, "Computer-Integrated Flexible Manufacturing: Organizational, Economic, and Strategic Implications," *Interfaces* 15 (May–June 1985): 94–115.

9. The basis for these distinctions is the concept of relational exchange, developed most fully by the legal scholar Ian Macneil in *The New Social Contract: An Inquiry into Modern Contractual Relations* (New Haven, Conn.: Yale University Press, 1980), and a seminal study of the dynamics of customer relationships by Barbara Bund Jackson, *Winning and Keeping Industrial Customers* (Lexington, Mass.: D. C. Heath, 1985).

10. There is an important theoretical point in this description of many account relationships. Standard economic theory makes no allowance for safeguarding specialized exchange assets other than vertical integration. But this is not feasible for many firms. A common alternative to vertical integration is what has been labeled "dependence balancing" (i.e., mutual offsetting investments by each party in a business relationship).

For readers interested in pursuing this topic, see the following articles: Jan B. Heide and George John, "The Role of Dependence Balancing in Safeguarding Transaction-Specific Assets in Conventional Channels," *Journal of Marketing* 52 (January 1988): 20–35; Jeffrey Bradach and Robert C. Eccles, "Price, Authority, and Trust: From Ideal Types to Plural Forms," *Annual Review of Sociology* 15 (1989): 97–118; and Patrick J. Kaufmann and Rajiv P. Dant, "The Dimensions of Commercial Exchange," *Marketing Letters* 3 (May 1992): 175–185.

11. This view of relationship development is adapted from J. Scanzoni, "Social Exchange and Behavioral Interdependence," in *Social Exchange in Developing Relationships,* R. L. Burgess and T. L. Huston, eds. (New York: Academic Press, 1979): 125–142; and F. Robert Dwyer, Paul H. Schurr, and Sejo Oh, "Developing Buyer-Seller Relationships," *Journal of Marketing* 51 (April 1987): 11–27.

12. For more on the evolution and interaction of channel design and account relations in this industry, see Frank V. Cespedes, "Formulating Channel Strategy in a Rapidly Changing Market," *Journal of Managerial Issues* 4 (Winter 1992): 476–493.

13. Susan Helper, "Strategy and Irreversibility in Supplier Relations: The Case of the U.S. Automobile Industry," *Business History Review* 65 (Winter 1991): 783.

14. Ibid., 811.

15. See Linda Platzer, *Managing National Accounts* (New York: The Conference Board, 1984), and Jerome Colletti and Gary S. Tubridy, "Effective Major Account Sales Management," *Journal of Personal Selling and Sales Management* 7 (August 1987): 1–12.

16. For a more detailed discussion of the research on which these observations are based, see Frank V. Cespedes, Stephen X. Doyle, and Robert J. Freedman, "Teamwork for Today's Selling," *Harvard Business Review* 67 (March–April 1989): 44–58; and Frank V. Cespedes, "Sales Coordination: An Exploratory Study," *Journal of Personal Selling and Sales Management* 12 (Summer 1992): 13–29.

CHAPTER 8

1. Under assumptions about the salesperson's objective function (to maximize income), constraints under which the salesperson operates, and the firm's knowledge of the individual salesperson's sales response function (i.e., how effort and results are related), these studies develop models for considering how the firm can set compensation to maximize profits across a line of products or accounts. Important studies of this area include: John U. Farley, "An Optimal Plan for Salesmen's Compensation," *Journal of Marketing Research* 1 (1964): 39–43; Charles B. Weinberg, "Jointly Optimal Sales Commissions for Non-Income Maximizing Sales Force," *Management Science* 24 (1978): 1252–1258; Rajiv Lal and Richard Staelin, "Salesforce Compensation Plans in Environments with Asymmetric Information," *Marketing Science* 5 (1986): 179–198; and Anne T. Coughlan and Subrata K. Sen, "Salesforce Compensation: Theory and Managerial Implications," *Marketing Science* 8 (1989): 324–342.

2. Surveys of practice in this area include Charles A. Peck, *Compensating Field Sales Representatives*, Report No. 828 (New York: The Conference Board, 1982); Rolph E. Anderson, Joseph F. Hair, and Alan J. Bush, *Professional Sales Management* (New York: McGraw-Hill, 1988); John K. Moynahan, ed., *Sales Compensation Handbook* (New York: American Management Association, 1991); and David J. Good and Robert W. Stone, "How Sales Quotas Are Developed," *Industrial Marketing Management* 20 (1991): 51–55.

3. A review of attribution theory and empirical evidence for it are available in Bernard Weiner, *Human Motivation* (New York: Holt, Rinehart and Winston, 1980). For its relevance to the sales context, see Harish Sujan, "Smarter Versus Harder: An Exploratory Attributional Analysis of Salespeople's Motivation," *Journal of Marketing Research* 23 (1986): 41–49, and Alan J. Dubinsky, Steven Skinner, and Thomas Whittler, "Evaluating Sales and Personnel: An Attribution Theory Perspective," *Journal of Personal Selling and Sales Management* 9 (1989): 9–21.

4. For the theories and assumptions underlying these models, see Leonard Lodish, "'Vaguely Right' Approach to Sales Force Allocation," *Harvard Business Review* 52 (January–February 1974): 119–174; and Anders Zoltners and Prabash Sinha, "Inte-

ger Programming Models for Sales Resource Allocation," *Management Science* 26 (1980): 242–260.

Most statistical packages based on these models depend on linear equations while, in most sales situations, the relevant variable relationships are probably nonlinear. For an example of an approach that incorporates nonlinear multiplicative relationships, see Adrian B. Ryans and Charles B. Weinberg, "Territory Sales Response Models: Stability Over Time," *Journal of Marketing Research* 24 (May 1987): 226–235.

5. Although not concerned with sales situations per se, a classic analysis of reward systems that pay off for one behavior while the rewarder hopes for another is Steven Kerr, "On the Folly of Rewarding A, While Hoping for B," *Academy of Management Journal* 18 (1975): 769–783.

6. The notion of "transaction-specific assets" is developed most fully by Oliver E. Williamson in "The Economics of Organization: The Transaction Cost Approach," *American Journal of Sociology* 87 (1981): 548–577 and his book, *The Economic Institutions of Capitalism* (New York: The Free Press, 1987). Applications of Williamson's theory to sales compensation include Erin Anderson and Richard L. Oliver, "Perspectives on Behavior-Based Versus Outcome-Based Salesforce Control Systems," *Journal of Marketing* 51 (October 1987): 76–88; and George John and Barton Weitz, "Salesforce Compensation: An Empirical Investigation of Factors Related to Use of Salary versus Incentive Compensation," *Journal of Marketing Research* 26 (1989): 1–14.

7. B. D. Dunn and S. E. Morrison, "Incentive Compensation Programs for Private Banking," *The Bankers Magazine* (July–August 1989): 16–19.

8. A missionary salesperson attempts to build goodwill and/or educate the potential user about the company's product line. This salesperson may never book an order personally. Instead, he or she focuses on building sales volume by persuading users to order from the firm's wholesalers or other stocking points. Examples would be a salesperson for a pharmaceuticals firm, soft drink company, or distillery who calls on a doctor, restaurant, or bar, respectively, even though the customer in each instance buys from a pharmacy, bottler, or distributor, not from the salesperson.

9. For discussions of how these factors affect the salary-incentive mix, see Coughlan and Sen, "Salesforce Compensation"; John and Weitz, "Salesforce Compensation"; or Gary Tubridy, "How to Pay National Account Managers," *Sales and Marketing Management* (January 13, 1986): 50–54.

10. I am indebted to Robert J. Freedman, formerly a specialist in sales and executive compensation at TPF&C, for the example provided as Exhibit 8-3.

CHAPTER 9

1. Ron Winslow, "Four Hospital Suppliers Will Launch Common Electronic Ordering System," *The Wall Street Journal* (April 12, 1994), B6.

2. For a seminal discussion of the role of pre- and postsale services in augmenting and differentiating commodities, see Theodore Levitt, "Marketing Success Through

Differentiation—of Anything," *Harvard Business Review* 58 (January–February 1980): 83–91.

3. For more on this study, see Frank V. Cespedes, "General Electric: Customer Service," Case No. 9-588-059 (Boston: Harvard Business School, 1988).

4. This analogy is borrowed from G. Lynn Shostack, "Planning the Service Encounter," in *The Service Encounter,* John A. Czepiel, Michael R. Soloman, and Carol F. Suprenant, eds. (Lexington, Mass.: D. C. Heath, 1985), 243–253.

5. This point is discussed at greater length in Benson P. Shapiro, V. Kasturi Rangan, and John J. Sviokla, "Staple Yourself to an Order," *Harvard Business Review* 70 (July–August 1992): 113–122.

6. For a discussion of the benefits of the case management approach, see Michael Hammer and James Champy, *Reengineering the Corporation* (New York: HarperBusiness, 1993), Chapter 3. For a discussion of the issues that must be confronted in implementing this approach, see Thomas H. Davenport and Nitin Nohria, "Case Management and the Integration of Labor," *Sloan Management Review* 35 (Winter 1994): 11–24.

7. See Valarie A. Zeithaml, Leonard L. Berry, and A. Parasuraman, "Communication and Control Processes in the Delivery of Service Quality," *Journal of Marketing* 52 (April 1988): 35–48.

8. A useful review of these factors, and their historical impact on Japanese service practices, is William A. Mahon and Richard E. Dyck, "Japanese Quality Systems from a Marketing Viewpoint," *Industrial Management and Data Systems* 5 (September–October 1982): 8–14.

9. For more details about service initiatives at this company, see Melvyn A. J. Menezes and Jon Serbin, "Xerox Corporation: The Customer Satisfaction Program," Case No. 9-591-055 (Boston: Harvard Business School, 1991).

10. Robert J. Berling, "The Emerging Approach to Business Strategy: Building a Relationship Advantage," *Business Horizons* 36 (July–August 1993): 16–27.

11. For an excellent discussion of these issues and how they affect cost accounting systems, see the series of articles by Robin Cooper, "The Rise of Activity-Based Costing," Parts 1–4, in *Journal of Cost Management* (Summer 1988): 45–54; (Fall 1988): 41–48; (Winter 1989): 34–46; and (Spring 1989): 38–49.

12. See Robert D. Buzzell and Bradley T. Gales, *The PIMS Principles: Linking Strategy to Performance* (New York: The Free Press, 1987), Chapter 5; Claes Fornell, Michael J. Ryan, and Robert A. Westbrook, "Customer Satisfaction: The Key to Customer Retention," *MOBIUS* 5 (Summer 1990): 14–17; Frederick F. Reichheld and W. Earl Sasser, "Zero Defections: Quality Comes to Services," *Harvard Business Review* 68 (September–October 1990): 105–113; and Valerie A. Zeithaml, A. Parasuraman, and Leonard L. Berry, *Delivering Quality Service* (New York: The Free Press, 1990).

CHAPTER 10

1. This noninvolvement of front-line personnel is built into reengineering doctrine and not simply, as is now often argued, one of the many types of "misunder-

standings" of reengineering. See Michael Hammer and James Champy, *Reengineering the Corporation: A Manifesto for Business Revolution* (New York: HarperBusiness, 1993), 207:

> It is axiomatic that reengineering never, ever happens from the bottom up . . . no matter how great the need or how prodigious the talent [of] frontline employees and middle managers. . . . [T]he push for reengineering must come from the top of an organization [because] the people near the front lines lack the broad perspective that reengineering demands.

While acknowledging the often useful rethinking of business processes spurred by this perspective, I have clearly taken a different tack in this book. Top-down "manifestos" are risky in a world that is getting more diverse and complex. Particularly in marketing, such an approach can be a disaster because it ignores or fails to capture vital local knowledge about customers.

2. Richard P. Rumelt, "Inertia and Transformation," in *Resources in an Evolutionary Perspective: Towards a Synthesis of Evolutionary and Resource-Based Approaches to Strategy,* Cynthia A. Montgomery, ed. (Norwell, Mass.: Kluwer Academic Publishers, 1995).

3. For a complementary argument that it is better to teach individuals how to handle complex, inconsistent demands than it is to expect organizational systems to eliminate these demands, see Richard D. Boettger and Charles R. Greer, "On the Wisdom of Rewarding A, While Hoping for B," *Organization Science* 5 (November 1994): 569–582. I do take issue with one of their conclusions: this fact of organizational life is *not* an argument for maintaining the inconsistent reward systems so ably diagnosed by Steven Kerr, "On the Folly of Rewarding A, While Hoping for B," *Academy of Management Journal* 18 (1975): 769–783.

4. Gary Samuels, "What Profits?" *Forbes* (October 24, 1994), 74.

5. Peter F. Drucker, *The Practice of Management* (New York: Harper & Brothers, 1954), 37.

Index

■

About the Author

■

Frank V. Cespedes is a managing partner at The Center for Executive Development in Cambridge, Massachusetts, where he provides management education and consulting services to companies in North America, South America, Europe, and Asia. Cespedes was a member of the Harvard Business School faculty for fifteen years, specializing in marketing, organizational design, and strategy implementation. He also developed and taught various courses in the MBA program and led the Strategic Marketing Management program for senior executives. Cespedes is the author of numerous articles and six books, including *Organizing and Implementing the Marketing Effort* and *Going to Market: Distribution Systems for Industrial Products* (HBS Press).